ESSENTIALS FOR design

JAVASCRIPT

level two

Michael Brooks
Drew Kinney

PEARSON
Prentice Hall

Prentice Hall
Upper Saddle River, New Jersey 07458

Library of Congress Cataloging-in-Publication Data
Brooks, Michael.
JavaScript, level two/Michael Brooks, Drew Kinney.
    p.cm. — (Essentials for design)
ISBN 0-13-146830-8
1. JavaScript (Computer programming language) I. Kinney, Drew. II. Title. III. Series

QA76.73.J39B76 2005
005.13'3—dc22   2004065407

Publisher and Vice President: Natalie E. Anderson
Executive Editor, print: Stephanie Wall
Executive Editor, media: Jodi McPherson
Acquisitions Editor: Melissa Sabella
Editorial Assistants: Alana Meyers, Brian Hoehl, Sandra Bernales, and Bambi Dawn Marchigano
Senior Media Project Manager: Cathleen Profitko
Senior Marketing Manager: Emily Knight
Marketing Manager: Sarah Davis

Marketing Assistant: Lisa Taylor
Senior Editorial Project Manager: Anne Garcia
Project Manager, Production: Vanessa Nuttry
Manufacturing Buyer: Vanessa Nuttry
Interior Design: Thistle Hill Publishing Services, LLC
Cover Design: Blair Brown
Cover Printer: Coral Graphics
Printer/Binder: Von Hoffman Press

10 9 8 7 6 5 4 3 2 1

ISBN 0-13-146830-8

ABOUT THE SERIES EDITOR

Ellenn Behoriam is president and founder of Against The Clock, Inc. (ATC), one of the nation's leading content providers. Ellenn and her staff have successfully produced many of the graphic arts industry's most popular and well-received books and related series. These works include the *Electronic Cookbook, Workflow Reengineering, Teams and the Graphic Arts, Adobe Photoshop Creative Techniques, Adobe Illustrator Creative Techniques,* and *QuarkXPress 6: Creating Digital Documents,* the foundation for the QuarkXPress Trainer certification programs. The Against The Clock series, published in concert with Prentice Hall/Pearson Education, includes more than 26 titles that focus on applications for the graphic and computer arts industries.

Against The Clock also worked with Pearson to develop the *Companion for the Digital Artist* series. These titles focus on specific and fundamental creative concepts, including design, Web-site development, photography, typography, color theory, and copywriting. These concise and compact works provide core concepts and skills that supplement any application-specific education, regardless of which textbooks are used to teach program skills.

Under Ellenn's leadership and direction, ATC is currently developing more than 20 titles for the new *Essentials for Design* series. Her staff and long-established network of professional educators, printers, prepress experts, workflow engineers, and business leaders add significantly to ATC's ability to provide current, meaningful, and effective books, online tutorials, and business-to-business performance and workflow-enhancement programs.

ABOUT THE AUTHORS

Michael Brooks is an instructor in the Interactive Media Design Department at The Art Institute of Charlotte; he is also a co-owner of Web-Answers, a multimedia design firm. Michael has an MPA from Appalachian State University. His professional duties require a great deal of time working in JavaScript and Flash. He has an intimate knowledge of the business and strategic aspects of Web design.

Raised in the foothills of Western North Carolina, Michael enjoys photography and occasionally teaches classes in business management and political science.

Drew Kinney designed and wrote Portfolio Builder exercises for every project, and various end-of-project exercises. He also contributed significantly to sections on cookies and XHTML compliance. Drew is a former art director for several well known movies and TV shows and is currently an instructor at the Art Institute of Charlotte's Interactive Media Design Department.

ACKNOWLEDGMENTS

We would like to thank the professional writers, artists, editors, and educators who have worked long and hard on the *Essentials for Design* series.

And thanks to the dedicated teaching professionals: John Griffin; Kyle Tait, Department Chair, Art Institute of Charlotte; Warren Kendrick, Professor and Department Chair, Florida Technical College; Lindsey Allen; and Dean Bagley. Your insightful comments and expertise have certainly contributed to the success of the *Essentials for Design* series.

We would also like to thank Julian Rickards and Dean Bagley for their technical assistance; John Dunning for his artwork contributions; and the students at The Art Institute of Charlotte, who tested exercises and provided excellent feedback.

Thank you to Laurel Nelson-Cucchiara, copy editor and final link in the chain of production, for her help in making sure that we all said what we meant to say.

And a very special thank you to Erika Kendra, production designer, technical consultant, partner in crime, and friend.

And to Melissa Sabella, Anne Garcia, Jodi McPherson, and Vanessa Nuttry — we appreciate your patience as we begin this new venture together.

CONTENTS AT A GLANCE

TABLE OF CONTENTS

HOW TO USE THIS BOOK

Essentials courseware from Prentice Hall is anchored in the practical and professional needs of all types of students. The *Essentials* series presents a learning-by-doing approach that encourages you to grasp application-related concepts as you expand your skills through hands-on tutorials. As such, it consists of modular lessons that are built around a series of numbered step-by-step procedures that are clear, concise, and easy to review.

Essentials books are divided into projects. A project covers one area (or a few closely related areas) of application functionality. Each project consists of several lessons that are related to that topic. Each lesson presents a specific task or closely related set of tasks in a manageable chunk that is easy to assimilate and retain.

Each element in the *Essentials* book is designed to maximize your learning experience. A list of the *Essentials* project elements, and a description of how each element can help you, begins on the next page. To find out more about the rationale behind each book element and how to use each to your maximum benefit, take the following walk-through.

WALK-THROUGH

Project Objectives.   Starting with an objective gives you short-term, attainable goals. Each project begins with a list of objectives that closely match the titles of the step-by-step tutorials. ▶

OBJECTIVES

In this project, you learn how to

- Use string methods
- Create and populate an array
- Sort an array
- Incorporate array methods
- Split and join strings
- Use multi-dimensional arrays

Why Would I Do This?   Introductory material at the beginning of each project provides an overview of why these tasks and procedures are important.

Visual Summary.   A series of illustrations introduces the new tools, dialog boxes, and windows you will explore in each project. ▼

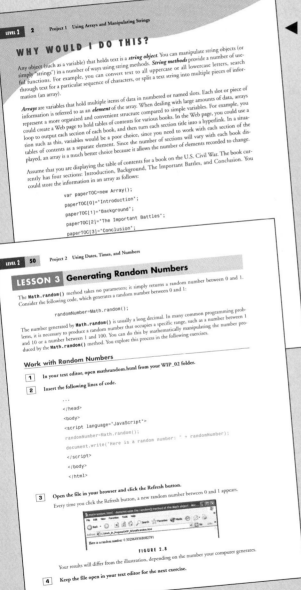

Step-by-Step Tutorials.   Hands-on tutorials let you learn by doing and include numbered, bold, step-by-step instructions.

◄ **If You Have Problems.** These short troubleshooting notes help you anticipate or solve common problems quickly and effectively.

◄ **Careers in Design.** These features offer advice, tips, and resources that will help you on your path to a successful career.

To Extend Your Knowledge. These provide extra tips, shortcuts, alternative ways to complete a process, and special hints about using the software. ►

To Extend Your Knowledge...

MILLISECOND CALCULATIONS FROM INDEX DATES

Dates can also be constructed and manipulated using milliseconds from an index date. This type of date manipulation is more complex than the examples presented in this book. The ability to manipulate dates in this fashion is useful for synchronizing events across different regions or making very precise time measurements. The index date is 12 a.m., January 1, 1970, Greenwich Mean Time (GMT).

When manipulating dates in terms of the index date, date and time information is returned in terms of the amount of time the date occupies from the index date. This can prove very confusing to novice programmers, since a day has 84,400,000 milliseconds, and a day before the index date would return as -84,400,000. A day after the index date would return as 84,400,000.

Manipulating dates using the index date is quite complex and only useful in very technical problem-solving situations. For the sake of simplicity, we describe the most common methods of the **date** object in this project and avoid using the index date. Additionally, we work with standard dates wherever possible, such as January 1, 1983, and avoid working with milliseconds.

toLocaleString() BROWSER COMPATIBILITY

The text string generated by the **toLocaleString()** method is slightly different in every browser. For this reason, your output may appear slightly different than the screen shots shown in this project.

End-of-Project Exercises. Extensive end-of-project exercises emphasize hands-on skill development. You'll find three levels of reinforcement: Skill Drill, Challenge, and Portfolio Builder. ▼

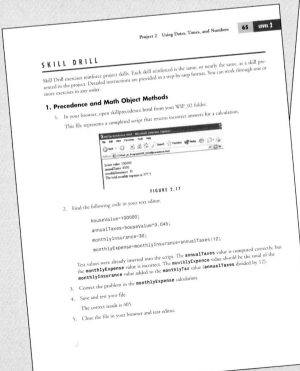

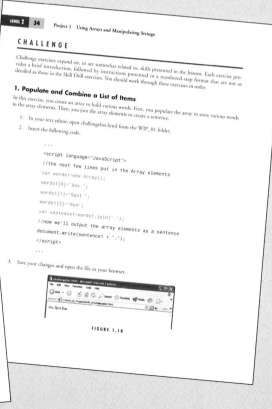

Portfolio Builder. At the end of every project, these exercises require creative solutions to problems that reinforce the topic of the project. ▶

Integrating Projects. Integrating projects are designed to reflect real-world graphic-design jobs, drawing on the skills you have learned throughout this book.

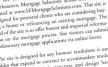

Task Guides. These charts, found at the end of each book, list alternative ways to complete common procedures and provide a handy reference tool. ▶

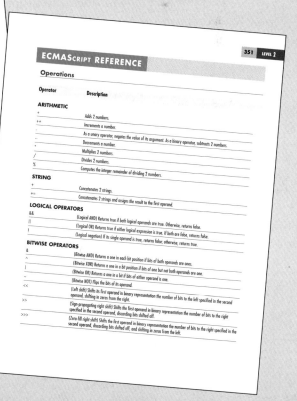

STUDENT INFORMATION AND RESOURCES

Companion Web Site (www.prenhall.com/essentials). This text-specific Web site provides students with additional information and exercises to reinforce their learning. Features include: additional end-of-project reinforcement material, online Study Guide, easy access to *all* resource files, and much, much more!

Before completing the projects within this text, you need to download the Resource Files from the Prentice Hall Companion Web site. Check with your instructor for the best way to gain access to these files or simply follow these instructions:

1. From an open Web browser, go to http://www.prenhall.com/essentials.

2. Select your textbook or series to access the Companion Web site. We suggest you bookmark this page, as it has links to additional Prentice Hall resources that you may use in class.

3. Click the Student Resources link. All files in the Student Resources area are provided as .sea files for Macintosh users and .exe files for those using the Windows operating system. These files do not require any additional software to open.

4. Click the Start Here link for the platform you are using (Macintosh or Windows).

5. Once you have downloaded the proper file, double-click that file to begin the self-extraction process. You will be prompted to select a folder location specific for your book; you may extract the file to your hard drive or to a removable disk/drive.

   The Start Here file contains two folders:

   ■ **RF_JavaScript_L2.** You can place this folder on your hard drive, or on a removable disk/drive.

   ■ **Work_In_Progress.** You can place this folder on your hard drive, or on a removable disk/drive.

6. Locate the project files you need from the list of available resources and click the active link to download. There is a separate file for each project in this book (e.g., Project_01, Project_02, etc.).

7. Once you have downloaded the proper file, double-click that file to begin the self-extraction process. You will be prompted to select a folder location specific to your book. You should extract the project-specific folders into the RF_JavaScript_L2 folder that was extracted from the Start Here file.

Resource CD.   If you are using a Resource CD, all the fonts and files you need are provided on the CD. Resource files are organized in project-specific folders (e.g., Project_01, Project_02, etc.), which are contained in the RF_JavaScript_L2 folder. You can either work directly from the CD, or copy the files onto your hard drive before beginning the exercises.

Before you begin working on the projects or lessons in this book, you should copy the Work_In_Progress folder from the Resource CD onto your hard drive or a removable disk/drive.

Resource Files.   Resource files are organized in project-specific folders, and are named to facilitate cross-platform compatibility. Words are separated by an underscore, and all file names include a lowercase three-letter extension. For example, if you are directed to open the file "graphics.eps" in Project 2, the file can be found in the RF_JavaScript_L2> Project_02 folder. We repeat these directions frequently in the early projects.

The Work In Progress Folder.   This folder contains individual folders for each project in the book (e.g., WIP_01, WIP_02, etc.). When an exercise directs you to save a file, you should save it to the appropriate folder for the project on which you are working.

The exercises in this book frequently build upon work that you have already completed. At the end of each exercise, you will be directed to save your work and either close the file or continue to the next exercise. If you are directed to continue but your time is limited, you can stop at a logical point, save the file, and later return to the point at which you stopped. In this case, you will need to open the file from the appropriate WIP folder and continue working on the same file.

Typeface Conventions.   Computer programming code appears in a monospace font that **looks like this**. In many cases, you only need to change or enter specific pieces of code; in these instances, the code you need to type or change appears in a second color and `looks like this`.

Technical Note.   Microsoft currently plans various security upgrades to Windows and Internet Explorer to address security concerns in client-side scripting languages (including JavaScript), which it refers to as Active X Controls. Some of these upgrades can significantly interfere with legitimate scripting code. It may be necessary to adjust the security settings of your browser to complete the exercises presented in this book.

INSTRUCTOR'S RESOURCES

Instructor's Resource Center.   This DVD-ROM includes the entire Instructor's Manual for each application in Microsoft Word format. Student data files and completed solutions files are also on this DVD-ROM. The Instructor's Manual contains a reference guide of these files for the instructor's convenience. PowerPoint slides with more information about each project are also available for classroom use.

Companion Web site (www.prenhall.com/essentials).   Instructors will find all of the resources available on the Instructor's Resource CD-ROM available for download from the Companion Web site.

TestGen Software.   TestGen is a test generator program that lets you view and easily edit test bank questions, transfer them to tests, and print the tests in a variety of formats suitable to your teaching situation. The program also offers many options for organizing and displaying test banks and tests. A built-in random number and text generator makes it ideal for creating multiple versions of tests. Powerful search and sort functions let you easily locate questions and arrange them in the order you prefer.

QuizMaster, also included in this package, enables students to take tests created with TestGen on a local area network. The QuizMaster utility built into TestGen lets instructors view student records and print a variety of reports. Building tests is easy with TestGen, and exams can be easily uploaded into WebCT, Blackboard, and CourseCompass.

Prentice Hall has formed close alliances with each of the leading online platform providers: WebCT, Blackboard, and our own Pearson CourseCompass.

OneKey.   OneKey lets you in on the best teaching and learning resources all in one place. OneKey for *Essentials for Design*
is all your students need for out-of-class work, conveniently
organized by chapter to reinforce and apply what they've
learned in class and from the text. OneKey is also all you need to plan and administer your
course. All your instructor resources are in one place to maximize your effectiveness and
minimize your time and effort. OneKey for convenience, simplicity, and success.

WebCT and Blackboard.   Each of these custom-built distance-
learning courses features exercises, sample quizzes, and tests in
a course-management system that provides class-administra-
tion tools as well as the ability to customize this material at the
instructor's discretion.

CourseCompass.   CourseCompass is a dynamic, inter-
active online course management tool powered by
Blackboard. It lets professors create their own courses in 15 minutes or less with preloaded
quality content that can include quizzes, tests, lecture materials, and interactive exercises.

Performance-Based Training and Assessment: Train & Assess IT.
Prentice Hall offers performance-based training and assessment
in one product — Train & Assess IT.

The Training component offers computer-based instruction that a student can use to
preview, learn, and review graphic-design application skills. Delivered via Web or CD-
ROM, Train IT offers interactive multimedia and computer-based training to augment
classroom learning. Built-in prescriptive testing suggests a study path based not only on
student test results but also on the specific textbook chosen for the course.

The Assessment component offers computer-based testing that shares the same user interface as Train IT and is used to evaluate a student's knowledge about specific topics in
software, including Photoshop, InDesign, Illustrator, Flash, and Dreamweaver. It does
this in a task-oriented, performance-based environment to demonstrate students' profi-
ciency and comprehension of the topics. More extensive than the testing in Train IT,
Assess IT offers more administrative features for the instructor and additional questions
for the student. Assess IT also enables professors to test students out of a course, place students in appropriate courses, and evaluate skill sets.

INTRODUCTION

The incredible growth and widespread acceptance of the Internet often obscures the technology that lies behind all of the useful, entertaining, compelling, and (in some cases) disturbing Web pages. One fact, however, is certain: today's site visitor expects visual quality, navigational integrity, and — to an increasingly greater degree — interactivity.

The real world of designing, building, populating, publishing, and maintaining world-class Web sites is far more complex than most people might imagine. Rather than a single process, many smaller procedures and tasks form a workflow, which is usually divided between two distinct groups. The first group includes designers, copywriters, artists, illustrators, photographers, videographers, and other individuals responsible for the creative side of the equation. The other group is technical in nature — those who take care of the coding, testing, database setup, and ongoing site management. While there are certainly some individuals who can design compelling sites and write/test code, that group is relatively small. Generally, the creative side of the house determines how a site should look, and the technical side turns the design into a working reality — which is where JavaScript comes into play.

JavaScript is a universally accepted scripting language responsible for much of the active and interactive technology you encounter on the Web. Before you can use Macromedia Dreamweaver, Microsoft FrontPage, or Adobe GoLive to apply JavaScript code to a page design, you must understand the language itself. Familiarity with JavaScript is critical for those who need to exercise total control over the functionality of their sites.

As this is an advanced (Level 2) book, we assume you have mastered the concepts in *Essentials for Design: JavaScript Level 1*. If you have basic knowledge of both HTML and Web site construction, you will find the lessons in this book easy to follow and understand.

Despite widespread standardization of the JavaScript language, cross-platform incompatibilities remain. While writing completely compatible code that works correctly on every available browser is an admirable goal, it is currently impossible to attain. We worked diligently to provide code compliant across the widest possible selection of browsers, but some users will undoubtedly encounter compatibility problems. We apologize in advance for this inconvenience. To ensure the best results, we recommend you use Windows XP Professional and Internet Explorer 6.0, the platform we used when writing this book.

PROJECT 1

Using Arrays and Manipulating Strings

OBJECTIVES

In this project, you learn how to

- Use string methods
- Create and populate an array
- Sort an array
- Incorporate array methods
- Split and join strings
- Use multi-dimensional arrays

WHY WOULD I DO THIS?

Any object (such as a variable) that holds text is a ***string object***. You can manipulate string objects (or simply "strings") in a number of ways using string methods. ***String methods*** provide a number of useful functions. For example, you can convert text to all uppercase or all lowercase letters, search through text for a particular sequence of characters, or split a text string into multiple pieces of information (an array).

Arrays are variables that hold multiple items of data in numbered or named slots. Each slot or piece of information is referred to as an ***element*** of the array. When dealing with large amounts of data, arrays represent a more organized and convenient structure compared to simple variables. For example, you could create a Web page to hold tables of contents for various books. In the Web page, you could use a loop to output each section of each book, and then turn each section title into a hyperlink. In a situation such as this, variables would be a poor choice, since you need to work with each section of the tables of contents as a separate element. Since the number of sections will vary with each book displayed, an array is a much better choice because it allows the number of elements recorded to change.

Assume that you are displaying the table of contents for a book on the U.S. Civil War. The book currently has four sections: Introduction, Background, The Important Battles, and Conclusion. You could store the information in an array as follows:

```
var paperTOC=new Array();

paperTOC[0]="Introduction";

paperTOC[1]="Background";

paperTOC[2]="The Important Battles";

paperTOC[3]="Conclusion";
```

As you continue to add sections to the paper, the number of sections will continue to change. Using an array makes it easy to determine the number of sections. For example, you can access the number of elements in the array using the **length** property, which works for any array.

```
paperTOC.length;
```

A number of methods allow you to manipulate arrays in a variety of ways. Arrays are most often used as a convenient way to store and manipulate lists. For example, JavaScript uses arrays to keep track of HTML tags, including links and images. Using array methods, you can manipulate these objects in the same way as other arrays. For example, you could access properties of the first image shown in a Web page or delete the last hyperlink created on a Web page.

As you complete the lessons in this project, you learn how to create arrays, manipulate arrays, apply array methods, and add arrays to your JavaScript code. The ability to use arrays often makes it easier to integrate large chunks of data into Web pages in an orderly, easy-to-understand manner. You will master these techniques throughout this project.

V I S U A L   S U M M A R Y

 Think of variables as boxes that temporarily hold information. Using this analogy, you can think of an array as a stack of boxes (variables). Each box can hold a different item, but the items are probably related in some form or fashion. As an abstract example, assume you are working at a pizza parlor and your boss asks you to create and box four different pizzas, as represented in the following diagram.

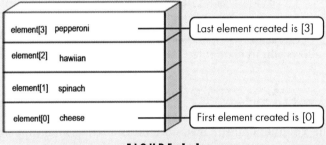

FIGURE 1.1

Each pizza box holds a different item. In programming terminology, the first element created (the cheese pizza) is referred to as **element[0]**. The last element created is **element[3]**, but this value will vary, depending on how many pizzas are waiting to be delivered. You could choose to manipulate the array in a number of ways by using various array methods:

- If you **pop** the array, you remove the last element — in this case, **element[3]**. The array length becomes shorter by one element, since only three pizzas would then be waiting for delivery.

- If you **push** the array, you add another element to the top of the stack. For example, an anchovy pizza may come out of the oven and become **element[4]**.

- You can **shift** the array by removing the item on the bottom of the stack. In this example, if you remove the cheese pizza, all the array elements are renumbered. The spinach pizza would become **element[0]**, and then every box would move down one space in the stack.

- You can **unshift** the stack by sliding in a pizza at the bottom of the stack. This new pizza would become **element[0]**, and then all the other pizzas would be renumbered to indicate that they were moved up in the stacking order.

- You can **reverse** the order of the array so that the first pizzas out of the oven are the first pizzas delivered. In this scenario, the cheese pizza would become **element[3]** and the pepperoni pizza would become **element[0]**.

Multi-dimensional arrays store an array as an element of another array. Think of a multi-dimensional array as boxes stored within a box.

LESSON 1 Using String Methods

In programming terms, a string is simply text. Strings are usually enclosed within quotes (single or double). In *Essentials for Design: JavaScript Level 1*, you worked with strings and string methods in a limited capacity in statements such as:

```
myVar-"Hi World!";

document.write(string.toUpperCase());
```

Any string in JavaScript is considered an object that can be manipulated with methods and properties. The string object in JavaScript allows you to manipulate strings for a variety of common purposes.

toUpperCase() and toLowerCase()

As you may remember, the **toUpperCase()** method returns a string in all uppercase letters. You probably already guessed that you can use the **toLowerCase()** method to return a text string in all lowercase letters.

```
name="ELLEN";

lowerName=name.toLowerCase();
```

charAt()

The **charAt()** method returns a single character from a specified position in a text string. The **charAt()** method takes a single argument, which is the position of the letter to be returned. The following statement assigns the third character from the variable named **invoiceNumber** into a new variable named **deptNumber**:

```
deptNumber=invoiceNumber.charAt(2);
```

Remember that JavaScript numbers letters in a text string beginning with position zero (0). In the string "**hat**," the letter in position **0** would be "**h**," the letter in position **1** would be "**a**," and position **2** would be "**t**."

indexOf()

The **indexOf()** method allows you to search through a string for a substring of characters. For instance, the following lines of code look for the phrase "**Axis of Evil**" in the variable named **articleTitle**.

```
articleTitle="Bush and the Axis of Evil: a New World View";

var phraseLocation=articleTitle.indexOf("Axis of Evil");

document.write("phrase found at location " + phraseLocation);
```

If the substring is found, this method returns the location of the substring. If the substring is not found, the method returns a value of negative one (**-1**). Using the above code in a simple script yields the following result.

FIGURE 1.2

lastIndexOf()

The **lastIndexOf()** method is virtually identical to the **indexOf()** method with one significant difference: it starts at the end of the string and searches backward for the specified substring. This point is important if the substring appears more than once in the specified text. The **indexOf()** method returns the first instance of the substring in the text, and **lastIndexOf()** returns the last instance of the substring in the text.

```
var phraseLocation=articleTitle.lastIndexOf("Axis of Evil");
```

Both the **indexOf()** method and the **lastIndexOf()** method return the location of a phrase or character in a string. The methods start at opposite ends of the specified string, but the location returned is always specified as the location starting from the beginning of the string, and both methods stop when they find the specified substring.

substring()

The **substring()** method extracts a substring from a larger string. To use this method, you must pass the beginning point of the substring to extract, or you must pass the beginning and ending points of the substring to extract. Assume you are creating a variable, as shown in the following line of code:

```
var bookTitle="All the Presidents Men";
```

You can use the **substring()** method to extract a new string from the original string, starting at the eighth position:

```
document.write(bookTitle.substring(7));
```

This statement outputs the text "**Presidents Men**." You can also extract all the text from position 8 to position 18 with the following statement:

```
document.write(bookTitle.substring(7,17));
```

This statement outputs the text "**Presidents**." You can assign the same text to a new variable:

```
var newString=bookTitle.substring(7,17);
```

Use the charAt() Method

1   **Copy the content of the RF_JavaScript_L2>Project_01 folder into the Work_In_Progress>WIP_01 folder.**

From now on, we refer to the RF_JavaScript_L2>Project_01 folder simply as the Project_01 folder, and we refer to the Work_In_Progress>WIP_01 folder simply as the WIP_01 folder.

2   **In your text editor, open charat.html from the WIP_01 folder.**

The file creates three variables using the following statements:

```
firstName="Kyle";

middleName="Alfred";

lastName="Tait";
```

3   **Create three more variables to hold the first initial of each variable by adding the following statements below the first three variables.**

```
...
firstName="Kyle";

middleName = "Alfred";

lastName = "Tait";


// **** insert code here ****
firstInitial=firstName.charAt(0);

middleInitial=middleName.charAt(0);

lastInitial=lastName.charAt(0);

</script>

</body>

...
```

To Extend Your Knowledge...

THE CONCAT() METHOD

The **concat()** method is a method that concatenates the contents of an array into a single text string.

4   **Add the following statement to output the results to the user.**

```
...
firstInitial=firstName.charAt(0);
middleInitial=middleName.charAt(0);
lastInitial=lastName.charAt(0);
document.write("Your initials are " + firstInitial + middleInitial +
lastInitial);
</script>
</body>
...
```

5   **Save your changes and open the document in your Web browser.**

FIGURE 1.3

6   **Close the file in your Web browser and text editor.**

LESSON 2 Creating and Populating Arrays

An array is similar to a variable because it serves as a temporary storage space for information. Simply stated, an array is a variable that can hold multiple values. You already know that JavaScript creates arrays for various objects. For instance, the **window** array represents all instances of the **window** object. If you want to send text to the second **window** object created, you could write a statement such as:

```
window[1].document.write("some text");
```

When creating arrays for internal use, JavaScript always starts with **[0]** as the first entry in the array. Each entry is represented by a number called an **index** that is always placed within brackets. JavaScript also allows you to create your own arrays, which is similar to creating variables. Using pseudo-code, you can create a blank array by writing the following statement:

```
arrayName=new Array(number of elements);
```

Arrays are useful when you want to store a large number of items in a simple, easy-to-find location, such as a grocery list, a list of email addresses, or a list of available item numbers.

array() Constructor Method

In *Essentials for Design: JavaScript Level 1*, you considered the **array()** constructor method — the method that creates a new **array()** object. If you specify no parameters, this method simply creates an empty **array()** object. It is not necessary to specify the length of the array, which is advantageous, since you may not be able to accurately predict the size you need. You can create an array with no specified length by including no parameters in the new array statement:

```
groceryList=new Array();
```

When you specify the length, the method creates a new **array()** object with the specified number of elements:

```
groceryList=new Array(10);
```

You can also insert values into elements when you create the **array()** object, as shown in the following statement:

```
groceryList=new Array("milk","butter","soy beans");
```

Arrays can consist of text or numbers (with or without decimal places). An array entry can also consist of a Boolean (**true** or **false**) value. Since JavaScript is designed to allow flexibility when using data, you can mix multiple types of data within the same array. In other words, within the same array, one element can be text and another can be a number.

An array is considered an object in JavaScript. Similar to other objects, arrays have properties, such as length. Arrays also have methods that allow you to easily manipulate the array in a number of ways, including adding data to an array. The process of inserting data into an array is known as ***populating*** an array.

Using Numbered Array Elements

Assuming you want to fill an array with values, you could enter statements such as:

```
groceryList[0]="milk";

groceryList[1]="butter";

groceryList[2]="soy beans";

groceryList[3]="tofu";

groceryList[4]="chicken feet";
```

Similar to a variable, you can change a list item at any time by assigning a new value:

```
groceryList[2]="ice cream";
```

You can also output the data within an array element with a simple statement such as:

```
document.write(groceryList[1]);
```

The **length** property allows you to identify the number of elements within an array. For instance, the following statement returns the number "**5**" because there are five elements within the **groceryList** array.

```
document.write(groceryList.length);
```

Up to this point, you have assigned text strings to array elements. It is a simple matter to place a number into an array element by writing a statement such as:

```
testScore[1]=96;
```

You can also enter several values when you create a new array:

```
var testScores=new Array(89,63,99,78,45);
```

Even if you don't specify the location of each element, the first element will be placed in location **[0]**, the second element in location **[1]**, and so forth. This method simply represents a shorter way to enter data into the array.

Applying Named Array Elements

Rather than index array elements using numbers, you can name array elements. For instance:

```
groceryList["meat"]="beef";
groceryList["items"]=10;
groceryList["vegetable"]="carrots";
```

You could output the information in one of the fields by writing a statement such as:

```
document.write(groceryList["meat"]);
```

In general, people can remember names easier than numbers, but naming array elements can be disadvantageous. For instance, you may want to design a loop to print every element in the array. Using named elements makes this task more difficult.

Most programmers typically prefer to work with numbered elements instead of named elements. It is also common for programmers to set aside one numbered element for the element name and one numbered element for the value.

Create and Use a Simple Array

1 In your text editor, open simplearray.html from your WIP_01 folder.

2 Find the comment that says `// **** insert code here ****`.

3 Create a new array by inserting the following statement.

```
...
<body>
<script language="JavaScript">
// **** insert code here ****
var testScores=new Array();
</script>
</body>
...
```

4 Assign numbers to various array elements with the following assignment statements.

```
...
<body>
<script language="JavaScript">
// **** insert code here ****
var testScores=new Array();
testScores[0]=56;
testScores[1]=88;
testScores[2]=100;
</script>
</body>
...
```

5   Add the following code to output the values of the array elements.

```
...
testScores[0]=56;
testScores[1]=88;
testScores[2]=100;
document.write("Test score one is "+testScores[0]+"<br>");
document.write("Test score two is "+testScores[1]+"<br>");
document.write("Test score three is "+testScores[2]+"<br>");
</script>
</body>
...
```

6   Save the file in your text editor and open it in your browser.

FIGURE 1.4

7   Delete the following lines of code from your script.

```
testScores[0]=56;
testScores[1]=88;
testScores[2]=100;
```

In the next step, you assign the values in a different way.

To Extend Your Knowledge...

ARRAY SUPPORT IN BROWSERS

Arrays were not supported in JavaScript 1.0 and may not work in older browsers (such as version 2 of Netscape or version 3 of Internet Explorer).

8   **Find the line of code that creates the array and change it to the following.**

```
...
<body>
<script language="JavaScript">
// **** insert code here ****
var testScores=new Array(56,88,100);
document.write("Test score one is "+testScores[0]+"<br>");
document.write("Test score two is "+testScores[1]+"<br>");
document.write("Test score three is "+testScores[2]+"<br>");
...
```

9   **Save your changes and refresh your browser. The results should be the same as before.**

10   **Close the file in your text editor and browser.**

LESSON 3   Sorting Arrays

The **sort()** method allows you to sort the content of an **array()** object using whatever sorting process you choose. Even though the **sort()** method is generally more complex than the other methods described (it requires some knowledge of JavaScript functions and conditional statements), using the **sort()** method can be quite simple. For example, assume you create and populate an array with the following lines of code:

```
var myArray=new Array();
myArray[0]=68;
myArray[1]=77;
myArray[2]=94;
myArray[3]=12;
myArray[4]=32;
```

You can quickly sort the array elements from lowest to highest number by writing the following statement:

```
myArray.sort();
```

If the array consisted of text strings, this statement would also sort the elements into alphabetical order. The **sort()** method compares each item in the list to the next item in the list. If the items are out of order, the method swaps their positions in the array. The process continues until each item is in the correct position.

The most interesting feature of the **sort()** method is that it allows the developer to modify the sorting process, which allows various types of sorts to be written. To modify the sorting process, a developer must specify the sorting function in the **sort()** method. For example, consider the following line of code:

```
myArray.sort(arranger);
```

In this line of code, a function named **arranger** specifies how to sort the items. To arrange the items in smallest-to-largest order (or in alphabetical order), you can use the following function:

```
function arranger(item1, item2) {
        var result = 0;
        if (item1 > item2) {
                result = true;
        }
        if (item1 < item2) {
                result = false;
        }
        if (item1 == item2) {
                result = false;
        }
    return result;
        }
```

This code reveals how the **sort()** method works when used in a default fashion. Specifically:

- Two elements are compared each time.
- If the items should be switched, **true** should be returned from the function.
- If the items should not be switched, **false** should be returned from the function.

By changing the conditional statements in the sorting function, you can specify other methods for sorting the data. For example, you could easily create a function that sorts the data from highest to lowest values or reverse alphabetical order.

Sort Array Elements in Numeric Order

1 **In your text editor, open arraysortnumbers.html from your WIP_01 folder and examine the source code.**

This file creates a simple array (named **testScores**) and enters data into the array to represent five test scores.

2 **Open the file in your browser.**

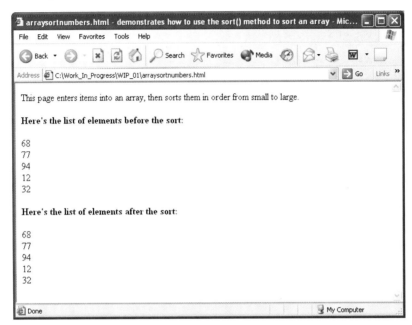

FIGURE 1.5

The step for sorting the arrays has not yet been inserted, so the array does not change through the course of the script.

3 **Find the following lines of code in the document.**

```
<title>arraysortnumbers.html - demonstrates how to use the sort()
method to sort an array</title>

<script language="JavaScript">

</script>
```

This script creates the function to sort the array.

4   **Insert the following code.**

```
...

<head>

<title>arraysortnumbers.html - demonstrates how to use the sort()
method to sort an array</title>

<script language="JavaScript">

// the function is used to set up the sorting criteria

// this one is designed to sort the elements in number order

// it would work whether the elements are numbers or text

function arranger(item1, item2) {

        var result = false;

        if (item1 > item2) {

                result = true;

        }

        if (item1 < item2) {

                result = -1;

        }

        if (item1 == item2) {

                result = false;

        }

        return result;

}

</script>

</head>

<body>

...
```

This function sorts the elements.

5   Insert the following code to sort the array.

```
...
document.write(testScores[4]);

document.write("<br>");

// insert code to sort the array elements

testScores.sort( arranger);

// output the list elements after the sort

document.write("<p><strong>Here's the list of elements after the
sort:</strong></p>");

//now we'll output the array elements after the sort

...
```

6   Save the file in your text editor and refresh the file in your browser.

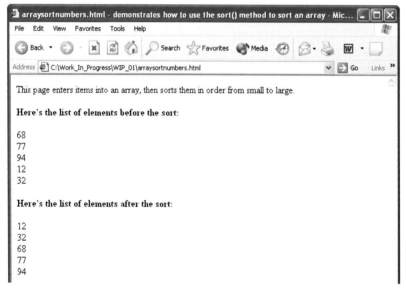

FIGURE 1.6

7   Close the file in your text editor and browser.

To Extend Your Knowledge...

SORTING AND OLDER BROWSERS

Early browser versions may not allow the **sort()** method or may require a sorting function to be present for the sort to work properly. IE versions 4 and higher should not have difficulty using the **sort()** method without specifying a sorting function.

LESSON 4 Incorporating Array Methods

Array methods allow you to manipulate the **array()** object in a variety of ways. Various array methods allow you to remove items from the beginning, middle, or end of an array. They also allow you to insert new elements into an array. Advanced methods allow complex manipulation, such as the ability to combine multiple arrays into a single array. In this lesson, you consider many basic methods for manipulating arrays.

pop()

The **pop()** method returns the last element from an array. The **pop()** method also removes the last element from an array. As an analogy, think about a stack of papers on your desk. If your manager demands that you complete the entire stack before leaving the office, you might take the top sheet of paper from the stack and complete it, complete the next piece of paper in the stack, and continue until you reach the last piece of paper in the stack. Assuming the sheet on the bottom of the stack is the first sheet, you might refer to it as **paper[0]**. If the top sheet is the 100th sheet of paper, you might refer to it as **paper[99]**. Every time you "pop" the stack, you remove the last (top) piece of paper from the stack.

For instance, to place the value of the last item from your **groceryList** array into a variable named **lastItem**, you would write the following statement:

```
var lastItem=groceryList.pop();
```

push()

The **push()** method adds an element to the end of an array. The following statement creates a new element at the end the **groceryList** array and places the text "**pork chops**" as the value of the new element:

```
groceryList.push("pork chops");
```

reverse()

The **reverse()** method reverses the order of the elements in an **array()** object. To reverse the order of the **groceryList** array, you would write the following statement:

```
groceryList.reverse();
```

shift()

The **shift()** method is similar to the **push()** method, but it removes an item from the beginning of the array instead of from the end. If you again consider the analogy of a stack of papers, the **shift()** method takes the paper from the bottom of the stack. The paper removed by the **shift()** method always **item[0]**, and the other elements move up by one position in the array.

The following statement removes **groceryList[0]** from the stack:

```
groceryList.shift();
```

The item referred to as **groceryList[1]** would then become **groceryList[0]**. The item referred to as **groceryList[2]** would become **groceryList[1]**, and so forth.

unShift()

The **unShift()** method adds a new element to the start of the array and moves other elements up by one position, which increases the length of the array by one. The following statement enters the string "**milk**" as the value of the first element. In addition, the prior first element becomes the second element, and so forth.

```
groceryList.unshift("milk");
```

Reverse the Order of Array Elements

1 In your browser, open reverse.html from your WIP_01 folder.

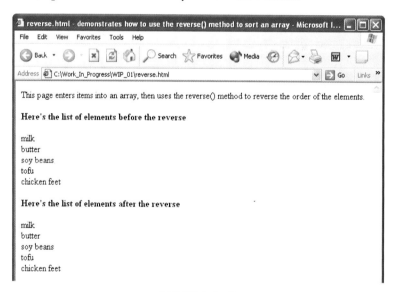

FIGURE 1.7

This file creates a simple array with five elements, reverses the array elements, and then outputs the results. In this exercise, you create the code to reverse the array.

2   Open the file in your text editor. Insert the following line of code.

```
...

document.write(groceryList[4]);

document.write("<br>"); //add a new line

// and now we reverse the order of the elements

groceryList.reverse();

document.write("<p><strong>Here's the list of elements after the
reverse</strong></p>");

//now we'll output the array elements after the sort

...
```

3   Save your changes and refresh the file in your browser.

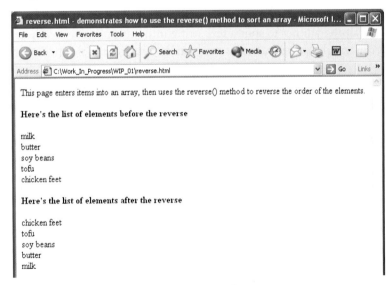

FIGURE 1.8

The order of the array elements is reversed.

4   Close the file in your browser and text editor.

To Extend Your Knowledge...

ARRAY METHODS

The Macintosh version of Internet Explorer 5 doesn't support **pop()** or several other methods of manipulating arrays, including **push()**, **shift()**, **splice()**, and **unShift()**.

LESSON 5 | Splitting and Joining Strings

When storing data, a ***delimiter*** is a character or sequence of characters marking the beginning or end of a unit of data. For example, early databases used text files to store information, and added commas, spaces, or tab characters to separate the data. Consider the following line of text, which could represent a comma-delimited database of student names:

```
Joe, Sue, Bill, Brian
```

When the data is read by a computer program, it is often assigned to a text variable, such as in the following statement:

```
myData="Joe, Sue, Bill, Brian";
```

split()

To make this information useful, it is often necessary to extract individual pieces of data. The **split()** method splits a string into an array — allowing easy manipulation of individual pieces of data. Simply stated, the **split()** method allows a programmer to split a text string into multiple pieces. The programmer must specify a delimiter to split the text. In this case, a new array can be created to hold the information extracted from the text string.

```
myStudents=myData.split(",");
```

After this information is extracted, it can be manipulated in the same way as any other array. For example, you could write the following line of code to determine the number of students:

```
numberStudents=myStudents.length;
```

join()

The **join()** method combines individual text elements in an array into one string. For instance, to create an array and insert all of the array elements into a single text string, you would write:

```
var  wordsArray=new Array("This","is","a","brave","new","world");
var sentence=wordsArray.join(" ");
```

The **join()** method can take a single parameter (the delimiter), which you can place between each element inserted into the string. In the example shown above, you are inserting a single space between each array element. You can output the new string as a sentence by writing the following simple statement:

```
document.write(sentence + ".");
```

Inserting these commands into a script in an HTML page yields the following result.

FIGURE 1.9

Split a Text String into an Array

1   **In your text editor, open split.html from your WIP_01 folder.**

```
split.html - Notepad
File  Edit  Format  View  Help
<html>
<head>
<title>split.html - demonstrates the split() method to manipulate a text
string</title>
</head>
<body>
<script language = "JavaScript">
//this script demonstrates the split() method which is used to split a text string
into an array

//the split() method requires you to specify a character that separates the
information
in the string
//our string uses commas as the delimiter

//output the contents of the array
document.write(glArray[0]+"<br>");
document.write(glArray[1]+"<br>");
document.write(glArray[2]+"<br>");
document.write(glArray[3]+"<br>");
</script>
</body>
</html>
```

FIGURE 1.10

2   **Insert the following line of code.**

```
...

<body>

<script language = "JavaScript">

//this script demonstrates the split() method which is used to split
a text string into an array

groceryList = "milk,bread,bananas,ketchup";

//the split() method requires you to specify a character that
separates the information in the string

//our string uses commas as the delimiter
```

3   Insert the following line of code.

```
...
groceryList = "milk,bread,bananas,ketchup";

//the split() method requires you to specify a character that
separates the information in the string
//our string uses commas as the delimiter
var glArray=groceryList.split(",");
//output the contents of the array
...
```

This code splits the contents of the **groceryList** variable into the **glArray**.

4   Save your changes and open the file in your browser.

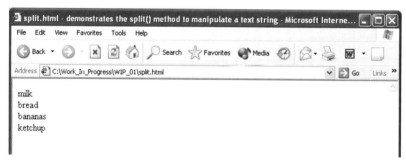

FIGURE 1.11

The script outputs each element in the array.

5   Close the file in your browser and text editor.

To Extend Your Knowledge...

ARRAY TERMINOLOGY

In many computer science applications, an array is often referred to as a "stack" or a "queue." In many computer programs, the term **stack** often refers to a section of memory where the most recently stored item is the first to be retrieved. This is known as a Last In, First Out (LIFO) method of storing and retrieving data.

The term **queue** refers to an array where the first item to be retrieved is the one stored earliest. This is known as a First In, First Out (FIFO) method of storing and retrieving data. Think of a stack as parts waiting to be assembled where the next part needed is always on top. Think of a queue as a "To Do" list where the next item to be completed is the oldest item on the list.

LESSON 6 Using a Multi-Dimensional Array

In general terms, a multi-dimensional array is an array stored within an array. Multi-dimensional arrays are useful when you have large chunks of data that need to be divided into subcategories. For example, imagine that you need to record information about the inventory of the electronics section of a retail store:

```
var electronicsArray=new Array();

electronicsArray[0]="DVD Players";

electronicsArray[1]="TVs";

electronicsArray[2]="Stereos";
```

Now consider that you also need to create arrays for each section of the store (not just electronics) and that many sections exist, including gifts and books. The store organizes the products by section. You can use an array to keep track of the sections:

```
var sectionArray=new Array();
```

In addition, you can place the array for each section into the section array:

```
sectionArray[0]=electronicsArray;
```

Now imagine that you want to output the second element of the first section:

```
document.write(sectionArray[0][1]);
```

Adding this code to a script in an HTML document yields the following result.

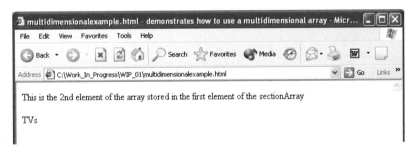

FIGURE 1.12

You can actually store an array within an array, and then call upon individual elements. Multi-dimensional arrays often seem overwhelming to new programmers, but they are reasonably easy to incorporate and use.

Use a Multi-Dimensional Array

In this exercise, you create a list of information within a larger list of information. Specifically, you create a list of student grades that will be stored as an array element of an array designed to store student information.

1   **In your text editor, open multidimensional.html from your WIP_01 folder.**

2   **Find the following lines of code.**

```
//create an array to hold student information
var studentArray=new Array();
studentArray[0]="Aaron";
```

This code creates an array to hold student information and assigns the name "**Aaron**" to the first array element.

3   **Insert the following line of code.**

```
...
//create an array to hold student information
var studentArray=new Array();
studentArray[0]="Aaron";
var gradeArray=new Array(99,88,77);
document.write("The first student is "+studentArray[0]+"<br>");
document.write("His (or her) first grade is ");
...
```

This code creates an array to hold the students' test scores.

4   **Insert the following line of code.**

```
...
studentArray[0]="Aaron";
var gradeArray=new Array(99,88,77);
studentArray[1]=gradeArray;
document.write("The first student is "+studentArray[0]+"<br>");
document.write("His (or her) first grade is ");
...
```

The array to store students' grades (**gradeArray**) is stored as the second element of the array that holds all the students' information (**studentArray**).

5   **Insert the following line of code.**

```
...
studentArray[1]=gradeArray;
document.write("The first student is "+studentArray[0]+"<br>");
document.write("His (or her) first grade is ");
document.write(studentArray[1][0]);
</script>
</body>
</html>
```

This code outputs the first student's first test grade.

6   **Save your changes and open the file in your browser.**

FIGURE 1.13

7   **Close the file in your browser and text editor.**

To Extend Your Knowledge...

BOOLEAN VALUES AS NUMBERS

Many methods, such as **indexOf()** and **lastIndexOf()**, may return "**-1**" to indicate a search string was not found. Other methods, such as **sort()**, return "**0**" or "**-1**" to indicate that two values do not need to be sorted. In JavaScript, as well as many other scripting languages, any number below **1** (such as **0** or **-1**) can be used interchangeably with the keyword **false**. Any positive integer can be used interchangeably with the keyword **true**.

SUMMARY

In this project, you learned how to use various string methods. Whenever text is used or stored in JavaScript, the text is considered a string object. JavaScript offers a variety of methods for the string object that allow you to manipulate text in various ways. For example, you can search through a text string for specific information, such as a name.

You also discovered how to use arrays as temporary storage spaces for information. The information can take a variety of forms, including text, Boolean values, or numbers. Arrays offer a simple way to store large or varying amounts of information. Array methods offer simple ways to manipulate information stored in arrays, such as allowing you to remove the first item from the array or the last item from the array and shift the remaining elements.

KEY TERMS

Array	Multi-dimensional array	Stack
Delimiter	Pop	String method
Element	Populating	String object
FIFO	Push	Queue
Index	Reverse	Unshift
LIFO	Shift	

CHECKING CONCEPTS AND TERMS

MULTIPLE CHOICE

Circle the letter that matches the correct answer for each of the following questions.

1. In the statement `var myAr=newArray(30)`, what does the number "30" represent?
   a. The value assigned to the first element in the array
   b. The number of elements to be used in the array
   c. The number of dimensions created in a multi-dimensional array
   d. All of the above
   e. None of the above

2. If you use the `indexOf()` method to search for a text string that is not found, what value will the method return?
   a. 0
   b. -1
   c. undefined
   d. code 3

3. If you use the **lastIndexOf()** method to search for a text string that is not found, what value will the method return?

  a. 0

  b. -1

  c. undefined

  d. code 3

4. When you use the **lastIndexOf()** method to search a text string, the method begins searching the string from the _____ of the text.

  a. beginning

  b. end

  c. middle

  d. None of the above

  e. All of the above

5. What characters are often used for delimiters in simple databases?

  a. Commas

  b. Spaces

  c. Tabs

  d. All of the above

  e. None of the above

6. When you "pop" an array, which element/s is/are deleted?

  a. The last element added to the array

  b. The first element created in the array

  c. Every element in the array

  d. None of the above

  e. All of the above

7. When you "shift" an array, which element/s is/are deleted?

  a. The last element added to the array

  b. The first element created in the array

  c. Every element in the array

  d. None of the above

  e. All of the above

8. Which of the following statements is/are true when creating an array?

  a. The length of the array must be specified

  b. The length of the array can be specified

  c. The length of the array does not have to be specified

  d. b and c

9. Can the **sort()** method be used without specifying a function name, such as **myArray.sort()**?

  a. Yes, and items will sort from lowest to highest order

  b. Yes, and items will sort from highest to lowest order

  c. No, the items will not sort

  d. None of the above

10. Why is it useful to specify a sorting function, such as **myArray.sort(arranger)**, when sorting an array?

  a. This is required to sort an array on newer browsers.

  b. You can customize the way array elements are sorted.

  c. Neither of the above

  d. Both a and b

DISCUSSION QUESTIONS

1. Why are arrays useful? When would it be more practical to use an array instead of several variables?

2. If a stack of papers on a desk represents an array of information, how would various array methods, such as **shift()**, **pop()**, **push()**, and **unshift()**, change the stack?

3. JavaScript uses arrays to record information about HTML tags. For example, **<a>** tags are recorded as elements of the **links** array. Without writing a script to test your ideas, how do you think you could use an array method such as **reverse()** to manipulate the **links** or **images** arrays?

4. When would it make sense to use a multi-dimensional array?

SKILL DRILL

Skill Drill exercises reinforce project skills. Each skill reinforced is the same, or nearly the same, as a skill presented in the project. Detailed instructions are provided in a step-by-step format. You should work through these exercises in order.

1. Use lastIndexOf()

In the first Skill Drill, you use the **lastIndexOf()** method. This tool allows you to search a text string, starting from the last character in the string. In this exercise, you practice using string methods to search for particular items in string objects. The exercise shows the differences between the **indexOf()** method and the **lastIndexOf()** method.

1. In your text editor, open skilllastindexof.html from your WIP_01 folder.

2. Find the following lines of code in the source code of the document.

```
articleTitle = "Bush and the Axis of Evil: a New World View";

var phraseLocation = articleTitle.indexOf("Axis of Evil");

document.write("phrase found at location " + phraseLocation);
```

The **indexOf()** method is used to find the phrase "**Axis of Evil**" in the larger text string.

3. Open the file in your browser and examine the result.

FIGURE 1.14

The phrase is found at location 13, which represents the fourteenth character in the complete string.

4. Return to your text editor and replace the **indexOf()** method with the **lastIndexOf()** method.

5. Change the **articleTitle** to make it equal to "**Bush and the Axis of Evil: Does the Axis of Evil Really Exist?**"

6. Save the file in your text editor and refresh your browser.

    Note the output. Is the result the same as before? Is the position of the string noted from the beginning or end of the text?

7. Close the file in your text editor and browser.

2. Populate an Array

In this exercise, you practice the most basic aspect of using an array. First, you create the array using the **new Array()** constructor function; then, you populate the array elements with information.

1. In your text editor, open skillsortnumbers.html from your WIP_01 folder.

2. Find the following line of code.

    ```
    //create the Array called testScores
    ```

3. Insert the following line of code to create an array named **testScores** using the **array()** constructor method.

    ```
    ...
    <p><strong>Here's the list of elements before the sort:</strong></p>
    <script language="JavaScript">
    //create the Array called testScores
    var testScores=new Array();
    //we'll output the list elements before the sort
    document.write(testScores[0]);
    document.write("<br>"); //add a new line
    ```

4. Modify the line of code you inserted in Step 3 as follows.

```
var testScores=new Array(68,77);
```

This statement populates **element[0]** as **68** and **element[1]** as **77**.

5. Modify the line of code you manipulated in Step 4 to insert **94** into **element[2]**, **12** into **element[3]**, and **32** into **element[4]**.

6. Save the file in your text editor and open the file in your browser.

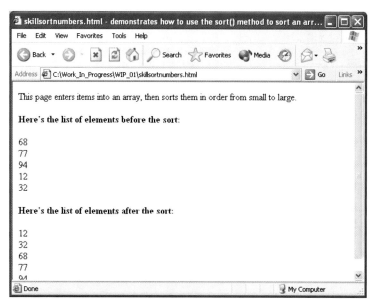

FIGURE 1.15

Your file should match the screen shot shown above.

7. Keep the file open in your text editor and browser for the next exercise.

3. Sort an Array from Highest to Lowest Values

In this exercise, you create a custom sorting function. To do so, you start with a sorting function that sorts items from lowest to highest, and then you modify the function to sort elements from highest to lowest.

1. In the open skillsortnumbers.html in your browser, examine the output of the page. The page sorts numbers from lowest to highest.

2. In your text editor, find the following code (it comprises the **arranger** function).

```
function arranger(item1, item2) {
        var result = 0;
        if (item1 > item2) {
                result = 1;
        }
        if (item1 < item2) {
                result = -1;
        }
        if (item1 == item2) {
                result = 0;
        }
        return result;
}
```

3. Find the following **if** statement.

```
if (item1 > item2) {
                result = 1;
}
```

This **if** statement returns the number **1** if the two array entries should be switched.

4. Change the **if** statement you found in the previous step to set the result to the number **1** if the first item is less than the second item, instead of setting the result to **1** if **item1** is greater than **item2**.

5. Find the following **if** statement.

```
if (item1 < item2) {
                result = -1;
}
```

This statement returns **-1** if the two array elements do not need to be switched.

6. Change the **if** statement you found in Step 5 to return **-1** if **item1** is greater than **item2**.

7. Save the file in your text editor and refresh the file in your browser.

   The numbers should now be sorted in order from highest to lowest.

8. Close the file in your browser and text editor.

4. Use shift()

In this exercise, you use the **shift()** method. When working with arrays, this method is useful for removing items from the bottom of the stack. In other words, this method allows you to delete the content of **element[0]** and move other items down the stack.

1. In your browser, open skillshift.html from your WIP_01 folder.

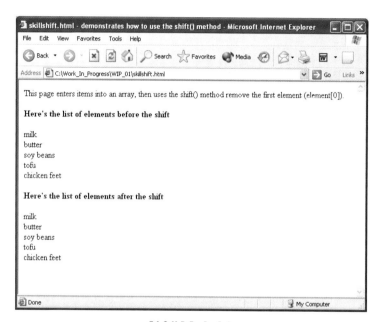

FIGURE 1.16

2. Open the file in your text editor. Find the following line of code.

```
// and now we shift the elements
```

3. Insert the following line of code to shift the array elements.

```
...
document.write(groceryList[4]);

document.write("<br>");

// and now we shift the elements

groceryList.shift();

document.write("<p><strong>Here's the list of elements after the
shift</strong></p>");

//now we'll output the array elements after the sort

document.write(groceryList[0]);

...
```

4. Scroll to the bottom of the source code and insert the following comment directly before the **</body>** tag.

```
...

document.write(groceryList[4]);

document.write("<br>");

</script>

<p>Since the first element is deleted and the others shifted, the
last element will be reported as undefined</p>

</body>

</html>
```

5. Save your changes and refresh your browser.

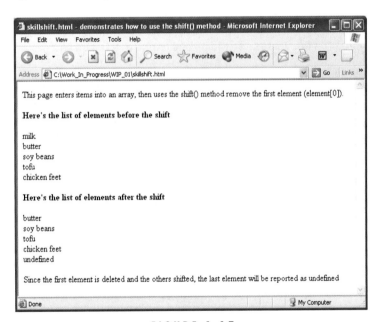

FIGURE 1.17

The **shift()** method removes the first element of the array. For this reason, **element[4]** is now undefined.

6. Close the file in your browser and text editor.

CHALLENGE

Challenge exercises expand on, or are somewhat related to, skills presented in the lessons. Each exercise provides a brief introduction, followed by instructions presented in a numbered-step format that are not as detailed as those in the Skill Drill exercises. You should work through these exercises in order.

1. Populate and Combine a List of Items

In this exercise, you create an array to hold various words. First, you populate the array to store various words in the array elements. Then, you join the array elements to create a sentence.

1. In your text editor, open challengelist.html from the WIP_01 folder.

2. Insert the following code.

```
...
<script language="JavaScript">
//the next few lines put in the Array elements
var words1=new Array();
words1[0]="See ";
words1[1]="Spot ";
words1[2]="Run";
var sentence1=words1.join(" ");
//now we'll output the array elements as a sentence
document.write(sentence1 + ".");
</script>
...
```

3. Save your changes and open the file in your browser.

FIGURE 1.18

4. Return to your text editor.

5. Insert three more array elements to add the words "to the store" to the sentence created by the array elements.

6. Save your changes and refresh your browser.

7. Close the file in your browser and text editor.

2. Sort Array Elements in Alphabetical Order

Assume you were asked to design a Web page to output class schedules of various students. You need to create custom sort functions to sort text strings stored in an array. To do so, use the **sort()** method to sort the array, and then modify sorting functions to change the sorting method.

1. In your text editor and browser, open skillsortstrings.html from your WIP_01 folder.

    This file stores a list of five classes in an array and outputs the list before and after a search. The code required to sort the array is incomplete.

2. Find the following line of code.

    ```
    // insert code to sort the array elements
    ```

3. After that line of code, insert the following statement to sort the array.

    ```
    myList.sort();
    ```

4. Save and test your file.

    The list should now be sorted in alphabetical order. Some browsers may require a sorting function to be specified to work correctly. You will specify a sorting function in the next step.

5. Return to your code and change the sorting method to use the **arranger** function defined in the **<head>** section of your document.

6. Change the **arranger** function to sort the elements in reverse alphabetical order.

    Hint: it is the same modification that sorts numbers in reverse order.

7. Save and test your file.

8. Close the file in your browser and text editor.

3. Search for Strings

Both the **indexOf()** and **lastIndexOf()** methods allow you to find specific characters in a larger string. These methods are often used to find where specific words start and end in a text string. In this exercise, you use the methods to detect the spaces between words in a string.

1. In your browser and text editor, open challengestrings.html from your WIP_01 folder.

   This file generates a prompt box that asks for a user's first and last names.

2. Insert the following code.

```
...
<script language = "JavaScript">
//this script demonstrates the substring() method that is used to
get the character location of a specified substring
var fullName=prompt("Enter your first and last name.");
firstSpacePosition=fullName.indexOf(" ");
document.write(firstSpacePosition);
</script>
</body>
</html>
```

3. Save your changes and refresh your browser.

4. Enter your first and last names.

   The browser should return the position of the first space found in the string.

5. Modify the prompt to ask for the first, middle, and last names of the user.

6. Create a variable named **lastSpacePosition** that will find the position of the last space within the document.

   Hint: use the **lastIndexOf()** method and the code you entered in Step 2 to figure out the proper line of code.

7. Remove the **document.write()** statement that you created in Step 2.

8. Create a **document.write()** statement to output the position of the last space in the document.

9. Save and test your file.

10. Keep the file open in your browser and text editor for the next exercise.

4. Extract Text from within Strings

In the previous Challenge, you used various methods to detect the positions of the first and last spaces in a text string. In this exercise, you use this information to extract the individual words from the information entered.

1. In the open challengestrings.html, remove any **document.write()** statements from your document.

2. Insert the following lines of code.

```
...
var fullName=prompt("Enter your first and last name.");

firstSpacePosition=fullName.indexOf(" ");

lastSpacePosition=fullName.lastIndexOf(" ");

firstName=fullName.substring(0,firstSpacePosition);

document.write("Your first name is "+firstName+"<br>");

</script>

</body>

</html>
```

3. Save your changes and refresh your browser.

4. Enter your first, middle, and last names into the prompt box, and then click OK.

   Your first name should be extracted.

5. Insert the following line of code.

```
...
lastSpacePosition=fullName.lastIndexOf(" ");

firstName=fullName.substring(0,firstSpacePosition);

document.write("Your first name is "+firstName+"<br>");

lastPosition=fullName.length;

</script>

</body>

</html>
```

6. After the line of code you created in the Step 5, create a variable named **lastName**. Assign the results of a substring search that extracts every character from **lastSpacePosition** and **lastPosition**.

7. Create a **document.write()** statement that outputs the **lastName** variable to the user.

8. Save and test your file.

   Your file should output the first and last names to the user.

9. Create a variable named **middleName** to hold the middle name entered into the string.

   Hint: it is the substring found between the first space and last space.

10. Output the **middleName** variable to the user.

11. Close the file in your browser and text editor.

5. Split Tab-Delimited Text

Many simple databases use text files to store data. The files are usually written with spaces, tabs, or commas separating each item of data. This technique works well for simple databases. When computer programs read these files, the language often reads one line at a time and splits the data into components that it can manipulate. In this exercise, you create a simple program to read financial transactions that have been delimited with tabs.

1. In your text editor, open challengesplit.html from your WIP_01 folder.

2. Find the following line of code.

   ```
   transactions = "$47.99    $58.22    $64.04    $99.98";
   ```

   This code creates a variable that uses tab characters to seperate transactions. Tab characters are often used to delimit pieces of information.

3. Find the following line of code.

   ```
   //our string uses tabs as the delimiter
   ```

4. Create an array named **transArray** and assign the tab-delimited content of the **transactions** variable.

   Hint: use the **split()** method.

5. Save your changes and open the file in your browser.

   Your file should output the information as shown below.

FIGURE 1.19

6. Close the file in your browser and text editor.

P O R T F O L I O   B U I L D E R

Create a Navigation Array

When you browse the Web, you may be using arrays without even realizing it. Arrays can be extremely useful in the creation and execution of a successful Web site. For example, consider that most Web sites use a navigation structure with a sequence of links. The links are essentially the same on every page. If you add a link, you must do so on every page of the site. This can become tedious, and it is difficult to ensure that the navigation structure is exactly the same on every page. In this exercise, you use an array to control the navigation structure of an entire Web site. To complete this Portfolio Builder, follow these steps:

■ Open navigation_array.html from the RF_JavaScript_L2>Project_01>Portfolio_Builder_01 folder in your browser. On the left side of the browser window is a navigation area. Currently, there are no links. (The links are generated by the **generateNav** function in the included JavaScript file.)

■ Open the included JavaScript file named generateNav.js and look for the following lines of code. In the code, an array is created for you.

```
// create a new array for navigation links

// new array creates navigation labels

linkText = new Array("home","products","services",
"locations","about us", "contact");
```

P O R T F O L I O   B U I L D E R

Create a Navigation Array (continued)

■ Create a variable named **linkURL**, and then set it equal to a new array. The new array will pass the link values to the browser.

■ Associate these links with their respective labels, as shown below:

home = index.html	products = products.html
services = services.html	locations = locations.html
about us = about_us.html	contact = contact.html

■ When creating the new array, enter the values for the page links in the same order that the labels are created within the **linkText** array.

■ After you create the new array, test the page in your browser. Click every link to ensure that they all work correctly. Notice that the navigation appears with the additional array. In order to function, **generateNav** needs both values for the hyperlink — **linkText** and the visible **linkLabel** text. With the values available, the script executes, and the navigation array writes to the page.

Using Dates, Times, and Numbers

O B J E C T I V E S

In this project, you learn how to

- Use operators and precedence
- Use Math object methods
- Generate random numbers

- Incorporate math properties
- Get and set time units
- Create timers

WHY WOULD I DO THIS?

JavaScript has many built-in objects and methods that allow you to work with dates, times, numbers, and timers. Understanding how to manipulate dates, times, and numbers is essential for writing many JavaScript programs. Many objects, methods, and properties are designed to facilitate the use of complex calculations that include dates and numbers. For example, you can use methods to simplify the following calculations:

- Financial transactions that require you to round dollar amounts to two decimal places

- Converting a number from one form to another, such as meters to feet

- Computing calculations based on units of time, such as the date and amount of a car payment

Learning how to use these objects and methods allows you to complete complex programming tasks in much less time and with reduced effort.

In this project, you examine how mathematical calculations are completed in JavaScript and other object-oriented programming languages. As part of the discussion, you consider the methods and properties of the **Math** object, which are used to simplify computations. You also learn how to create and manipulate **date** objects to complete calculations involving time and dates. In addition, you explore the use of timers, which you can use to delay the execution of a JavaScript statement or to tell a JavaScript statement to repeat at various intervals.

V I S U A L   S U M M A R Y

When processing complex formulas, programming languages incorporate *rules of precedence* that determine how the formulas are computed. The term *precedence* simply means the order in which operations are completed. Consider the following formula; it computes a temperature in Fahrenheit when given a Celsius value.

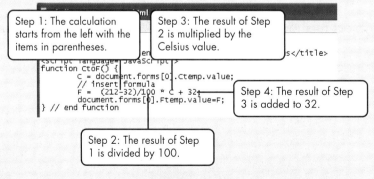

Step 1: The calculation starts from the left with the items in parentheses.

Step 3: The result of Step 2 is multiplied by the Celsius value.

Step 4: The result of Step 3 is added to 32.

Step 2: The result of Step 1 is divided by 100.

```
<script language="JavaScript">
function CtoF() {
        C = document.forms[0].Ctemp.value;
        // insert formula
        F = (212-32)/100 * C + 32;
        document.forms[0].Ftemp.value=F;
} // end function
```

FIGURE 2.1

If you were to remove the parentheses, the calculation would change, causing a subsequent error in the calculation.

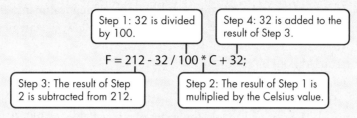

Step 1: 32 is divided by 100.

Step 4: 32 is added to the result of Step 3.

$$F = 212 - 32 / 100 * C + 32;$$

Step 3: The result of Step 2 is subtracted from 212.

Step 2: The result of Step 1 is multiplied by the Celsius value.

FIGURE 2.2

Calculations may often involve the manipulation of dates or time. The **date** object offers a comprehensive set of methods that you can use to calculate specific dates or times. Methods of the **date** object can be used in a number of ways. For example, you can insert the current date and time into a Web page or script. You can also calculate the exact amount of time that has elapsed since a specific date.

Consider the following script as an example of the **date** object and its associated methods.

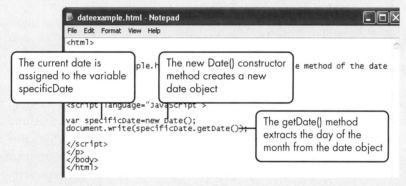

The current date is assigned to the variable specificDate

The new Date() constructor method creates a new date object

The getDate() method extracts the day of the month from the date object

FIGURE 2.3

In this example, the current day of the month is returned to the user. If the current date is January 12, the script will output the number 12 back to the user.

JavaScript also has methods designed to create timers. For example, you may want to create a page that reloads automatically every 15 seconds.

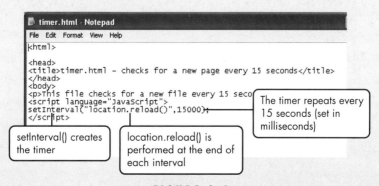

setInterval() creates the timer

location.reload() is performed at the end of each interval

The timer repeats every 15 seconds (set in milliseconds)

FIGURE 2.4

LESSON 1   Understanding Operators and Precedence

In *Essentials for Design: JavaScript Level 1*, you considered basic mathematical manipulation in terms of variables and assignment operators, an example of which is shown in the following statement:

```
var calculation=64/5+87*4;
```

At this point in your JavaScript studies, a discussion of mathematical precedence is warranted. If you use the above statement in a script, JavaScript will report the value of the variable as **360.8**. Assuming you want to double-check the code, you could do the math yourself to check the logic in the formula. Let's start by performing the following calculation:

```
65/5=12.8
```

Next, add 87 to the previous total.

```
12.8+87=99.8
```

Lastly, multiply the result by 4.

```
99.8*4=399.2
```

This value is different than the JavaScript calculation. Obviously, this could cause a significant problem if you were calculating an important value, such as a mortgage payment or the amount of refund due to a customer. The answer to the discrepancy lies in the operator precedence of the calculations. Rules of precedence require that certain operators be evaluated before others. In general, calculations are made from left to right in the following order:

- Calculations in parentheses, dots, and brackets ((), .., []) are evaluated first.
- Increment, decrement operations (++, --) are calculated next.
- Multiplication, division, modulus operations (*, /, %) are evaluated next.
- Addition, subtraction operations (-, +) are calculated last.

Returning to the previous example, you can now see how JavaScript completes the calculation:

```
var calculation=64/5+87*4;
```

JavaScript starts at the left, first evaluating the following:

```
64/5=12.8
```

Since multiplication has precedence over addition, the next part evaluated is:

```
87*4=348
```

JavaScript then completes the addition of the two calculations:

```
12.8+348=360.8
```

Understanding the rules of precedence is simple, but can create problems when devising and entering complex formulas. Memorizing the rules of precedence will help you to debug and understand complicated formulas. Remember that you can always break down the steps of a complex formula into smaller steps, and then output the values at each step. This process will help you to find errors.

Assignment Operators

As you learned in *Essentials for Design: JavaScript Level 1*, an assignment operator is a character (or characters) that assigns a value to a variable. In the statement **variableName="value"**, the equal sign is the assignment operator. This is the simplest assignment statement in JavaScript. Other assignment operators are shown in the following statements:

> **A-=B;** which is the same as **A=A-B;**
>
> **A+=B;** which is the same as **A=A+B;**
>
> **A*=B;** which is the same as **A=A*B;**
>
> **A/=B;** which is the same as **A=A/B;**
>
> **A++;** which is the same as **A=A+1;**
>
> **A--;** which is the same as **A=A-1;**

The modulus operator requires a bit more explaining. You use the ***modulus operator*** to find the remainder after division. For instance, the following lines of code return a value of 1:

```
A=5;
B=2;
A=A % B;
document.write(A);
```

Other operators affect the status of a single bit of computer memory; these operators are referred to as ***bitwise operators***. Using bitwise operators is a complex process that is beyond the scope of our current discussion. Common bitwise operators include **&=**, **|=** and **^=**. You will occasionally see these operators in complex code examples.

Correct Precedence Errors

1 Copy the contents of your RF_JavaScript_L2>Project_02 folder into your Work_In_Progress>WIP_02 folder.

2 In your text editor, open precedence.html from your WIP_02 folder.

3 Insert the following code.

```
...
</head>
<body>
<script language="JavaScript">
commission=10+10*.05;
document.write("The sales commission is "+commission);
</script>
...
```

4 Save your changes and open the file in your browser.

FIGURE 2.5

The script returns the wrong amount because the multiplication took place before the two numbers were added.

5 Insert parentheses into your formula as shown below.

```
...
<body>
<script language="JavaScript">
commission=(10+10)*.05;
document.write("The sales commission is "+commission);
...
```

The parentheses correct the precedence problem.

6   **Save your changes and refresh your browser.**

FIGURE 2.6

The calculation executes correctly.

7   **Close the file in your browser and text editor.**

LESSON 2   Using Math Object Methods

The **Math** object is a built-in JavaScript object. It contains a variety of constant values used in mathematical calculations (such as pi), as well as a number of methods for calculating many common math functions.

The **Math** object uses various methods to simplify complex mathematical formulas. For instance, to raise 2 to the power of 9 and add 8 to the result, you could devise a statement such as:

```
result=(2*2*2*2*2*2*2*2*2)+8;
```

As an alternative, you could simplify the formula by using the **Math.pow()** method:

```
result=Math.pow(2,9)+8;
```

JavaScript supports a number of methods that are used to complete various calculations. The most common **Math** methods are listed below.

Math.abs()

The **Math.abs()** method returns the absolute value of any number you pass to it. The result is always positive, regardless of whether the original number is positive or negative. For example, the following code segment outputs the number **27** to the screen, not **-27**, as you might expect.

```
var myNumber=-27;
document.write(.Math.abs (myNumber));
```

Math.max() and Math.min()

These methods allow the programmer to compare multiple numbers and ask for the smallest (min) number or the largest (max) number. For instance, the following script returns the number **6** because **6** is the lowest number in the list.

```
var lowestNumber=Math.min(27,33,54,76,43,23,12,6,78,98);

document.write(lowestNumber);
```

To return the largest number in the list (**98**), you would write the following:

```
var largestNumber=Math.max(27,33,54,76,43,23,12,6,78,98);

document.write(largestNumber);
```

Math.pow()

This method requires two numeric arguments to calculate the result of a specific number raised to a certain power. The first argument is your base number and the second is the exponent. For instance, to calculate **5** to the power of **2**, you would write the following statement:

```
calculation=Math.pow(5,2);
```

Math.round()

This method rounds whatever number it receives to the closest integer value. To round the number **4.343** to the nearest whole number and output the result to the user, you would write the following statement:

```
document.write("The number 4.343 rounded is " + Math.round(4.343));
```

Math.sqrt()

This method returns the square root of whatever number it receives. The following statement returns **2** to the user:

```
document.write("The square root of 4 is " + Math.sqrt(4));
```

Notice how the method is written with all lowercase letters as **sqrt()**. Similar methods are written differently. For instance: **SQRT2()** returns the square root of the number 2, which is often used in calculations.

Use Math Object Methods

1   In your text editor, open mathmethods.html from your WIP_02 folder.

2   Insert the following code.

```
...
</head>
<body>
<script language="JavaScript">
theRoot=Math.sqrt(20);
document.write("The square root of 20 is " + theRoot+"<br>");
document.write("The number rounded is "+Math.round(theRoot));
</script>
</body>
</html>
```

3   Save your changes and open the file in your browser.

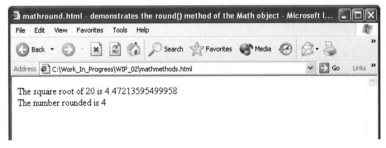

FIGURE 2.7

4   Close the file in your text editor and browser.

To Extend Your Knowledge...

THE MATH OBJECT

The **Math** object must be spelled as "**Math**" rather than "**math**" to work in most browsers.

LESSON 3 Generating Random Numbers

The **Math.random()** method takes no parameters; it simply returns a random number between 0 and 1. Consider the following code, which generates a random number between 0 and 1:

```
randomNumber=Math.random();
```

The number generated by **Math.random()** is usually a long decimal. In many common programming problems, it is necessary to produce a random number that occupies a specific range, such as a number between 1 and 10 or a number between 1 and 100. You can do this by mathematically manipulating the number produced by the **Math.random()** method. You explore this process in the following exercises.

Work with Random Numbers

1   In your text editor, open mathrandom.html from your WIP_02 folder.

2   Insert the following lines of code.

```
...
</head>
<body>
<script language="JavaScript">
randomNumber=Math.random();
document.write("Here is a random number: " + randomNumber);
</script>
</body>
</html>
```

3   Open the file in your browser and click the Refresh button.

Every time you click the Refresh button, a new random number between 0 and 1 appears.

FIGURE 2.8

Your results will differ from the illustration, depending on the number your computer generates.

4   Keep the file open in your text editor for the next exercise.

Return a 1 or 0 (True or False) Value

1   In the open mathrandom.html, insert the following code.

```
...
<script language="JavaScript">
randomNumber=Math.random();
document.write("Here is a random number: " + randomNumber);
document.write("<br>");
randomNumber=Math.round(randomNumber);
document.write("Rounded version is "+randomNumber);
</script>
...
```

The script returns either 0 or 1, which could later be used to represent a true (**1**) or false (**0**) value.

2   Save your changes and refresh the file in your browser.

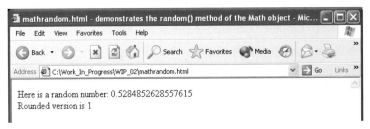

FIGURE 2.9

Every time you click the Refresh button, the number changes between 0 and 1.

3   Insert the following code to generate a number between 1 and 10.

```
...
randomNumber=Math.random();
document.write("Here is a random number: " + randomNumber);
document.write("<br>");
randomNumber*=10;
randomNumber=Math.round(randomNumber);
document.write("Rounded version is "+randomNumber);
...
```

This statement takes the current value of the number and multiplies it by 10.

4 | Save the file in your text editor.

5 | Repeatedly click the Refresh button in your Web browser.

FIGURE 2.10

The code generates random numbers between 1 and 10.

6 | Close the file in your browser and text editor.

To Extend Your Knowledge...

RANDOM NUMBER GENERATION

Computers don't really produce "random" numbers. In order to operate correctly, a computer processor has an internal clock that completes a full cycle billions or trillions of times each second. When asked for a random number, computer languages check the status of the processor clock and report the position of the processor clock in its current cycle. Since the processor clock completes billions or trillions of cycles per second, the generated number is virtually impossible to predict. This simple fact allows programmers to create complex video games and apply digital encryption.

LESSON 4   Incorporating Math Properties

Math object properties are different from the properties of most objects because **Math** object properties cannot be changed. In JavaScript, a property that cannot be changed is referred to as a ***constant property***. Constant properties hold numeric constants that are used frequently in mathematical calculations. JavaScript supports many constant properties, a few of which are described below.

Math.E

Math.E is the constant value **2.718281828459045**, which is used in many common calculations. To compute the value of the number **5** multiplied by the constant "**E**" and store it in a variable named **result**, you would write the following statement:

```
var result=5*Math.E;
```

Math.PI

Math.PI is the constant value **3.141592653589793**. For example, consider the following statement that multiplies the number **5** with the constant **PI** and stores the calculation in a variable named **result**:

```
var result=5*Math.PI;
```

Math.SQRT2

Math.SQRT2 is the constant value given to the square root of **2**, which is **1.414213562373091**. To calculate the result of the number **8** divided by the constant number represented by **SQRT2**, you would write the following statement:

```
var result=8/Math.SQRT2;
```

Use Math Properties

1   **In your text editor, open mathpi.html from your WIP_02 folder.**

2   **Insert the following code.**

```
...
</head>
<body>
<script language="JavaScript">
diameter=prompt("Enter the diameter of the circle","");
diameter=parseInt(diameter);
var circumference=Math.PI*diameter;
document.write("The circumference of the circle is " + circumference);
</script>
</body>
</html>
```

The **prompt()** method returns information as a string, so you need to use **parseInt()** to ensure that the value is converted to an integer.

3 | Save your changes and open the file in your browser.

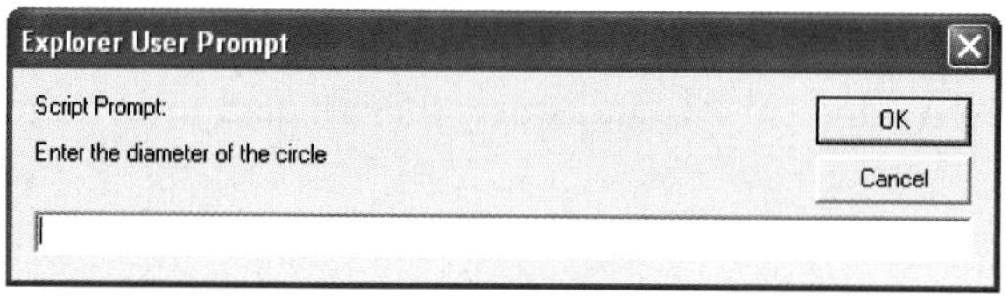

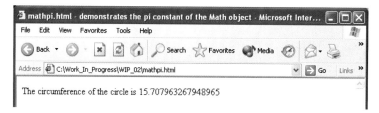

FIGURE 2.11

A prompt box appears.

4 | Enter "5" as the diameter and click OK.

FIGURE 2.12

5 | Refresh the file in your browser and enter different diameters.

The responses you receive depend on the numbers you enter.

6 | Close the file in your browser and text editor.

To Extend Your Knowledge...

MATH PROPERTIES

In most browsers, the constant properties of the **Math** object are case sensitive. Typing **Math.PI** as **Math.pi** causes the script to stop working in many browsers.

LESSON 5   Getting and Setting Time Units

The **date** class in JavaScript allows you to create objects that hold date and time information. To insert the current date and time into a variable named **currentTime**, you would write the following statement:

```
var currentTime=new Date();
```

The **newDate()** method is a constructor method that creates a new instance of the **date** object. You can then output the variable to the screen with the following simple statement:

```
document.write(currentTime);
```

It is often necessary to pass a specific date to a **date** object. You can do this by writing the following statement:

```
var specificDate=new Date("October 18, 1969 15:40:00");
```

This code creates a new variable named **specificDate** that creates a new **date** object, as well as stores the date October 18, 1969 and the time 3:40 p.m. Notice that the time must be specified in a 24-hour format. If you prefer, you can specify the date in numeric format. The following pseudo-code shows you how to enter the date in numeric format:

```
var specificDate=new Date(year, month, day, hours, minutes,
seconds);
```

More specifically, you could use the following statement to enter the date and time shown above:

```
var specificDate=new Date(1969, 9, 18, 3, 40, 0);
```

Months start with the number **0** (similar to many other objects in JavaScript), so October is referenced as **9** instead of **10**. If you leave off the hours, minutes, and seconds, the computer assumes that you mean midnight, as shown below:

```
var specificDate=new Date(1969, 9, 18);
```

Methods of the Date Class

The **date** class includes a large number of methods for manipulating dates. These methods allow programmers to create new dates and change existing dates. Methods of the **date** object are designed to change an aspect of a particular date (such as the hour setting) and are often entered as strings or numbers.

Depending on the specific method (when entering the information as a number), you can enter the information in terms of a time (such as the 14 of December) or in milliseconds that have elapsed from a certain point (such as add 14,523 milliseconds). You can output dates in several ways, depending on the amount of information needed and how user-friendly you need the output to be. You explore several of the most common methods of the **date** object in the following sections.

getDate(), setDate()

The **getDate()** and **setDate()** methods apply to the day of the month in a particular **date** object. For instance, the following code outputs **18** as the day in the **date** object:

```
var specificDate=new Date("October 18, 1969 15:40:00");

document.write(specificDate.getDate());
```

The **setDate()** method changes the day of the month in a **date** object. To change the date in the code example to **21**, you would write the following statement:

```
specificDate.setDate(21);
```

getDay()

The **getDay()** method returns the day of the week of the day stored in the **date** object. The day of the week returns as a numeric value from **0** (Sunday) to **6** (Saturday). Using the **date** object created in the previous section, you can request the day of the week by writing the following statement:

```
document.write(specificDate.getDay());
```

Using the date October, 25, 1969, the number **6** returns, which indicates that this particular day was a Saturday.

get FullYear(), setFullYear()

These methods allow you to return the year or set the year within the **date** object. The number is specified as a four-digit number (hence, the word "full" in the method name). To return the year from a **date** object named **myDate**, you would write:

```
document.write(myDate.getFullYear());
```

To set the year in the same **date** object, you would write:

```
myDate.setFullYear(1971);
```

getHours(), setHours()

As you might imagine, these methods get and set the hour stored in the **date** object. Hours are expressed as **0** for midnight and extend to **23** for 11 p.m. To change the hour to 2 p.m., you would write the following statement:

```
myDate.setHours(14);
```

To check the current hour specified in the **date** object, you would write:

```
document.write(myDate.getHours());
```

getMinutes(), setMinutes()

To set the **minute** property in a **date** object, you can use the **setMinutes()** method, as shown in the following statement:

```
myDate.setMinutes(10);
```

The previous statement changes the **minute** setting to **10**. It's important to note that minutes start at **0** for the first minute and end at **59** for the last minute in the hour, which is the way we usually note time (rather than noting the 60th minute at the end of the hour). To check the **minute** setting in a **date** object, you would write:

```
myDate.getMinutes();
```

getMonth(), setMonth()

At this point, the **getMonth()** and **setMonth()** methods are probably obvious to most readers. Remember that months start with **0** for January and end with **11** for December. To change the month to November in a **date** object named **myDate**, and then output the month to the user, you would write the following statements:

```
myDate.setMonth(10);
document.write(myDate.getMonth());
```

toLocaleString()

The **toLocaleString()** method returns the time from a **date** object as an easy-to-understand text string. Browsers often output this information in slightly different fashions, but this method usually offers the most user-friendly version of the date, which includes the day of the week. To create a **date** object and return the object to the user, you would write the following statements:

```
var specificDate=new Date("October 18, 1969 15:40:00");
document.write(specificDate.toLocaleString());
```

Incorporating this code into a Web page with some explanatory copy yields the following result in a browser.

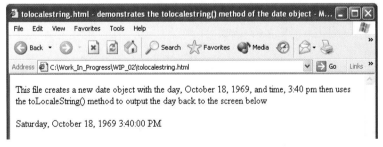

FIGURE 2.13

To Extend Your Knowledge...

THE DATE OBJECT

The **newDate()** constructor method and many of the other methods of the **date** object allow programmers to manipulate dates and time in milliseconds. One day is equal to 84,400,000 milliseconds. This level of precision is very useful when working with extremely technical and precise calculations.

Instantiate a Date Object

1 **In your text editor, open date.html from your WIP_02 folder.**

2 **Insert the following code.**

```
...

<body>

<p>This file creates a new date object with the current day and
time, and then outputs it back to the screen below</p><p>

<script language="JavaScript">

var currentTime=new Date();

document.write("The current time is "+currentTime);

</script>

</p>

</body>

...
```

3 **Save your changes and open the file in your browser.**

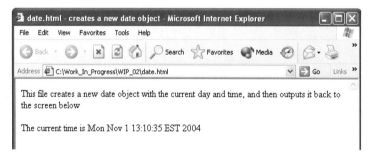

FIGURE 2.14

The current date and time display.

4 **Close the file in your browser and text editor.**

To Extend Your Knowledge...

MILLISECOND CALCULATIONS FROM INDEX DATES

Dates can also be constructed and manipulated using milliseconds from an index date. This type of date manipulation is more complex than the examples presented in this book. The ability to manipulate dates in this fashion is useful for synchronizing events across different regions or making very precise time measurements. The index date is 12 a.m., January 1, 1970, Greenwich Mean Time (GMT).

When manipulating dates in terms of the index date, date and time information is returned in terms of the amount of time the date occupies from the index date. This can prove very confusing to novice programmers, since a day has 84,400,000 milliseconds, and a day before the index date would return as -84,400,000. A day after the index date would return as 84,400,000.

Manipulating dates using the index date is quite complex and only useful in very technical problem-solving situations. For the sake of simplicity, we describe the most common methods of the **date** object in this project and avoid using the index date. Additionally, we work with standard dates wherever possible, such as January 1, 1983, and avoid working with milliseconds.

toLocaleString() BROWSER COMPATIBILITY

The text string generated by the **toLocaleString()** method is slightly different in every browser. For this reason, your output may appear slightly different than the screen shots shown in this project.

LESSON 6 Creating Timers

Programs often require *timers* to set a waiting period before an action executes. Some JavaScript methods are designed to create a timer, and then carry out a JavaScript statement when the timer expires. Depending on the method used, the method may execute the statement once when the interval expires, or it may start the timer again and repeatedly execute the statement at the end of each interval. Additional methods may also be used to stop the timer (once it starts) and keep the statement from executing. You explore these methods in the following sections.

setTimeout() and ClearTimeout()

The **setTimeout()** method requires two parameters. The first is a valid JavaScript statement, and the second parameter is a number that represents the number of milliseconds that should pass before the command executes. The first parameter passes as a string, and the second parameter passes as a number. Using pseudo-code, the **setTimeout()** method takes the following form:

```
setTimeout("statement",time in milliseconds);
```

To display a welcome message after 5 seconds, you would write a statement such as:

```
setTimeout("document.write('Hi!')",5000);
```

Every timer created by the **setTimeout()** method creates a unique ID that is returned by the method. This ID can be used by the **clearTimeout()** method to stop the counter before the command in the **setTimeout()** method executes. For instance, examine the following code:

```
var timer=setTimeout("document.write('Hi!')",5000);

document.write(timer);

clearTimeout(timer);
```

These code statements create a timer that writes the string "**Hi!**" after 5 seconds. The timer is created using the **setTimeout()** method, which also places the ID of the timer into the variable named **timer**. The **clearTimeout()** method uses this ID to keep the **document.write()** statement from executing. Placing this code into a script yields the following result in a browser.

FIGURE 2.15

setInterval() and clearInterval()

The **setInterval()** method is virtually identical to the **setTimeout()** method with one exception: when the time runs out, the command executes and the timer restarts. The code executes repeatedly until the **clearInterval()** method stops the timer.

The **setTimeout()** method executes the statement once (when the timer is finished). The **setInterval()** method loops at the specified interval by executing the statement and restarting the timer.

Timers are used for a variety of purposes in various scripts. Programmers often use timers to allow their users enough time to read a message before an event occurs. In the following exercise, you give the user enough time to read a message before redirecting the browser to another page. Programmers often use this technique when a Web page has been moved to new location/URL.

Create a Timer

1 In your text editor, open timer.html from your WIP_02 folder.

2 Insert the following code.

```
...
</head>
<body>
<script language="JavaScript">
setInterval("location.reload()",15000);
</script>
</body>
</html>
```

This code executes the **reload()** method every 15 seconds. If a new version of the page has been saved, the page automatically reloads.

3 Open the file in your browser.

A blank page displays, since the page does not yet have any visible content.

4 In your text editor, insert the following code.

```
<body>
<script language="JavaScript">
setInterval("location.reload()",15000);
</script>
<p>This file checks for a new file every 15 seconds</p>
</body>
</html>
```

This code creates a noticeable change in the file that can be detected when it reloads.

5 Save your changes in the text editor.

6   **Return to your browser and wait.**

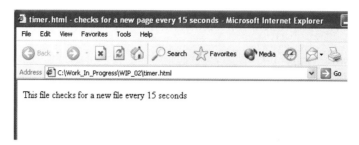

FIGURE 2.16

The file should reload within a few seconds.

7   **Close the file in your browser and text editor.**

To Extend Your Knowledge...

MILLISECONDS

A *millisecond* is 1/1000th of a second. Therefore, 5000 milliseconds equals 5 seconds.

SUMMARY

In Project 2, you discovered how JavaScript programmers work with dates, times, and numbers. When working with numbers, it is important to remember that calculations in JavaScript follow a strict precedence. In general, calculations are completed from left to right. You now know that items in parentheses or brackets are calculated first; multiplication or division is completed next; and addition or subtraction is completed last.

You also considered the **date** object and **Math** object in this project. Strictly speaking, you can work without either of these objects and still manipulate dates and complete complex calculations — but the programming would be quite difficult. The **Math** object, in particular, provides methods that convert numbers to absolute values, round numbers to the nearest integer, generate random numbers, raise numbers to powers, take square roots, and pick the largest or smallest number from a list of numbers. The **Math** object also has constant properties that hold constant values, such as the number represented by pi.

The **date** object allows you to easily store and manipulate dates. Various methods of the **date** object allow you to add or subtract time from a date, as well as change a part of a date and time, such as the month, day, or hour. In this project, you also considered the **setInterval()** and **setTimeout()** methods, which allow you to execute a command after a specific amount of time or to repeatedly perform a command at a specific interval.

CAREERS IN DESIGN

TARGETED DESIGN SOLUTIONS

Professional portfolio Web sites show a variety of design solutions, each of which is tailored for a specific audience. For example, if you were designing a site for a company that creates custom jewelry, you might use colors, graphics, and fonts that suggest a luxurious, high-class lifestyle; you might apply a white background and a crisp, clean layout that emphasizes the simple elegance of the jewelry. However, if you were building a Web site for four-wheel-drive off-road driving enthusiasts, you might choose a combination of dark, earth-tone colors and closely cropped, imposing pictures of modified vehicles in action at an off-road course. Clearly, these sites have different target audiences, and therefore, have different presentational (design) requirements.

Novice designers often favor one particular style, color palette, and font, such as using dark blues and grays on a white background, an image in the top-left corner, and the content layed out in a table-like structure. Experienced designers have personal preferences, too, but they have learned to broaden their scope and their creative abilities. Experienced designers generate effective design solutions based on the needs of the client — which can include the full gamut of color palettes, fonts, styles, layouts, and image choices.

Rather than limit your portfolio Web site to your favorite styles, colors, and fonts, include as wide a variety of choices as possible. When you allow potential clients and employers to see your versatility, you will enjoy far greater success.

KEY TERMS

Bitwise operators	Millisecond	Rules of precedence
Constant property	Modulus operator	Timer
Index date	Precedence	

CHECKING CONCEPTS AND TERMS

MULTIPLE CHOICE

Circle the letter that matches the correct answer for each of the following questions.

1. Which list represents the normal order of precedence of mathematical operations in JavaScript?

a. +, -, /, *, ()

b. -, +, *, /, ()

c. (), *, /, +, -

d. /, *, +, -, ()

2. **Math** properties are different from the properties of most objects because they _____.

a. represent large text strings

b. represent very large numbers

c. represent values (such as pi) that cannot be changed

d. None of the above

3. Which **Math** method can you use to ensure a positive value returns?

   a. `Math.abs()`

   b. `Math.pos()`

   c. `Math.unNeg()`

   d. `Math.makePos()`

4. What is the purpose of the **Math.round()** method?

   a. To calculate the circumference of a round object

   b. To calculate the diameter of a round object

   c. To calculate the area of a round object

   d. To round off a number to the nearest integer

5. What arguments are required by the **Math.pow()** method?

   a. The number to be raised

   b. The number to be raised and the power to raise it to

   c. Four numbers to be multiplied

   d. This method requires no information.

6. How does the **getDay()** method of the **date** object return information?

   a. As a day of the week, represented by a text string (e.g., "Saturday")

   b. As a day of the week, represented by a number (e.g., "2")

   c. As a day of the current month (e.g., "25th")

   d. None of the above

7. What is the purpose of the modulus (%) operator?

   a. To convert a string to an integer value

   b. To multiply two numbers

   c. To return the rounded amount after division without a decimal

   d. To return the amount left over after division

8. What type of number does the **Math.random()** method generate?

   a. An integer between 0 and 1000

   b. An integer between 0 and 100

   c. A long decimal between 0 and 1

   d. An integer between 0 and 10000

9. Which method can you use to clear a repeating loop of actions?

   a. `setInterval()`

   b. `setTimeout()`

   c. `clearInterval()`

   d. `clearTimeout()`

10. Which method can you use to create a repeating loop of actions?

   a. `setInterval()`

   b. `setTimeOut()`

   c. `clearInterval()`

   d. `toLocaleString()`

DISCUSSION QUESTIONS

1. Why is the **date** object useful? How can you perform complex time calculations when using **date** objects?

2. Why is the order of precedence important in complex calculations?

3. When would it be useful to work in milliseconds when computing dates?

4. From a conceptual standpoint, what are the steps to calculate a random number between 1 and 10 using JavaScript?

SKILL DRILL

Skill Drill exercises reinforce project skills. Each skill reinforced is the same, or nearly the same, as a skill presented in the project. Detailed instructions are provided in a step-by-step format. You can work through one or more exercises in any order.

1. Precedence and Math Object Methods

1. In your browser, open skillprecedence.html from your WIP_02 folder.

    This file represents a completed script that returns incorrect answers for a calculation.

FIGURE 2.17

2. Find the following code in your text editor.

```
houseValue=100000;

annualTaxes=houseValue*0.045;

monthlyInsurance=30;

monthlyExpense=monthlyInsurance+annualTaxes/12;
```

Test values were already inserted into the script. The **annualTaxes** value is computed correctly, but the **monthlyExpense** value is incorrect. The **monthlyExpense** value should be the total of the **monthlyInsurance** value added to the **monthlyTax** value (**annualTaxes** divided by 12).

3. Correct the problem in the **monthlyExpense** calculation.

4. Save and test your file.

    The correct result is 405.

5. Close the file in your browser and text editor.

2. Generate Random Numbers within a Range

In this exercise, you generate random numbers in a given range. To do so, you create a simple function. You can use this function to generate numbers within any boundaries, such as a number between 50 and 100.

1. In your text editor, open skillrandom.html from your WIP_02 folder.

2. Find the following code in the **<head>** section of the document.

    ```
    ...
    <script language="JavaScript">
    // insert function here


    </script>
    ...
    ```

3. Create a function named **getBetween**. The function should accept two numbers: **number1** and **number2**.

4. Insert the following code into the function.

    ```
    ...
    <script language="JavaScript">
    // insert function here
    function getBetween(number1,number2){
    if (number2>number1) {
        return (Math.round(Math.random()*(number2-number1))+number1);
    }
    else {
    return (Math.round(Math.random()*(number1-number2))+number2);
    }
    }
    </script>
    ...
    ```

5. Insert the following code in the **\<body>** section of the document to trigger the function.

```
...
</head>
<body>
<script language="JavaScript">
result=getBetween(3,7);
document.write(result);
</script>
</body>
</html>
```

6. Save your file.

7. Test the file in your browser.

    It should return a number between 3 and 7 each time.

8. Change the code to return a number between 10 and 20, and then test the file.

9. Close the file in your browser and text editor.

3. Use Numbered Time Units

1. In your text editor, open datenumbers.html from your WIP_02 folder.

2. Insert the following code.

```
...
<p>This file creates a new date object with the day, October 18,
1969, and time, 3:40 pm, by entering the date as a sequence of num-
bers, and then outputs it back to the screen below</p><p>
<script language="JavaScript">
// note: months start with month 0 (January) so 9 means October.
var currentTime=new Date(1969, 9, 18, 3, 40, 0);
document.write(currentTime);
</script>
</p>
</body>
...
```

3. Save your changes in the text editor and open the file in your browser.

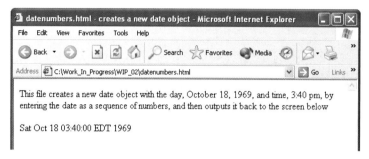

FIGURE 2.18

4. Return to your text editor and change the code to use **January 12, 1985** at **2:30 pm**.

5. Change the explanatory text to match the date you assigned in Step 4.

6. Save and test your file.

7. Close the file in your browser and text editor.

4. Use a Timer Before Redirecting a User to Another Page

1. In your text editor, open skilltimer.html from the WIP_02 folder.

2. Find the following line of code.

```
document.location="http://www.againsttheclock.com";
```

This file uses the **location** property to redirect users to the Against The Clock Web site.

3. Open the file in your Web browser.

Your browser should immediately redirect to the Against The Clock Web site. Users who own computers with fast Internet access may not have seen the initial page — it may not have remained visible long enough to read. You correct this problem by adding a timer that allows you to read the explanatory text on the initial page before being redirected.

4. Return to your text editor. Change the line that starts with **document.location** to the following:

```
setTimeout("document.location='http://www.againsttheclock.com'",5000);
```

Notice that the code uses single quotes for the location property, nested inside double quotes for the timer.

5. Add some explanatory text to tell the user that the page will redirect after 5 seconds.

6. Save and test your file.

7. Change the code and explanatory text to redirect the user to a Web site of your choice after 4 seconds.

8. Close the file in your browser and text editor.

CHALLENGE

Challenge exercises expand on, or are somewhat related to, skills presented in the lessons. Each exercise provides a brief introduction, followed by instructions presented in a numbered-step format that are not as detailed as those in the Skill Drill exercises. You should work through these exercises in order.

1. Use Precedence

For a class assignment, you are writing a script to change temperature values from Fahrenheit to Celsius and Celsius to Fahrenheit. You partially completed the script. To finish the assignment, you must write the formula that computes the Fahrenheit value when given the Celsius value.

1. In your browser, open challengetemperature.html from the WIP_02 folder.

2. Enter **212** for the Fahrenheit temperature and click elsewhere on the page. The Celsius temperature should compute as **100**.

3. Open the file in your text editor.

4. Find the following code.

    ```
    ...
    function CtoF() {
            C = document.forms[0].Ctemp.value;
            // insert formula


            document.forms[0].Ftemp.value=F;
    } // end function
    ...
    ```

    You use this function to convert Celsius values to Fahrenheit.

5. Insert the following code to start a calculation for the variable **F**. This variable represents the Fahrenheit value.

    ```
    ...
    function CtoF() {
            C = document.forms[0].Ctemp.value;
            // insert formula
            F =
            document.forms[0].Ftemp.value=F;
    } // end function
    ...
    ```

6. Use the following flowchart to write the formula to compute the Fahrenheit value (**F**) that you started in the previous step.

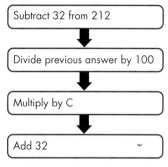

```
Subtract 32 from 212

Divide previous answer by 100

Multiply by C

Add 32
```

FIGURE 2.19

7. Save your changes and refresh your browser.

8. Enter **100** as the Celsius value and click elsewhere on the page.

   If you entered the formula correctly, a value of **212** should return as the Fahrenheit temperature.

9. Close the file in your browser and text editor.

2. Determine Maximum and Minimum Values

In this Challenge, you use methods of the **Math** object to determine the largest or smallest number in a string of numbers.

1. In your text editor, open challengemax.html from the WIP_02 folder.

2. Insert the following code.

```
...
<body>
<p>This page uses a simple script to find the largest number in a
list using the Math.max() method.</p>
<script language="JavaScript">
var largestNumber=Math.max(27,33,54,76,43,23,12,6,78,98);
document.write("The largest number is "+largestNumber+"<br>");
</script>
</body>
</html>
```

3. Save the file in your text editor and open the file in your browser.

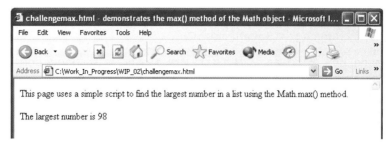

FIGURE 2.20

4. Insert additional code to determine the minimum value from the same list of numbers.

    Hint: use the **Math.min()** method.

5. Save and test your file.

6. Close the file in your browser and text editor.

3. Use Timers to Create a Clock

In this Challenge, you create an online clock, and then place the clock in the title bar of a Web page. This script requires complex use of timers that are triggered by event handlers when the page loads and unloads. You use the **toLocaleString()** method to format the time and date.

1. In your text editor, open challengeclock.html from your WIP_02 folder.

2. Insert event handlers to start the clock when the page loads and stop the clock when the page unloads.

```
...
</script>
</head>
<body onload="startClock()" onunload="stopClock()" >
<p>This page creates a clock in the title bar.</p>
</body>
</html>
```

3. Insert the code to initialize the timer and create the function to start the clock.

```
...
<script language="JavaScript">
// made by: Nicolas - http://www.javascript-page.com
var clockID = 0;

function startClock() {
   clockID = setTimeout("updateClock()", 500);
}
</script>
</head>
<body onload="StartClock()" onunload="StopClock()">
...
```

4. Insert the function to update the clock.

```
...
function StartClock() {
   clockID = setTimeout("UpdateClock()", 500);
}
function updateClock() {
   if(clockID) {
      clearTimeout(clockID);
      clockID  = 0;
      } // end if

      var tDate = new Date();
      document.title = tDate.toLocaleString();
      clockID = setTimeout("UpdateClock()", 1000);
} // end function
</script>
</head>
<body onload="StartClock()" onunload="StopClock()">
...
```

5. Insert the function to stop the timer when the user closes the page.

```
...
document.title = tDate.toLocaleString();
clockID = setTimeout("UpdateClock()", 1000);
} // end function

function stopClock() {
   if(clockID) {
      clearTimeout(clockID);
      clockID  = 0;
   }
}
</script>
</head>
<body onload="startClock()" onunload="stopClock()">
...
```

6. Save your changes in the text editor.

7. Open the file in your browser and inspect the title bar to ensure your script is working properly. The clock should change every second.

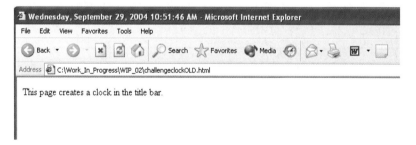

FIGURE 2.21

8. Keep the file open in your browser and text editor for the next Challenge.

4. Use Date Object Methods

In the previous exercise, you used timers to constantly create new **date** objects. Using the **toLocaleString()** method, you were also able to output the current date and time as a text string. In this Challenge, you use **date** object methods and decision statements to exercise greater control over the information returned to the user.

1. In the open challengeclock.html, find the following line of code in the **updateClock()** function.

    ```
    document.title = tDate.toLocaleString();
    ```

2. Modify this line of code as follows to use **date** methods to format the output of the clock.

    ```
    document.title = ""+ tDate.getHours() + ":" + tDate.getMinutes() +
    ":" + tDate.getSeconds();
    ```

3. Save the file in your text editor and refresh your browser.

    The title bar should be formatted with the hours, minutes, and seconds only.

4. Write a statement to create a variable to hold the current day. Use the **getDay()** method to assign the day to the variable you create.

5. Use **if** statements to translate the day from a number to the name of the day. For example, if the day is **3**, convert the day into the string "**Wednesday**".

6. Modify the output to include the day of the week. The formatting of your output should match the following.

FIGURE 2.22

7. Save and test your file.

8. Close the file in your browser and text editor.

P O R T F O L I O   B U I L D E R

Calculate a Pizza Order

Designers commonly build forms to calculate e-commerce transactions. This requires programmers to build forms that compute the cost of the transactions. To illustrate such a form, open the file named pizzecalculator.html from the Project_02>Portfolio_Builder_02 folder in your browser. On the left side of the window, you see a form that allows a user to choose the following options when ordering a pizza:

> What size of pizza?   What type of pizza?   How many pizzas?

You need each of these items to accurately calculate the total cost of the order. Simulate a typical user and make some choices on the form, and then click the Calculate Total button. An alert dialog box appears. Notice that the values are incorrect.

In this Portfolio Builder, your task is to create mathematical calculations that allow a typical user to see accurate values.

- As you create your calculations, remember to control the order of operation. The correct order of operation will generator correct results — which will in turn allow users to trust the site and its processes.

PORTFOLIO BUILDER

Calculate a Pizza Order (continued)

- Use the following pseudo-code to create the actual calculations:

```
subtotal = (type * 4) + (size * quantity)
total = subtotal + delivery
```

- The value type is multiplied by the value of 4, which represents a fixed mark-up based upon the type of pizza. Depending upon business profit margins, this value could change, so a variable should be used to represent the fixed mark-up in the code.

- After creating both the subtotal and total calculations, the alert dialog box should display the correct values.

- The alert should also tell you whether you are paying a delivery fee.

- Use a calculator to check the result to ensure that your script is functioning correctly.

PROJECT 3

Flow of Control and Debugging

OBJECTIVES

In this project, you learn how to

- Choose options with switch and break

- Perform actions using "while" loops

- Perform actions using "do while" loops

- Incorporate "for" statements

- Find errors in your code

- Identify common scripting errors

WHY WOULD I DO THIS?

Computer programs often need to make decisions about whether to perform specific actions. As you know, a conditional statement allows a computer program to perform a function if a condition evaluates to **true**. Consider the following example, which could be used to score an online test:

```
if (answer==true) {

        // add 1 to the score

        score++;

}

else {

        // subtract 1 from the score

        score--;

}
```

Conditional (**if**) statements are easy to understand. The computer stops the execution of the command long enough to evaluate a condition, and then follows specific commands based on the result. These types of statements are also referred to as *flow-of-control* statements because they alter the natural flow of the program. As an analogy, consider that you are driving a car and come to a fork in the road. Based on your objective, such as which path offers the quickest route to your destination, you make a choice.

An **if** statement is the simplest type of conditional (flow-of-control) statement. Other flow-of-control statements are more complex. For example, you may want to repeat an action until a condition becomes true, instead of simply evaluating the condition once. Using the previous example, assume that you want to modify the online test so the user continues to answer until he arrives at the correct answer. Using pseudo-code, you can see how to change the program from a simple statement to one that is a bit more complex:

```
if (the answer is true) {

        go to the next question;

}

else {

        repeat the question and perform this comparison again;

}
```

Reaching this level of complexity often results in coding errors, which, of course, must be located and corrected. In fact, many programmers spend more time correcting the problems in their programs than writing new code! The process of finding and correcting errors in code is known as *debugging*. In this project, you not only learn how to use a number of additional keywords to create loops and flow-of-control statements, you also learn how to find and correct errors in your code. In addition, you discover many common errors made by even the most experienced programmers — and learn how to avoid these pitfalls.

V I S U A L   S U M M A R Y

The **for** statement is one of the most useful flow-of-control (conditional) statements. This type of statement allows developers to easily create loops that execute a specified number of times. Consider the following script that illustrates a **for** statement.

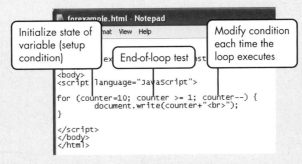

FIGURE 3.1

For statements use a variable to determine how many times the loop executes. The variable is initialized to a starting value. An end-of-loop test is a conditional statement that determines when the loop stops executing. The modify condition portion of the loop changes the variable each time the loop executes. The code shown above returns the following result in a browser.

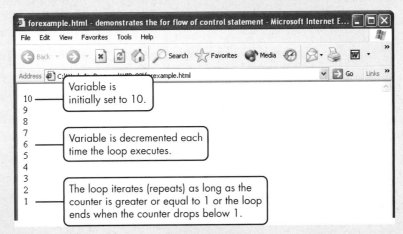

FIGURE 3.2

LESSON 1 Choosing Options with Switch and Break

The **switch** keyword offers the same type of flexibility as an **if** statement; **switch** works well when you have several known values of a variable. For example, consider that you are designing a program for a weight-loss business. At every 10 pounds of weight lost, you want to congratulate the user on his success.

```
weightLost=30;

switch (weightLost) {

    case 10:

        {

        document.write("You've lost 10 pounds!");

        break;

        }

    case 20:

        {

        document.write("You've lost 20 pounds!");

        break;

        }

    case 30:

        {

        document.write("You've lost 30 pounds!");

        break;

        }

    case 40:

        {

        document.write("You've lost 40 pounds!");

        break;

        }

}  // this marks the end of the switch statement
```

To write a **switch** statement, you simply specify a variable in the statement, in this case **weightLost**, and identify the code to execute for various values. Notice the colon (**:**) at the end of each **case** statement; placing a semicolon at the end of a **case** statement would create an error in the code. The keyword **break** tells the interpreter that no more comparisons are necessary. Whenever the interpreter encounters the keyword **break**, it immediately goes to the end of the code in the **switch** statement.

Statements that use the **switch** keyword offer several advantages:

- They work well for situations where you are looking for several known values.

- They are easy to write.

- They are easy to understand.

- The interpreter typically executes this type of statement very quickly.

Use Flow-of-Control Statements

1 Copy the contents of your RF_JavaScript_L2>Project_03 folder into your Work_In_Progress>WIP_03 folder.

2 In your browser, open switch.html from your WIP_03 folder.

FIGURE 3.3

A prompt box appears.

3 Enter the number "4" and click OK.

FIGURE 3.4

4 In your text editor, find the following code.

```
// insert switch here
```

5   Insert the `switch` statement.

```
...
var tickets=prompt("How many tickets do you have?","");;
document.write("You have "+tickets+" tickets."+"<br>");


// insert switch here
switch (tickets) {
    case "1":

        {
        document.write("You got a ticket!"+"<br>");

        break;

        }
    case "2":

        {
        document.write("If you get 3 tickets, your license will
be suspended. "+"<br>");

        break;

        }
    case "3":

        {
        document.write("Your license is suspended!"+"<br>");

        break;

        }
    case "4": {
        document.write("You drove without a license. The police
are taking you to jail!");

        break;

        }
} // end of switch
</script>
</body>
</html>
```

Notice how the **case** values use double quotes. This is necessary because the **prompt()** method always returns the value as a string.

6 | Save the file in your text editor and refresh your browser.

7 | In your browser, enter the number "1" and click OK.

FIGURE 3.5

8 | Refresh your Web browser.

9 | Repeat Steps 7 and 8; but this time, enter 2, 3, or 4 as the number of tickets.

The message should change with each value.

10 | Close the file in your browser and text editor.

To Extend Your Knowledge...

DEFAULT CASE VALUES

It is possible to specify a default value for a **switch** statement. The code executes if no case evaluates to **true**.

LESSON 2 Performing Actions Using "While" Loops

In Lesson 1, you discovered how to use **if** statements to choose a particular code segment to execute, based on an evaluated condition. This feature is useful in certain situations, but not as commonly used as code segments that must repeat until a condition changes. You can use **while** and **do while** statements to create such code segments. **While** and **do while** statements allow you to loop certain code segments until a value changes. For example, let's examine a loop that continues to execute until a car has traveled 10 miles.

```
miles=0;
while (miles<=10) {
        document.write("You've traveled "+miles+" miles."+"<br>");
        miles++;
        }
document.write("You've arrived!");
```

If you execute the code in a script, the following results display in a browser.

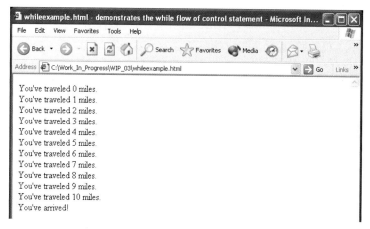

FIGURE 3.6

Create a "While" Loop

1   In your text editor, open while.html from your WIP_03 folder.

2   Find the following lines of code.

```
answer=0;

// insert while statement
```

This code creates and initializes the **answer** variable at a value of **0**.

3   Insert the following code.

```
...
<script language="JavaScript">
answer=0;
// insert while statement
while (answer!="Alaska") {
    answer=prompt("What is the correct answer?","");
} // end while
document.write("That is correct!");
</script>
...
```

The **prompt** statement in the **while** loop continues to execute until the user enters the correct answer.

4 Save your changes in the text editor and open the file in your browser.

FIGURE 3.7

A prompt box appears.

5 Enter the name of any state except Alaska and click OK.

The prompt box reappears.

6 Enter "Alaska" as your answer and click OK.

FIGURE 3.8

7 Close the file in your browser and text editor.

To Extend Your Knowledge...

LOOPING THROUGH ARRAYS

Loops are often useful when working with array values. For example, you could devise a loop to output the value stored in each array element by using the **counter** variable to reference the array, as in `document.write(myArray[counter])`. You can use the **length** property of the array to determine the correct number of times to execute the loop.

LESSON 3 Performing Actions Using "Do While" Loops

While effective in many situations, the **while** statement has one limitation: if the condition is **false**, the code never executes, which might cause a problem if you want the code to execute at least once, regardless of the condition. The **do while** statement offers a solution to this problem. Continuing with the example from Lesson 2, if the driver has already arrived, you may want to tell her the number of miles traveled. To do so, you can use a **do while** statement, as shown below:

```
miles=10;

do {

document.write("You've traveled "+miles+" miles."+"<br>");

        miles++;

        } while (miles<=10)

document.write("You've arrived!");
```

Inserting this code into an HTML page yields the following result.

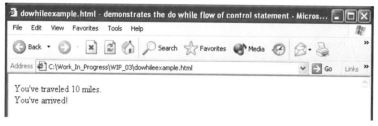

FIGURE 3.9

In the previous lesson, you used a **while** loop to ensure that a user entered the correct answer for a test question. Imagine that you included additional questions in the test and that you encountered a problem in your script. Through careful analysis, you realized the script does not work correctly when two questions, asked in consecutive order, have the same answer.

For example, if the correct answer to the first question is **Alaska**, the variable named **answer** is set to that value. Then, the next set of code statements is encountered, which asks for the answer to the second question:

```
while (answer!="Alaska") {

        answer=prompt("What is the correct answer?","");

} // end while

document.write("That is correct!");
```

In this situation, the condition in the **while** loop evaluates to **true**, which means the second question is never asked. This creates an obvious error because you want to ask the second question regardless of the answer to the first question. In the following exercise, you use a **do while** statement to correct this error.

Use "Do While" Statements in a Script

1 In your browser, open dowhile.html from your WIP_03 folder.

FIGURE 3.10

The code inside the **while** loop has not yet executed.

2 Open the file in your text editor and find the following code.

```
...
// the following code asks for the answer to question 2
while (answer!="Alaska") {
        answer=prompt("What is the correct answer?","");
} // end while
...
```

3 Modify the code as follows.

```
...
// the answer to question 1 is set
answer="Alaska";

// the following code asks for the answer to question 2
do {
        answer=prompt("What is the correct answer?","");
} while (answer!="Alaska")
document.write("That is correct!");

</script>
</body>
...
```

4   Save your changes in the text editor and refresh your browser.

FIGURE 3.11

5   Enter "Alaska" as the answer and click OK.

The script asks for the answer to the second question, regardless of the previous answer.

6   Close the file in your browser and text editor.

To Extend Your Knowledge...

"DO WHILE" LOOPS

Programmers tend to use **do while** loops less often than regular **while** statements, since fewer situations require a **do while** loop. **Do while** loops work best in situations where the content of the loop needs to execute at least once, regardless of the status of the testing condition. It is possible to use **while** statements in these situations, but additional redundant code is necessary for the code to execute properly.

LESSON 4   Incorporating "For" Statements

For statements may be a bit more difficult to master than other flow-of-control statements, but they give the user additional control over the looping operations. **For** statements provide a streamlined method of creating the starting condition that will be evaluated, testing for the condition that will end the loop, and changing the condition as the loop progresses. This process is similar to the **while** and **do while** operations, but the **for** statement is more compact. The following pseudo-code describes how **for** statements work:

```
for (setupCondition; endofLoopTest; modifyCondition) {
        codeGoesHere;
}
```

The pseudo-code consists of the following parts:

- The *setup condition* refers to a variable that initializes to create the beginning state of the loop.

- The *end-of-loop test* is a condition that is evaluated to determine when the loop stops executing.

- The *modify condition* is a change that executes each time the loop executes.

If this seems a bit overwhelming, don't worry — a working example will make the pseudo-code example easier to understand. In the following exercise, you create a loop that counts from one to ten.

Create a "For" Loop Statement

1 In your text editor, open for.html from your WIP_03 folder.

2 Insert the following code.

```
...
<body>
<script language="JavaScript">
// insert for loop here
for (counter=1; counter <= 10; counter++) {
        document.write(counter+"<br>");
}
</script>
</body>
</html>
```

3 Save your changes in the text editor and open the file in your browser.

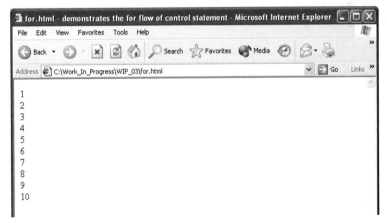

FIGURE 3.12

4 Close the file in your text editor and browser.

In this exercise, you created a variable named **counter** to control your loop. The **counter** was initialized to a value of **1**. The loop executed as long as the variable was less than or equal to **10**. Each time the loop executed, the variable was incremented by adding 1 to its current value.

To Extend Your Knowledge...

"FOR" LOOPS

`For` loops are particularly useful when you want to perform an action a specific number of times. In many common applications, you also need to nest certain actions. Consider the example of a class registration system: you need to register 100 students, with each student registering for 5 classes. In this situation, you would need one loop to register each student, as well as a nested loop to handle each of the 5 classes for each student.

LESSON 5 | Finding Code Errors

From your work in *Essentials for Design: JavaScript Level 1*, you know how to use the **window** object, the **document** object, and the **form** object, as well as use their properties, methods, event handlers, and subordinate objects. From earlier projects in this book, you know how to use variables and arrays, as well as create functions and flow-of-control statements. Using these skills, you can now write complex code that integrates all of the various aspects of JavaScript that you have learned.

As scripts become increasingly complex, it becomes progressively difficult to find errors (mistakes) in the code. Coding errors take two primary forms:

- *Syntax errors* refer to errors in the grammatical rules of JavaScript. Syntax errors are (usually) relatively easy to find.

- *Logic errors* mean the code does one thing, but it was intended to do something else. Logic errors are often more difficult to find and correct than syntax errors.

Consider the following line of code:

```
document.writ("hi world!");
```

Obviously, the "**e**" in "**write**" is missing. In many browsers, changing the case of a method generates an error or stops the code from executing. These types of syntax errors are often difficult to find, since the code may work fine in one browser but fail in another.

Throughout this lesson, you discover various techniques for avoiding errors, as well as ways to find errors you inadvertently placed in your code. The process of finding and correcting errors in your code is known as debugging. An early programmer coined this term when she found that an actual bug (an insect) had caused errors in the computer she was using.

Writing Clean Code

Writing code that is easy to read and understand is the best way to avoid making mistakes. Let's take a moment to review the steps involved in writing good (clean) code:

- Use whitespace to show nested loops in code.

- Place a semicolon at the end of each line of code, even when the interpreter doesn't require it. In most cases, you should not place a semicolon at the end of the right parenthesis of **while ( )**, **for ( )**, or **if ( )** conditions. You should, however, place a semicolon at the end of a **do while ( )** statement.

- Use programmer's comments to describe the purpose of each code segment, such as a function or a code segment that draws an HTML table.

- Use programmer's comments to describe the purpose of each variable when it is created.

- Use variable and function names that are easy to identify and understand.

- Use functions for code segments that are used repeatedly.

- Avoid using methods, objects, or properties that aren't supported in most commonly used browsers.

Writing clean code requires a bit of up-front work, rather than simply sitting down and writing a script as quickly as possible and resolving problems later. Good programmers break down complex problems into manageable chunks, and then they build one part of the solution at a time. This method ultimately saves a great deal of time that would otherwise be spent in painstaking searches for errors. As each section of the code is built (written), the programmer concentrates on simple, easy-to-understand scripts, tests them thoroughly, ensures they works perfectly, and then moves on to the next part. This work is often slow and tedious, but ultimately leads to far less frustration.

Interpreting Error Messages

In newer browsers, JavaScript error messages are often suppressed (hidden) from the user. Consider IE version 6, which ignores error messages. The following illustration shows the default options for IE. Notice that script debugging is turned off by default, and the browser does not display a notification about every script error.

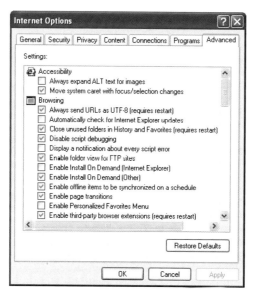

FIGURE 3.13

As with HTML, the browser is designed to ignore errors whenever possible and to display pages to the best of its ability. Consider the following error, which leaves off the ending parenthesis in the **alert()** method:

```
alert("This is a simple JavaScript command";
```

Using Internet Explorer 6.0 set to the defaults, the line of code is ignored, but an error icon may display in the lower-left corner of the status bar.

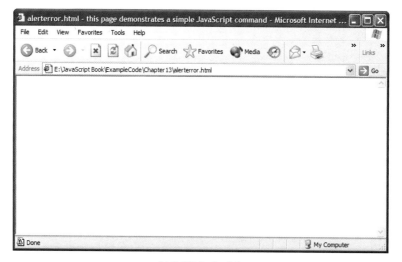

FIGURE 3.14

This error may not appear, depending on whether "Display an error about every script error" is turned on in the browser. Double-clicking the error icon generates an alert box that contains information about the error. The Hide Details button on the right side of the alert box allows you to hide or show the details of the error.

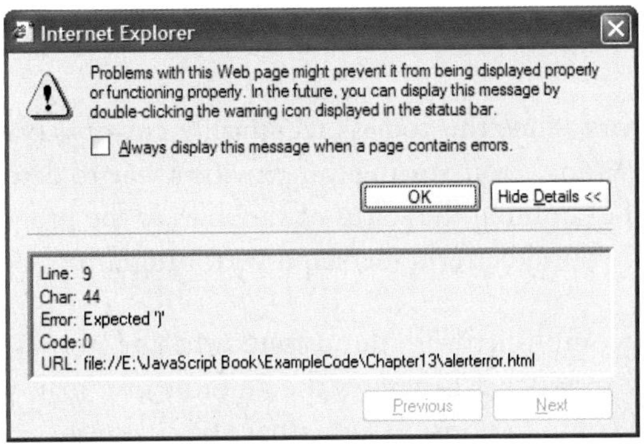

FIGURE 3.15

If you check the box that says "Always display this message when a page contains errors," the alert box appears automatically whenever an error occurs. In IE version 4 or higher, you can turn this message on or off by choosing Tools>Internet Options. In the Internet Options dialog, you can click the Advanced tab and activate the check box that says "Display a notification about every script error."

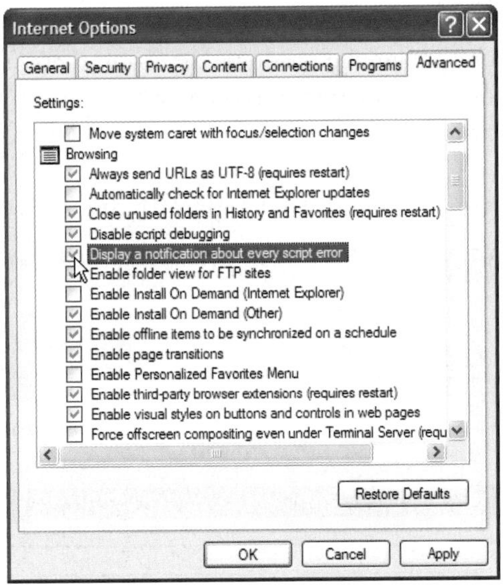

FIGURE 3.16

It is also important to remember that the line number listed may not be the actual source of the problem. For instance, imagine that the following line of code in your script uses variables to perform a calculation. Assume that you haven't yet defined the **taxAmount** variable.

```
total=subTotal*taxAmount;
```

If the interpreter sends you a message that an error occurred in Line 14, it may be unclear that the error was actually caused by an undeclared variable. In this case, the variable should have been declared in an earlier statement, which would have resolved the problem.

Tracing

Logic errors do not generate errors, since the code is technically correct. ***Precedence errors*** occur when the steps in a solution execute in the wrong error. Tracing can provide a way to determine the root cause of this type of error. ***Tracing*** is the process of examining the status of variables as the program executes. Tracing is a simple and powerful method that allows you to better understand your programs (code).

In JavaScript, tracing is usually accomplished with **document.write()** or **alert()** commands. For instance, assume you are trying to write a script that generates the amount of a loan payment, which involves several steps and complex mathematical computations. Assume that you wrote the steps on paper and figured out an example payment. After writing the script, you realize that it always arrives at the wrong answer. To find the problem, you can output the value of important variables at each step, using a simple statement such as:

```
document.write("After step 2, the value is "+loanAmount);
```

Use Tracing to Correct a Logic Error

In this exercise, assume that you are developing a Web page to display various products for an online store. You created an array to hold information about the products the store offers. You also created a loop to output information about the products. You are a conscientious programmer, so you test each part of your script as you write it. Your next step is to use tracing to find and correct an error in your code.

1   **In your browser, open logicerror.html from your WIP_03 folder.**

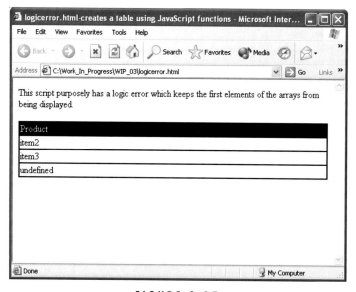

FIGURE 3.17

You do not receive an error message, but the first item does not display, and a value of "undefined" displays as the last value in the array.

2   **Find the following code in your document.**

```
...
// start section to draw table rows
v=0;
do {
        v++;
        document.write('<tr>');
        document.write('<td>'+productName[v]+'</td>');
        document.write('</tr>');
} while (v<productName.length)
...
```

This code creates an HTML table to display information about each product.

3   **Insert the following code.**

```
...
do {
        v++;
        document.write('<tr>');
        document.write("Counter is set to "+ v+"<br>");
        document.write('<td>'+productName[v]+'</td>');
        document.write('</tr>');
} while (v<productName.length)
...
```

This code traces the value of the counter (**v**) as the loop executes.

4 Save your changes in the text editor and refresh your browser.

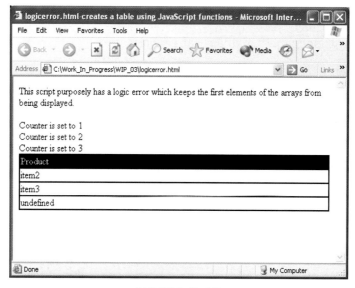

FIGURE 3.18

This reveals the problem with the script — if you had not already spotted it. Although the counter is initialized to **0**, it sets to **1** before the first product outputs to the screen.

5 Find and delete the following line of code.

```
v++;
```

6 Insert the line of code you deleted in Step 5 in the following location.

```
...
do {
        document.write("Counter is set to "+ v+"<br>");
        document.write('<tr>');
        document.write('<td>'+productName[v]+'</td>');
        document.write('</tr>');
v++;
} while (v<productName.length)
</script>
</table>
...
```

This change corrects the error.

7 Save your changes in the text editor and refresh your browser.

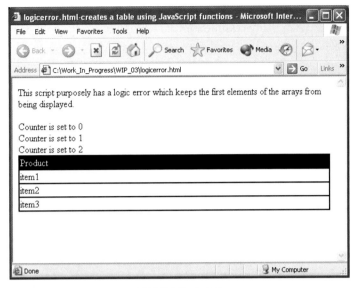

FIGURE 3.19

8 Find and delete the following line of code.

```
document.write("Counter is set to "+ v+"<br>");
```

This change removes the trace.

9 Save and close the file in your browser and text editor.

To Extend Your Knowledge...

ERROR MESSAGE NOTIFICATION

Error messages from JavaScript display the line number where the error occurs. It is important to note that the line number is counted from the beginning of the HTML document, not from the beginning of the `<script>` tag.

LESSON 6 Identifying Common Scripting Errors

JavaScript developers typically make many common errors while writing code. In this lesson, you examine the most common types of errors committed by JavaScript developers. Many languages, including Java, C++, and Flash ActionScript, use grammatical rules that are very similar to JavaScript's rules. The following list of common errors is relevant to these other programming languages, as well as to JavaScript.

1. Leaving off ending quote, bracket, or parenthesis, such as:

```
document.write("Hi everyone!);

j=x[32+1;

alert("You choose the luxury option.";
```

Corrected versions:

```
document.write("Hi everyone!");

j=x[32+1];

alert("You choose the luxury option.");
```

2. Using the assignment operator instead of the equality operator or vice versa, such as:

```
if (number=32)

var number==32;
```

Corrected version:

```
if (number==32)

var number=32;
```

3. Creating infinite loops, such as:

```
x=1;

while (x<32)

doSomething(x);
```

Corrected version:

```
x=1;

while (x<32) {

doSomething(x);

x++

} // end while
```

4. Using undefined variables, such as:

```
document.write(firstName);
```

Corrected version:

```
firstName="Joe";

document.write(firstName);
```

5. Inserting extra semicolons, such as:

```
if (paid==true);

makePayment();
```

Corrected version:

```
if (paid==true)

makePayment();
```

6. Omitting **break** statements in a **switch** statement. This usually causes latter parts of the **switch** statement to execute:

```
switch (payment) {

case "cash": {

doSomething();

}

case "credit":

doSomethingElse();

}
```

```
switch (payment) {

case "cash": {

doSomething();

break;

}

case "credit":

doSomethingElse();

break;

}
```

7. Calling non-existent methods, functions, or properties, such as:

```
window.screenSize;

window.makeSmaller();
```

Corrected versions:

```
screen.availWidth;

window.resizeBy(-200,-200);
```

8. Using a form element instead of the value of the element. When using the value stored in a form element, you must use the **value** keyword:

```
document.form1.email;

document.forms[1].state;
```

Corrected versions:

```
document.form1.email.value;

document.forms[1].state.value;
```

Mistakes involving the type of information used can create significant problems for developers. These mistakes are actually logic errors, rather than syntax errors. For example, consider the following statement:

```
total=2+"5";

document.write(total);
```

Since part of the information is a string, and part of the information is a number, JavaScript assumes that you want to concatenate the information into a single text string. This code outputs the string "**25**" to the screen.

Recall that JavaScript is loosely typed, which means that you do not have to declare the type of information stored in a variable. Instead, JavaScript decides how to deal with a variable based on the type of information you enter. Entering incorrect information into the variable can create unusual problems that are difficult to find. For example, consider the following script:

```
x=prompt("Enter a number");

result=x+32;

document.write("x plus 32 equals "+result);
```

Assuming you run this script in a browser and enter the number "**6**" at the user prompt, you receive "**326**" as the result of the calculation. The **parseInt()** method is needed to convert the value from a text string to a numeric value. For numbers using decimal values, you can use the **parseFloat()** method to convert a string to a floating-point decimal number.

Correct Common Scripting Errors

| **1** | **In your browser and text editor, open common.html from your WIP_03 folder.**

This is essentially the same file that you used in a previous exercise to create a counter. Common scripting errors are currently keeping the file from executing.

| **2** | **Find the following code.**

```
. . .

for (counter==1; counter = 10; counter++) {

        document.write(counter+"<br>");

}

. . .
```

| **3** | **Change the line of code to use the equal sign (=) instead of the equality operator (==) to initial-ize the variable.**

```
. . .

for (counter=1; counter = 10; counter++) {

        document.write(counter+"<br>");

}

. . .
```

4 Save your changes in the text editor and refresh your browser.

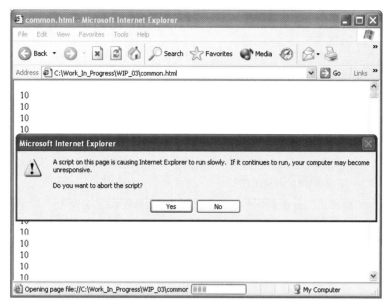

FIGURE 3.20

The script creates an infinite loop.

5 Click Yes to abort the script.

6 Change the condition to use the less than or equal to operator (<=).

```
...
for (counter=1; counter <= 10; counter++) {
        document.write(counter+"<br>");
}
...
```

To Extend Your Knowledge...

DEBUGGING PROGRAMS

Debugging programs typically include tracing windows that show the values of variables as the program executes. These programs usually allow you to "step" through the script, enabling developers to run one line of code at a time. As of this writing, the Microsoft Script Debugger is available as a free download from Microsoft. Other JavaScript debuggers are also available as free downloads, including versions by Netscape that are specifically designed to interact with Netscape browsers.

7   **Save your changes in the text editor and refresh your browser.**

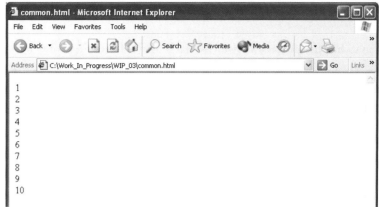

FIGURE 3.21

The code now executes correctly.

8   **Close the file in your browser and text editor.**

SUMMARY

In Project 3, you learned that flow-of-control statements use comparisons to decide if certain actions should execute. You discovered that an **if** statement simply asks whether a condition is **true** and, if so, carries out an action or a sequence of actions. Similarly, a **while** statement performs an action repeatedly until the condition becomes **false**. A **do while** statement, in contrast, performs a code statement at least once before the condition is evaluated.

You found that **switch** and **break** statements are useful when you are looking for certain known values. The **for** statement, in contrast, is specifically designed to provide an advanced loop that you control by specifying when the loop will end and exactly how many times it will execute.

In this project, you discovered how programmers can avoid making common coding errors. In addition, you learned how to use various debugging techniques to find errors in your JavaScript code. You also learned how to use tracing, a method commonly used to find programming errors in code. Even though writing clean and consistent code helps you to avoid many errors, some errors in complex scripts are unavoidable — even the most conscientious developers make mistakes from time to time.

KEY TERMS

Debugging	Logic error	Syntax error
Do while statement	Modify condition statement	Tracing
End-of-loop test	Precedence error	While statement
Flow-of-control statement	Setup condition	

CHECKING CONCEPTS AND TERMS

MULTIPLE CHOICE

Circle the letter that matches the correct answer for each of the following questions.

1. What term is often used to describe flow-of-control statements, such as **if** and **switch**?

   a. Conditional statement

   b. Function statement

   c. Method

   d. Constant modifier

   e. None of the above

2. What happens when you leave off the **break** keyword from a **switch** statement?

   a. The browser locks up and stops working.

   b. The switch creates an infinite loop.

   c. The code for conditions that do not test **true** may also execute.

   d. This does not affect the switch statement because the **break** keyword is optional.

3. Using a **switch** statement is useful in situations where you _____.

   a. want to execute lines of code at least once, regardless of a testing condition

   b. want to execute lines of code a certain number of times

   c. want to repeat lines of code until a condition is **false**

   d. have several known values

4. Using a **while** statement is useful in situations where you _____.

   a. want to execute lines of code at least once, regardless of a testing condition

   b. want to execute lines of code a certain number of times

   c. want to repeat lines of code until a condition is **false**

   d. have several known values

5. Using a **do while** statement is useful in situations where you _____.

   a. want to execute lines of code at least once, regardless of a testing condition

   b. want to execute lines of code a certain number of times

   c. want to repeat lines of code until a condition is **false**

   d. have several known values

6. What does the setup condition portion of a **for** statement do in a script?

   a. It does not affect the execution of the loop.

   b. It initializes a variable that will be used to create a counter.

   c. It tests for a condition to end the loop.

   d. It modifies a variable each time the loop executes.

7. What does the modify condition portion of a **for** statement do in a script?

   a. It does not affect the execution of the loop.

   b. It initializes a variable that will be used to create a counter.

   c. It tests for a condition to end the loop.

   d. It modifies a variable each time the loop executes.

8. What does the end-of-loop test portion of a **for** statement do in a script?

   a. It does not affect the execution of the loop.

   b. It initializes a variable that will be used to create a counter.

   c. It tests for a condition to end the loop.

   d. It modifies a variable each time the loop executes.

9. Which of the following is an example of a logic error?

   a. When you use mismatching brackets or quotes

   b. When you misspell method names

   c. When you omit semicolons from code statements

   d. When you place commands in the wrong order

10. Which one of the following is an example of a syntax error?

   a. When the code does something different than intended

   b. When you use the wrong variable in a code statement

   c. When you misspell method names

   d. When you place commands in the wrong order

DISCUSSION QUESTIONS

1. How are all flow-of-control statements (such as **for**, **while**, and **switch**) similar to **if** statements?

2. How could a programmer accidentally create an infinite loop when using flow-of-control statements?

3. How can tracing help you to find coding errors?

4. Name at least two common programming errors. Why do you think programmers make these particular errors?

SKILL DRILL

Skill Drill exercises reinforce project skills. Each skill reinforced is the same, or nearly the same, as a skill presented in the project. Detailed instructions are provided in a step-by-step format. You should work through the exercises in order.

1. Create a "For" Loop

In this exercise, you consider a situation that uses a nested **for** loop. You create a simple program to output multiplication tables. You need one loop to create the first number, and you need an inner loop to create the second number and multiply the values.

1. In your text editor, open fornested.html from the WIP_03 folder.

   First, you write the code for the outer loop to create and display the first number.

2. Add the following code within the script in the body of the page.

```
for (outNumber=1; outNumber<=10; outNumber++) {


} // end for
```

3. Insert a **document.write()** statement into the **for** loop that outputs the value stored in the **outNumber** variable and a blank space.

   This allows you to see how the loop works.

4. Save your changes in the text editor and open the file in your Web browser.

   Your output should match the following illustration.

FIGURE 3.22

5. Keep the file open in your text editor and browser for the next exercise.

2. Use Nested "For" Loops

1. In the open fornested.html, find and delete the code shown below.

   Your code may look slightly different, since this is the code you created in Step 3 of the previous exercise.

   ```
   document.write(outNumber+" ");
   ```

2. Insert the inner loop to create the second number. This loop should repeat 10 times for each execution of the outer loop. Inside the existing **for** loop, create a second **for** loop. This loop should use a variable named **inNumber**. The **inNumber** variable should be initialized to a value of **1**. The loop should continue until the **inNumber** variable is less than or equal to **10**. The loop should increment the **inNumber** variable by **1** each time the loop executes.

3. Insert the following code into the loop you created in the previous step.

   ```
                   result=outNumber*inNumber;

                   document.write(outNumber+"* " + inNumber+" =
   "+result+"<br>");

           } // end inner for

   } // end for

   </script>

   </body>

   . . .
   ```

4. Insert the following line of code between the brackets that mark the end of the **for** loops.

```
...
                result=outNumber*inNumber;
                document.write(outNumber+"* " + inNumber+" =
"+result+"<br>");
        }
        document.write("<br>");
} // end for
</script>
</body>
...
```

5. Save your changes in the text editor and refresh your browser.

Your file should match the following illustration.

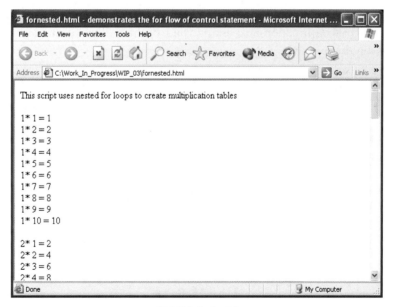

FIGURE 3.23

6. Close the file in your text editor and browser.

3. Test for Errors

In this exercise, you debug a travel agency's Web page. The page is designed to allow a user to enter her name, and then pick a destination. If the user chooses Cancun, Mexico, or the Dominican Republic, a confirmation box should appear, requiring the user to acknowledge that a birth certificate or passport is required. If the user chooses Monterrey, CA, no further confirmation is needed.

1. In your browser, open travelpackagecomplete.html from your WIP_03>travel folder.

    This is the finished version of the file. You will not debug this version of the file.

2. Leave the Name field blank and click Send.

    You receive an alert message, informing you that you must enter a name.

3. Click OK.

4. Type any name in the Name field and click Send.

    Since the package defaulted to Monterrey, CA, no further confirmation is necessary, and you should be redirected to a Thank You page.

5. Click the Back button to return to the form.

6. Choose Cancun, Mexico, from the pull-down menu, and then resubmit the form.

    You should receive a confirmation box, asking you to confirm that you understand a birth certificate or passport is required.

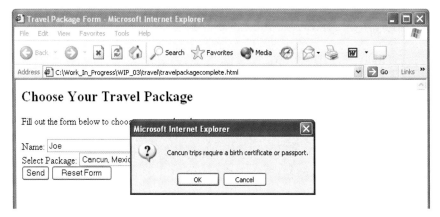

FIGURE 3.24

7. Click Cancel.

    An alert box informs you that the submission has been canceled.

8. Click OK to return to the form.

9. Close the file.

10. In your text editor and browser, open travelpackage.html from your WIP_03>travel folder.

    You debug this version of the file.

11. In the browser, leave the Name field blank and click Send at the bottom of the page.

     You should receive a message that tells you to enter a name; instead, you receive a confirmation message about trips to Cancun.

12. Click Cancel.

13. Click OK in the alert box that tells you the form submission has been canceled.

14. Leave the Name field blank and choose other destinations.

     The script should always generate an alert box when the Name field is blank. Note whether the error occurs whenever the field is blank or only when choosing certain destinations.

15. Keep the file open in your text editor and browser for the next exercise.

4. Correct a Logic Error

1. In the open file, return to your text editor and inspect the following code in the function.

```
...
if (travelForm.name =="")
        {
        alert("You must enter a name.");
        return false;
        }
        else
                switch (travelForm.package.value)
...
```

    Parts of the **switch** statement are executing in the browser. This suggests that the condition evaluated in the **if** statement always evaluates to **false**; the **switch** statement would only execute if this were the case.

2. Insert the following trace command directly before the **if** statement.

```
alert(travelForm.name);
```

3. Refresh the page in your browser.

4. Leave the Name field blank and click Send.

    The alert box displays a cryptic message that simply says "**[object]**." Other browsers may display an error message in this situation. This tells you that the value of the form object isn't being considered in the **if** statement.

5. Click OK.

6. Correct the **if** statement to refer to the **value** property stored in the **name** object and remove the tracing alert.

7. Save your changes in the text editor and refresh your browser. Leave the Name field blank and click Send. You should receive a warning message about leaving the Name field blank.

8. Click OK. Keep the file open in your browser and text editor for the next exercise.

5. Correct a Switch Statement

1. In the open file, type any name into the Name field, leave the package menu set to Monterrey, CA, and click Send.

    You should receive a message about Cancun trips requiring a birth certificate or passport.

2. Click Cancel, and then click OK.

3. Return to your text editor and find the following code.

```
...

switch (travelForm.package.value)

        {

            case "Monterrey":

                {

                ask=true;

                }

            case "Cancun":

                {

                ask=confirm("Cancun trips require a birth certifi-
cate or passport.");

                break;  }

            case "Dominican": {

                ask=confirm("Dominican Republic trips require a
passport");

                break;  }

} // end of switch

...
```

The **switch** statement contains a common error that causes the code to continue to execute, even though the first **case** evaluates to **true**.

4. Correct the following code segment.

```
case "Monterrey":

        {

        ask=true;

        }
```

5. Save the file in your text editor and refresh your browser.

6. Test the page thoroughly. The code should now work correctly.

7. Close the file in your browser and text editor.

CHALLENGE

Challenge exercises expand on, or are somewhat related to, skills presented in the lessons. Each exercise provides a brief introduction, followed by instructions presented in a numbered-step format that are not as detailed as those in the Skill Drill exercises. You should work through these exercises in order.

1. Create Cases for a Switch

A company that specializes in tour packages contracted you to design a page to interface with an existing software system. To complete the job, you must write a **switch** statement that converts the package name values from text to numbers.

1. In your browser and text editor, open challengedefault.html from your WIP_03 folder.

2. Find the following **switch** statement in the head of the document.

    This statement converts the value **Luxury** to a matching number.

```
...
        switch (travelForm.package.value)
            {
            case "Luxury":
                {
                package=1;
                break;
                }
        } // end of switch
...
```

3. Add another **case** statement for the value **Adventure**. If this **case** evaluates to **true**, the variable **package** should be set to a value of **2**.

4. Add another **case** statement for the value **Touring**. If this **case** evaluates to **true**, the variable **package** should be set to a value of **3**.

5. Keep the file open in your text editor and browser for the next exercise.

2. Use the Default Option in a Switch to Find Errors

During the construction of the tour package Web page, the development team noticed that the interface occasionally generates errors when a bug in the system allows users to pick a package that is not covered in the **switch** statement. In this exercise, you use the **default** option for a **switch** statement to detect when the software cannot translate a value to a number.

1. In the open challengedefault.html, find the following code in the head of the document.

```
switch (travelForm.package.value)
    {
    case "Luxury":
        {
        package=1;
        break;
        }
    case "Adventure":
        {
        package=2;
        break;
        }
    case "Touring":
        {
        package=3;
        }
    } // end of switch
```

2. Insert the following code. (This code creates a tracing alert when the switch is unable to resolve the text value to a numeric value.)

```
...
            case "Touring": {
                        package=3;
                        break;
                }
                default: {
                        alert("no case tested true in number assignment");
                }
            } // end of switch
            return false;
        } // end function
    ...
```

3. Save your changes in the text editor and refresh your browser.

4. Choose Other from the pull-down menu.

5. Click Send.

    An alert box appears.

6. Click OK.

7. Assume the software is designed to handle the errors. Set the **default** option to set the **package** variable to a value of **4** and remove the tracing alert you inserted in Step 2.

8. Save and test your file.

    No alerts should appear.

9. Close the file in your browser and text editor.

3. Use Tracing to Design a Script

Assume that you were asked to design a page that displays a random picture whenever the page loads. You were given 76 pictures to use for the project. The solution to this problem has two parts: 1) You know that you need to pick a random number between 1 and 76; and 2) You must dynamically generate the code to display the picture selected in Part 1. Start the script by writing the code to generate the random number.

1. In your text editor, open challengerandom.html from your WIP_03 folder and examine the code.

2. Open the file in your Web browser.

   The page doesn't yet output anything to the end user. At this point, you know the script doesn't generate any syntax errors, but you haven't verified that the script is working properly. You need to use tracing to see if the code has been designed correctly.

3. Find the following function in the head of the document.

   ```
   . . .

   function getPicNumber() {

               randomNumber=(Math.random());

               return randomNumber;

   } //end function

   . . .
   ```

4. Create a statement to trace the value of the **randomNumber** variable before the number returns from the function.

5. Save your changes in the text editor and refresh your browser.

FIGURE 3.25

Examining the file in the browser reveals a bug in the logic: the **Math.random()** method returns a number between **0** and **1**, but you need a number between **1** and **76**.

6. Change the assignment statement to the following.

```
randomNumber=Math.random() * 100;
```

7. Save your changes in the text editor and refresh your browser. You managed to get a two-digit number, but you need to discard the amount after the decimal point.

8. Create another statement that uses the **Math.round()** method to discard the decimal amount.

9. Save your changes and refresh your browser several times.

   With each refresh, you should see a new number between **1** and **100**.

10. Keep the file open in your browser and text editor.

4. Use Tracing to Debug a Script

In the previous exercise, you probably noticed that the browser returned many numbers that were greater than 76. In this exercise, you use tracing to correct this error and continue to develop this script.

1. Continue working in the open file. Since the largest number that can be generated is **76,** you need to multiply the result by **0.76** (76%), as shown in the following statement.

```
randomNumber=(Math.random() * .76) * 100;
```

2. Instead of multiplying the number by **0.76** and **100**, change the formula to simply multiply the number by **76**.

3. Save your changes and refresh the browser several times.

   Your script appears to be perfect, but it actually has one significant bug: if the **Math.random()** method returns a very small number, such as **.002832739482**, the result is **0** (zero).

4. To fix this problem, multiply by **75** instead of **76** and always add **1** to the result.

5. Save your changes in the text editor and refresh the browser several times to test your script.

   The script should always generate a number between **1** and **76**.

6. Close the file in your browser and text editor.

PORTFOLIO BUILDER

Debug a Complex Script

The ability to debug complex scripts is one of the most important skills a Web developer can bring to a project team. The most common code errors are syntax errors, which are usually simple typographic mistakes. In this Portfolio Builder, you debug a complex script, one step at a time, until it is error free.

- Open debug.html from your Work_In_Progress>WIP_03 folder in your browser. Be sure that error reporting is enabled.

- When the page attempts to load, an error displays in the browser window as either a warning box or an alert icon in the status bar. Read the error message. On what line does the error occur? Are there any notations of missing characters?

- Because scripting errors are so common, developers have learned to prioritize the debugging process. For example, knowing that quote mismatch is a very common mistake, the first task is to find and fix those errors. Then, programmers look for missing parentheses, brackets, and semicolons. Debug your script for these syntax errors.

- Follow the error reports to locate the errors in the script. Continue the process until the page is error free. When the page is "clean," you will receive a prompt and be presented with a list produced by an array.

- As you work through the debugging process, consider how you will develop a personal method of debugging. What process works best for you? Once you identify a process that works well, use it every time you debug your code. This method helps you to become a more efficient code debugger.

Adding Forms and Images

OBJECTIVES

In this project, you learn how to

- Use form elements and properties

- Validate form elements

- Use image properties

- Preload images

- Create rollover scripts

- Use advanced image scripts

WHY WOULD I DO THIS?

The **form** object and **image** object are probably the most useful objects within JavaScript's Document Object Model (DOM) because these objects allow you to manipulate HTML forms and images in ways not possible using HTML alone. Most practical applications of JavaScript usually incorporate one of these two objects.

HTML forms allow programmers to gather data from users for various purposes. Designing forms in HTML is particularly practical because it allows designers to create forms that are easy for end users to understand. JavaScript allows you to greatly extend the power and flexibility of HTML forms by allowing you to check the quality of the information entered and perform other tasks before the form data is sent to the server.

JavaScript allows you to use images in many ways, including rollover buttons (images that change in response to user choices). In HTML, you use the **<img>** tag to display images, as shown in the following example:

```
<img src="boy.jpg">
```

Using HTML, you can display an image; in contrast, JavaScript provides several new ways of manipulating images. For example, you can **preload** image files, which means you load the file before the user sees the image. In many situations, a preloaded image appears as soon as a user clicks on it. In this project, you learn how to use JavaScript to add and manipulate forms and images, allowing you to extend the complexity, depth, and functionality in your Web pages.

V I S U A L   S U M M A R Y

Recall from your work with HTML that you use the **<form>** tag to create a form. When you use this tag, JavaScript creates a matching **form** object that can be referenced from the **forms[]** array. For example, the first form in a page would be referred to as **forms[0]**, and the second form in a page would be referred to as **forms[1]**.

To create an element in a form, you could use the **<input>** tag. The **type** attribute specifies the type of **form** element that you want to create. The **type** attribute can include the following: **text**, **password**, **radio**, **checkbox**, **reset**, **button**, **submit**, **image**, and **hidden**. Consider the code for the following form, which allows a user to request a service appointment for her vehicle.

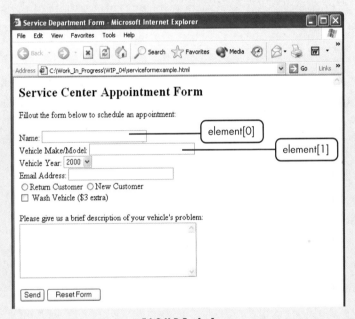

FIGURE 4.1

```
serviceformexample.html - Notepad
File  Edit  Format  View  Help
<html>
<head>
<title>Service Department Form</title>
</head>
<body>
<p><h2>Service Center Appointment Form</h2></p>
<p>Fillout the form below to schedule an appointment:</p>
<form method="POST" action="mail2.asp">
      <p>Name: <input name="name" type="text" size="30"><br>
      Vehicle Make/Model: <input name="carMake" type="text" size="30"><br>
      Vehicle Year:
      <select name="carYear">
      <option value="2000">2000</option>
      <option value="2001">2001</option>
      <option value="2002">2002</option>
      <option value="2003">2003</option>
      </select><br>
      Email Address: <input name="email" type="text" size="30"><br>
      <input type="radio" name="repeat" value="returnCustomer">Return Customer
      <input type="radio" name="repeat" value="newCustomer">New Customer<br>
      <input type="checkbox" name="washvehicle" value="checkbox">
      Wash Vehicle ($3 extra)<br>
      <p>Please give us a brief description of your vehicle's problem: <br>
      <textarea name="description" cols="40" rows="6"></textarea></p>
      <input type="hidden" name="redirect" value="thanks.html">
      <input type="submit" value="Send" name="submit">
      <input type="reset" value="Reset Form">
      </p>
</form>
</body>
</html>
```

FIGURE 4.2

In this form, the **<input>** tag creates various **form** elements. In the Email Address and Name fields, the **text** type is used. A **checkbox** type is used for the Wash Vehicle check box. The **radio** type is used to create the Return Customer and New Customer radio buttons, and the **<textarea>** tag is used to gather the description of the vehicle.

In this form, the information is sent to a server-side script named mail2.asp using the **post** method. The server-side script is an ASP script that accepts the information and sends an email to the service manager. A hidden field is also sent to the script; it contains the URL of a Thank You page that the user will see after the server-side script accepts the information.

Recall from HTML that you use the **post** or **get** method to submit a form. The **get** method appends the data to the end of the URL specified in the **action** attribute of the **<form>** tag. The **post** method sends the data as part of the HTTP protocol, which effectively hides the information from the end user.

If you do not specify a file in the **action** attribute, the information is sent back to the file that contained the **<form>** tag. If you do not specify a method for the **<form>** tag, the **get** method sends the information. Most server-side scripts are designed to receive information sent by the **post** method. (The ability to set up a server-side script to process form data requires an understanding of a server-side scripting language, as well as an understanding of the server's configuration. An explanation of these items is beyond the scope of this book. Most Web-hosting companies offer free scripts and detailed explanations on how to set up form-processing scripts on their servers.)

The **document** object represents the HTML code in a Web page. The **forms[]** array represents each **<form>** tag in the document. Similarly, the **elements[]** array represents each **form** element within the form. The first element in the **elements[]** array represents the first item in the form. For instance, to reference the first element in the first form, you would write:

```
document.forms[0].elements[0]
```

To reference the second element in the first form, you would write:

```
document.forms[0].elements[1]
```

The keyword **value** outputs the value stored in the **form** element. For instance, if you want to see what a user entered into the third element in the form, you would write the following:

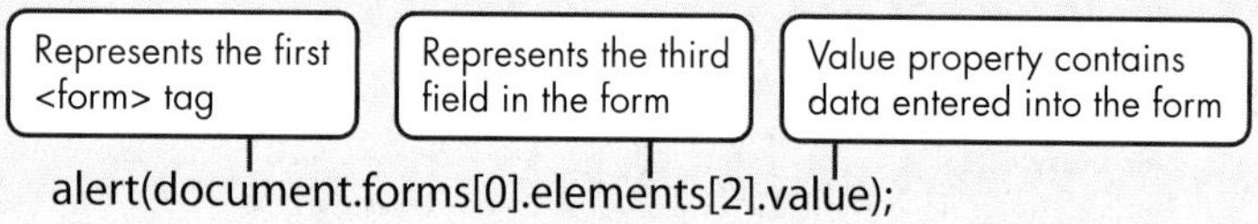

| Represents the first <form> tag | Represents the third field in the form | Value property contains data entered into the form |

```
alert(document.forms[0].elements[2].value);
```

FIGURE 4.3

Whenever you use an `<img>` tag, JavaScript creates an **image** object to represent the image. Similar to other JavaScript objects, an image can be represented by the name assigned to it in HTML. Similarly, **image** objects in JavaScript are represented by the **images[]** array. The **images[]** array is part of the **document** object. Each element in the **images[]** array contains an **image** object. One **image** object is created for every `<img>` tag found in the HTML code. This is consistent with the way that JavaScript handles other HTML tags, as you may remember from previous examples. For instance, if you assume the `<img>` tag example shown above is the first one in the HTML document, you could reference the image as:

```
document.images[0]
```

If the HTML tag includes the name of the image, you can also refer to the image by name in JavaScript. For instance, consider the following line of code:

```
<img src="boy.jpg" name="boyPic">
```

Knowing this, you can also refer to the image in the following ways within JavaScript:

```
document.images['boyPic']

document.boyPic
```

LESSON 1   Using Form Elements and Properties

As you know, JavaScript creates an entry in the **forms[]** array for each `<form>` tag encountered in the document. Each **form** element within a form creates an entry in an **elements[]** array for that form. As you have seen, the forms and elements are numbered in the order in which they appear in the HTML document.

You can also name forms and elements, and then refer to the objects by their assigned names or ids. For instance, you can name a form and an element in the following fashion:

```
<form action="" name="serviceForm" id="serviceForm">

Name: <input name="name" id="name" type="text" size="30">
```

In this situation, you can refer to the value of the element of the form as follows:

```
serviceForm.name.value
```

Assuming that **serviceForm** is the first form in the document, you could also refer to the value of this field as:

```
forms[0].name.value
```

Assuming that you are referring to the value stored in first element of the form, you could type:

```
serviceForm.elements[0].value
```

Depending on your specific needs, you can choose to use the **forms[]** array or the **elements[]** array to refer to any form or element. As you learned in previous lessons, referring to the number of the element is useful when creating loops, but it is usually easier to use the name of an individual element when checking the value of a single field.

If more than one element has the same name, JavaScript creates an array to hold the values. This is useful with radio buttons that must have the same name, since only one button can be chosen at a time. The following code establishes radio buttons that allow you to know whether a customer is new or returning.

```
<input type="radio" name="repeat" value="returnCustomer">Return
Customer

<input type="radio" name="repeat" value="newCustomer">New
Customer<br>
```

To access the value of the first radio button in the **repeat[]** array, you would type:

```
forms[0].repeat[0]
```

Similar to radio buttons, multiple check boxes can have the same name, too. In this case, you would create an array for all check boxes that have the same name.

The **form** object contains several properties that primarily contain the aspects assigned in the HTML **<form>** tag. These properties include the **name** property assigned to the **<form>** tag, as well as names assigned to individual **<input>** tags. They also include a property that allows you to find out if a particular check box or radio button has been selected. In the following sections, you examine the primary properties of the **form** object.

Name

The **name** property returns the name assigned to each **<form>** tag or each element within the form. Consider the following statements in an HTML form:

```
<form method="post" name="serviceForm" action="mail2.asp">
<p>Name: <input name="name" type="text" size="30">
```

To generate an alert box with the name of the first form in the HTML document, you would write:

```
alert(document.forms[0].name);
```

Similarly, if you want to determine the name of the first element in the first form, you would write:

```
alert(document.forms[0].elements[0].name);
```

Checked

With check boxes or radio buttons, you are usually only interested in the item that was checked (selected). Whenever you have multiple radio buttons or check boxes with the same name, HTML allows you to check only one of the items, and then JavaScript creates an associated array. You can use the **checked** property to discover which element was checked. For instance, to determine whether the first radio button in the example file was checked, you would write:

```
document.forms[0].repeat[0].checked;
```

If the first radio button was checked, a value of **true** returns. This creates interesting possibilities. For instance, you might want to trigger a specific action if the second radio button was checked:

```
if (document.forms[0].repeat[1].checked) {
        alert("You chose the second radio button.");
} // end if
```

Action

The **action** property of the **form** object holds the URL where the information in the form will be sent when the user clicks the Submit button. If a form named **serviceForm** sends the information to a server-side script named **formmail.pl**, your **<form>** tag might be written as:

```
<form name="serviceForm" action="formmail.pl">
```

In this situation, you could refer to the file in the **action** attribute within JavaScript in the following fashion:

```
document.serviceForm.action
```

In this example, the value of the **action** property is **formmail.pl**.

Method

The **method** property holds the same information specified in the **method** attribute of the **<form>** tag. You may recall from HTML that the **method** is specified as **post** or **get**. For instance, assume that the following **<form>** tag is within an HTML document:

```
<form name="serviceForm" method="post" action="formmail.pl">
```

In this situation, the **method** property of the document returns a value of **post**. You can reference this property as:

```
document.serviceForm.method
```

Access Form Elements in JavaScript

1 Copy the contents of the RF_JavaScript_L2>Project_04 folder into your Work_In_Progress>WIP_04 folder.

2 In your text editor, open seeelements.html from the WIP_04 folder.

This file is essentially the same form that was shown as an example in the preceding text. In the following steps, you write a function to display the content of each **form** element when the form is submitted. The function was started for you.

3 Insert the following code in the function in the head of the HTML document.

```
function seeElements() {

        alert(document.forms[0].elements[0].value);

} //end seeElements
```

This code will display the first value in the form when the form is submitted.

4 Add the following code to the **<form>** tag.

```
<form action="" method="post" onsubmit="return seeElements()">
```

This code triggers the function.

5 Save the file in your text editor and open it in your browser.

6 In the Name field, type your name and click the Send button at the bottom of the page.

An alert box appears with the name you entered into the field. If your name were Joe Smith, the alert would resemble the following illustration.

FIGURE 4.4

7 Click OK to close the alert box. Close your browser.

Next, you change the function to display all the elements.

8   Return to the text editor. Change the function to the following.

```
...
function seeElements() {
for (x=0; x<11; x++) {
        alert(document.forms[0].elements[x].value);
} //end for
        return false;
} //end seeElements
...
```

9   Save your changes in the text editor and reopen the file in your Web browser.

10   Enter information in the fields on the form, and then click the Send button.

As you click OK to move through each element, match the element value shown in the alert box with the element in the original HTML file. The value of the hidden element is thanks.html, which is the name of the redirect file shown after the form is submitted. The last element shown is the Reset button.

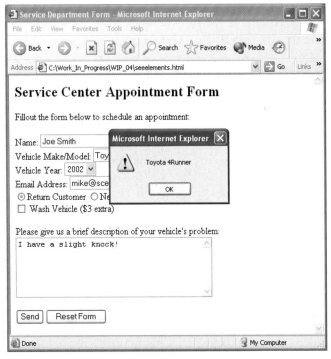

FIGURE 4.5

11   Close the file in your Web browser and text editor.

Your sample form contains a hidden element that also has an entry in the **elements[ ]** array.

To Extend Your Knowledge...

USING SCRIPTS TO CREATE EMAILS

Active Server Pages (ASP) and Perl are technologies often used to process form data. Students are often curious about how to set up a server-side script to send an email message with the content of an HTML form. You can accomplish this task in a number of ways using different technologies, including ASP and Perl. A Perl script, known as `formmail.pl`, is often used to accomplish this task, and the Common Gateway Interface (CGI) protocol is often used to communicate between the HTML form and a server-side script. CGI is a server-side technology that allows different languages to pass information to one another.

LESSON 2 Validating Forms

As you may remember from *Essentials for Design: JavaScript Level 1*, the ability to validate form data was one of the primary reasons that JavaScript was created. The term ***validate*** means to ensure that the user entered his information completely and correctly, and that the information is in the proper format. Form validation can take on a variety of different aspects. In many cases, you may simply want to ensure that the user entered a value in a required field.

Form validation methods vary according to the specific needs of the information you want to receive. In one case, you may want to ensure that the user entered an email address or a phone number into a form field. On another form, you may need to ensure that the user entered a number or value of a specific length.

The event handler usually calls on a function to validate the data. The function itself may call on various **form** properties, and then use Boolean logic with flow-of-control statements to analyze the information submitted.

Throughout the following sections, you examine a number of simple scripts that validate form data. These scripts demonstrate many basic validation methods that are useful in a number of programming situations.

Validating Email Addresses

Online users often choose to ask questions or investigate products because they like the anonymity associated with using the Internet. They may also buy products from another country or conduct business after hours. Using a Contact form is the method of choice for most users who investigate products online, and many businesses pay particular attention to leads generated from the Contact forms on their Web sites.

Many users inadvertently enter their email addresses incorrectly when filling out forms. When this happens, the user enters her email address and submits the form, but never receives a response. This error can result in a lost sale or other significant miscommunications.

Many simple forms gather user information. Consider the following form used for a new-user sign-up page.

```
<form action="">
<p>Name: <input name="name" type="text" size="30"><br>
Email Address: <input name="email1" type="text" size="30"><br>
<input type="submit" value="Send" name="submit">
        <input type="reset" value="Reset Form">
</form>
```

FIGURE 4.6

With JavaScript's ability to read and respond to form data, you can provide solutions to such problems as entering incorrect email addresses. First, you can ensure that the user entered a valid email address. Let's start by modifying the **<form>** tag so it uses a function when the form is submitted.

```
<form action="" onsubmit="return validEmail()">
```

By returning a **true** or **false** value to the **onsubmit** event, you can cancel the submission (if the value is **false**) or confirm the submission (if the value is **true**). When you create the function, design the code so that it ensures the email address is valid. You can do this by searching through the user's information for the "**@**" symbol and a final period for the associated domain. (Remember that you can use the **indexOf()** method to search through a string for a specific character or phrase.) If the character doesn't exist, a value of "**-1**" will return from the method. The following code searches for the "**@**" sign:

```
function validEmail() {
        var atLocation=document.forms[0].email1.value.indexOf("@");
        if (atLocation == -1) {
                alert("The email address entered isn't a valid email
address. Please resubmit.");
        } // end if
        return false;
} //end function
```

A valid email address also has a period after the "@" sign. You can search for the period by using the **lastIndexOf()** method. (Remember that the **indexOf()** and **lastIndexOf()** methods return a value of "-1" if the search string cannot be found.) The **lastIndexOf()** method works exactly like the **indexOf()** method, but the **lastIndexOf()** method starts searching at the end of the string, rather than the beginning. The **lastIndexOf()** method is the most appropriate method, since an email address can include more than one period.

```
var dotLocation=document.forms[0].email1.value.indexOf(".");
```

You also need to modify your **if** statement to make two comparisons instead of one, and perform actions if either statement evaluates to **true**. The logical OR (||) operator would satisfy this purpose.

```
if (atLocation == -1 || dotLocation == -1) {
```

This statement ensures that both characters are present in the text entered. If you try this in your browser, it will work well in most situations. If a user enters "joe.smith@massivecorporation" into the Email field, the script will not realize that the ".com" part of the address is missing, nor will it know that this is an invalid email address. Your current script will always fail in situations where the user enters a period before the "@" sign.

This may appear to be a lot of worry and work for a few rather unimportant details, but the opposite is actually true. Imagine that you work for a very large company whose Web site receives millions of inquiries every day. You submitted your form to the Webmaster who immediately placed it on the corporate Web site (he assumed it contained error-free code). Within an hour, over a thousand invalid email addresses had been received. The company had to hire two full-time employees to call those users to get their correct information. When the company's president asked the Webmaster what went wrong, he identified the new online form as the culprit.

The business of programming (or scripting) often means that you must consider every mistake a user can make and proactively prevent as many of those errors as possible. The following change to your **if** statement fixes the problem with the period in the email address:

```
if (dotLocation <= atLocation||atLocation==-1) {
```

In this example, the code works as follows:

Situation	Variable Values	Condition
Address entered without dot	`dotLocation = -1`	**true**
Field left blank	`dotLocation = -1; atLocation = -1`	**true**
Address entered without @	`atLocation = -1`	**true**
Dot entered before @	`dotLocation<atLocation`	**true**

Even if the user entered an email address that has the "**@**" sign and the final period (dot), the user can still create a typographical error when entering her email address. Knowing this to be true, many Web sites ask the user to enter the information twice, and then compare the two entries to ensure they are identical — which is as simple as using the equality operator (==). Assuming that you have two Email fields (named **email1** and **email2**), you could write a function such as:

```
function compareEmail() {
        if (document.forms[0].email1.value!=
        document.forms[0].email2.value) {

                alert("The email addresses entered don't match. Please
                resubmit.");

        } // end if

        return false;

} //end function
```

Checking for Blank Fields

Making sure that the user has entered information into a field is easy to do in JavaScript. You simply need to add a flow-of-control statement to ensure the value isn't blank. The **if** statement works well for this type of work, as demonstrated in the following example:

```
function checkBlank(field)

{

        if (field.value =="")

        {

        alert("You must enter a phone number.");

        return false;

        }

        else {

        return true; }

}
```

Here's the code to access the form validation:

```
<form action="" onsubmit="return checkBlank(this.phone)">

Phone: <input type="text" name="phone" id="phone">

<input type="submit" value="Submit">

<form>
```

Checking for Numeric Values

It is often necessary to check a value to ensure that it is a number. You can do this in a number of ways, including using the **isNaN()** method. This method returns **true** if the submitted value is a number, and it returns **false** if the submitted value is not a number. This method takes a single attribute, which is the value to be considered. The following simple script creates a form that allows a user to enter a number.

```
<form action="" onsubmit="return checkNumber()">
        <input name="number" type="text" size="12">
        <br>
        <input type="submit" value="Send" name="submit">
        <input type="reset" value="Reset Form">
</form>
```

Viewing this code in a Web browser yields the following result.

FIGURE 4.7

You create the necessary **isNaN()** method with the following code:

```
function checkNumber() {
        num=document.forms[0].number.value;
        if (isNaN(num)) {
                alert("You must enter a number. Please resubmit.");
        } // end if
        return false;
} //end function
```

The function simply assigns the value of the **form** element to the variable **num**, and then checks to see if the variable is a number. This script does not accept numbers with spaces or dollar signs. Elaborate scripts for number validation are available at no charge at various JavaScript-enthusiasts' Web sites.

Submitting and Resetting Forms

Methods of the **form** object allow you to manually trigger the actions of a form. The primary methods of the **form** object are **reset()** and **submit()**. As you might imagine, these actions allow you to reset or submit the content of a form. The **submit()** method does not cause the **onsubmit** event to fire. This is in contrast to the **reset()** method, which causes the **onreset** event to fire.

Reset()

The **reset()** method performs the same action as clicking a Reset button on a form. This method clears all values the user entered into the form and resets the default values. Clever readers might ask why this is necessary, since you can click the Reset button to perform the same action. This is true, but being able to manually trigger the event gives you more control over when the event triggers. To reset a form when the user clicks a Reset button, you would write:

```
<a href="#" onclick="document.serviceForm.reset();">Reset</a>
```

Submit()

The **submit()** method has the same effect as clicking the Submit button on a form with one minor exception: the **onsubmit** event doesn't fire. This may seem a little confusing, so let's take a minute to consider the method more carefully. The **onsubmit** event allows you to validate the form data before the data is actually submitted. In this situation, you can use the **onsubmit** event to call upon a function that will validate the form data. The **submit()** method is designed to be used within a form-validation script, after the data has been successfully validated.

Validate a Form Element

1   **In your text editor and browser, open checkforblank.html from your WIP_04 folder.**

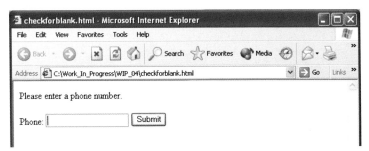

FIGURE 4.8

2   Find the following line of code.

```
<form action="">
```

3   Modify the code as follows.

```
<form action="" onsubmit="return checkBlank(this.phone)">
```

4   Insert the following function into the head of the document.

```
...
<title>checkforblank.html</title>
<script language="JavaScript">
function checkBlank(field) {
        if (field.value =="")
        {
        alert("You must enter a phone number.");
        field.focus();
        return false;
        }
        else {
                return true; }
} // end function
</script>
</head>
...
```

5   Save your changes in the text editor and refresh your browser.

To Extend Your Knowledge...

USING EVENT HANDLERS TO TRIGGER VALIDATION

You can use event handlers such as **onblur** or **onchange** with individual **form** elements to trigger a function, but the **onsubmit** handler is usually the easiest and most user-friendly way to trigger form validation.

6   **Leave the Phone Number field blank and click the Send button.**

FIGURE 4.9

An alert box appears.

7   **Click OK.**

The form submission is canceled.

8   **Enter a value into the field and click Send.**

The form clears, which indicates it was submitted.

9   **Close the file in your browser and text editor.**

To Extend Your Knowledge...

FORMMAIL SCRIPTS

The Perl script **formmail.pl** is often used to set up scripts that process information from an HTML form. You can download this script from Matt's script archive, located at www.scriptarchive.com/form-mail.html. Some knowledge of the hosting server is needed to configure this script.

LESSON 3   Using Image Properties

In HTML, **<img>** tags often accept many attributes. Consider the following code from an HTML page:

```
<img src="topslice0.jpg" width="720" height="121" border="0"
alt="Bridge Picture" name="bridgePic">
```

This statement includes many of the attributes common in **<img>** statements. Let's use pseudo-code to review the purpose of this statement.

```
Display the image topSlice0.jpg at a width of 720 pixels and a
height of 121 pixels. Name the picture bridgePic and make sure no
border appears around the image. The text "Bridge Picture" should be
shown if the image hasn't finished loading or if the user rolls his
mouse over the image.
```

The attributes shown in the code example represent the most common attributes used to display images, but additional attributes can also be used. You already know that every HTML **<img>** tag is represented by an **image** object in JavaScript. The attributes specified in the **<img>** tag are represented by an associated property of the **image** object. Conveniently, the property in JavaScript is named as it appears in the HTML code. For instance, the **align** property of the **image** object holds the value assigned in the **align** attribute of the HTML **<img>** tag. Take a moment to review the list of properties of the **image** object.

Property	*Description*
align	Can take on several different values, but is usually set to left or right.
alt	The alternative text shown if the image hasn't loaded or the user rolls over the image. Set by the **alt** attribute in the **<img>** tag.
border	The border (in pixels) shown around the image.
complete	A Boolean value that indicates whether the image has finished loading.
height	The height of the image in pixels. This can be a percentage value (of the table cell or browser window), but this is rare.
hspace	The horizontal space around the image.
longDesc	The **longdesc** attribute from the **<img>** tag, which represents a longer description than the **alt** attribute.
lowSrc	The **lowsrc** attribute of the **<img>** tag, which specifies a low-resolution file that can temporarily display while a higher-resolution file loads.
name	Represents the **name** attribute of the **<img>** tag.
src	The URL of the image.
useMap	The URL of the client-side image map if the **<img>** tag has a **useMap** attribute.
vspace	The vertical space in pixels around the image.
width	The width of the image in pixels. This can also be a percentage value (of the table cell or browser window), but this is rare.

Use Image Properties

1   **In your text editor and browser, open imageproperties.html from your WIP_04 folder.**

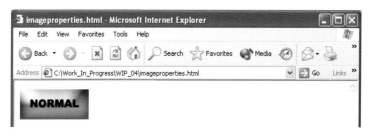

FIGURE 4.10

2 Insert the following code.

```
...
<a href="#">
<img name="imageOne" id="imageOne" src="normal.jpg" border="0"
width="120" height="50">
</a>
<br>
<script language="JavaScript">
document.write("name is " + document.images[0].name+"<br>");
document.write("ID is "+ document.images[0].id+"<br>");
document.write("src is "+document.images[0].src+"<br>");
document.write("width is "+document.images[0].width+"<br>");
</script>
</body>
</html>
```

3 Save your changes in the text editor and refresh the file in your browser.

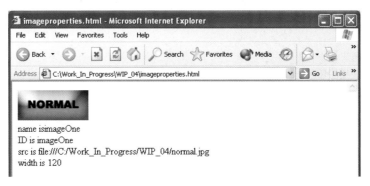

FIGURE 4.11

4 Close the file in your browser and text editor.

To Extend Your Knowledge...

TIPS FOR USING IMAGES

It's a good idea to include the `border="0"` statement in your `<img>` tags. If you omit this statement, some browsers display a border around the image by default.

The browser will make your pictures smaller or larger if you set the `width` or `height` attributes different than the actual picture. Doing so distorts the image, however, and should be avoided. If you need to resize an image, do so in an image-manipulation program such as Adobe Photoshop or Macromedia Fireworks, and then use a sharpen filter before adding the image to your Web page.

Even if your image is sized correctly, you should always include the `width` and `height` statements in the `<img>` tag. This allows the Web browser to format the page correctly (even if the picture hasn't finished loading) and allows users to read text and see most hyperlinks without waiting for the picture to load.

LESSON 4   Preloading Images

Most HTML users are familiar with the concept of image maps. Image maps allow designers to create areas of an image that contain hyperlinks (hotspots). Rollover effects are preferable to image maps because they provide a very visible method of letting the user know he can click an image to do something. If nothing happens when the user moves the mouse over an image, the user may not realize the image is a link. Most experienced Web users realize that when the mouse pointer turns into a pointing finger, a hyperlink is present; novice users often miss this detail.

Rollover effects are much more intuitive than image maps, but they have one major disadvantage: rollover effects add significantly to the size of a Web page because a different image must load each time the user rolls over the button.

The use of rollovers creates another issue in terms of usability and file size. Consider the sample rollover effect you created earlier. The `<img>` tag creates an **image** object in JavaScript that you can manipulate. The **image** object has a `src` property that holds the file name of the image represented by the **image** object. By changing the `src` attribute, you force the Web browser to download a new image to display.

In the current rollover script, you must wait for the rollover image to download once you move the mouse over the original image. When using complex images, the user must wait for several seconds before seeing the rollover effect, which creates the appearance of a sluggish browser or a problem with the page. Worse still, some browsers display a broken link alert box when it takes more than a few seconds to download an image.

An easy way to work around this problem is to create an **image** object for each image and to set the `src` attribute of each object. This causes the image to preload before the user rolls over the image. You typically add this code in the head section of an HTML document between the `<head>` and `</head>` tags.

Remember that you can create objects by using the keyword **new** and specifying the class to which the object belongs. The object is also created as a variable. For instance, to write a statement that creates a new **image** object named **homeOver**, you would write:

```
var homeOver = new Image();
```

Strictly speaking, it isn't necessary to pass any parameters to the constructor that creates the **image** object. However, it is considered good form to pass the **width** and **height** parameters in the following fashion:

```
var homeOver = new Image(width, height);
```

Assuming your image has a width of 120 pixels and a height of 25 pixels, you would write:

```
var homeOver = new Image(120, 25);
```

Next, you set the **src** attribute of the **image** object you created, which causes the image to preload:

```
homeOver.src = "images/homeover.gif";
```

Creating an **image** object and setting the **src** attribute forces the browser to load the image, even though it has not yet displayed. Assume you already created another image object by using an **<img>** tag in the HTML document. At this point, you can use JavaScript to change the src attribute of the **<img>** tag to force the browser to exchange the displayed image for the preloaded image. You explore this method in the following exercise.

Use Preloaded Images

1   In your text editor, open start.html from your WIP_04 folder.

2   Insert the following code in the head of the document.

```
<title>start.html</title>
<script language="JavaScript">
// preload the images
var offHome = new Image(44,20);
offHome.src = "images/homenormal.gif";
var onHome = new Image(44,20);
onHome.src = "images/homeover.gif";
// turn the button on
function buttonOn ()
...
```

This creates two **image** objects and preloads the files they contain.

3 **Find and examine the following code.**

```
// turn the button on
function buttonOn ()
{
document.images.home.src = onHome.src;
}
```

This code changes the source of the image on the page to the source file of the preloaded image when the user moves over the button. A similar function changes the button back when the user moves off the button. Event handlers were inserted to trigger the functions when needed.

4 **Save the file in your text editor.**

5 **Open the file in your browser and move your mouse across the button.**

The image changes. You explore techniques to create rollovers in the next lesson.

FIGURE 4.12

6 **Close the file in your browser and text editor.**

To Extend Your Knowledge...

IMAGE ROLLOVERS

Older browsers may not allow developers to use event handlers such as **onmouseover** and **onmouse-out** in **<img>** tags. You can circumvent this problem by enclosing the **<img>** tag within an **<a>** tag and placing the event handler code within the **<a>** tag.

LESSON 5   Creating Rollovers

Creating image rollovers is probably the most popular way to use JavaScript. A rollover effect is created when one image changes to another image when the user moves the mouse pointer over a button. Rollover buttons can have two or three states. A *state* is an image that displays when a particular event occurs.

When creating buttons using JavaScript, designers usually include a normal state and an over state. The *normal state* refers to the image that displays when the user is not interacting with the button. The *over state* refers to the image that displays when the user moves the mouse pointer over the image.

Using a combination of event handlers and **image** objects, you can change an image when the user clicks it, rolls over it, or rolls off it. For instance, consider the following simple rollover script:

```
<img name="imageOne" id="imageOne" src="normal.jpg"
border="0"  width="120" height="50"
onmouseover="document.imageOne.src='over.jpg'"
onmouseout="document.imageOne.src='normal.jpg'">
```

Although this script works correctly in most browsers, it has some negative aspects. In the event handler, there is a single quote inside a double quote, which is likely to result in typing errors. In versions 3 and 4 of the Netscape browser, **onmouseover** and **onmouseout** event handlers cannot be used, so this script would not work in those browsers.

Using functions for the normal and over states of the buttons would make the script easier to type and use:

```
function buttonOn()

    {

    //change button to over state

    document.imageOne.src = 'over.jpg'

    }  // end function

function  buttonOff()

    {

    // change button back to normal state

    document.imageOne.src='normal.jpg'

    }
```

Typically, you want the image rollover to act as hyperlink. You can accomplish this by enclosing the **<img>** tag within an **<a>** tag.

```
<a href='newpage.html'>
<img name="imageOne" id="imageOne" src="normal.jpg" border="0"
width="120" height="50" onmouseover="buttonOn()"
onmouseout="buttonOff()">
</a>
```

Using the `<a>` tag allows you to add a greater degree of compatibility by allowing you to use event handlers with the `<a>` tag instead of the `<img>` tag. This simple change allows older versions of the Netscape browser to work correctly with this rollover effect.

```
<a href='newpage.html' onmouseover="buttonOn()"
onmouseout="buttonOff()"><img name="imageOne" id="imageOne"
src="normal.jpg" border="0"  width="120" height="50"  ></a>
```

Our current rollover script works well, but you can make additional improvements. If you were to add multiple rollover buttons, you would need multiple rollover functions, since the functions are designed to work with only one button. Using variables, however, you can reuse the functions you already created. For instance, if you modify the functions in the following manner, you can pass information to the function as necessary.

```
function buttonOn(imageName,overImage)

    {

    //change button to over image

    document[imageName].src = overImage;

    }  // end function

function  buttonOff(imageName,normalImage)

    {

    // change button back to normal image

    document[imageName].src= normalImage;

    } // end function
```

This requires you to also change the HTML code in order to pass the information to the function.

```
<a href='newpage.html' onmouseover="buttonOn('imageOne',
'over.jpg')" onmouseout="buttonOff('imageOne','normal.jpg')">
<img name="imageOne" id="imageOne" src="normal.jpg" border="0"
width="120" height="50"  ></a>
```

Let's examine this code more closely. Consider the following statement:

```
onmouseover="buttonOn('imageOne','over.jpg')"
```

Using pseudo-code, you can describe the statement in the following fashion:

```
When the mouse rolls over the current image, call on the buttonOn()
function. For the first parameter, pass the name of the image as
specified in the name attribute of the <img> tag. For the  second
parameter, pass the name of the image to show when the mouse is over
the image.
```

Incorporating the script into an easily reusable function allows you to use as many rollover buttons as you prefer.

Create a Simple Rollover Effect

1   In your text editor and browser, open rollover.html from your WIP_04>rollover folder.

FIGURE 4.13

2   Find the following code.

```
<img name="imageOne" id="imageOne" src="normal.jpg" border="0"
width="120" height="50">
```

3   Insert the following into the code you found in the previous step.

```
<img name="imageOne" id="imageOne" src="normal.jpg"
border="0" width="120" height="50"
onmouseover="document.imageOne.src='over.jpg'"
onmouseout="document.imageOne.src='normal.jpg'">
```

Notice the file name is enclosed within a set of single quotes, but the entire sequene associated with the event is placed within double quotes.

4   Save your changes in the text editor and refresh your browser.

5   Move your mouse pointer over the button.

FIGURE 4.14

The button changes as you move the mouse pointer on and off.

6   Close the file in your browser and text editor.

To Extend Your Knowledge...

DEFINING DOWN STATES

It is possible to define a ***down state*** for a button in JavaScript, which is an image that displays when you click the button. This isn't necessary, however, since you usually go to another page when you click a button.

LESSON 6   Using Advanced Image Scripts

Advanced scripts using the **image** object can be incorporated into Web pages to create stunning effects. For example, you could create a slideshow, complete with Back and Forward buttons, within a single Web page. Using techniques that you learned in previous lessons, you could preload the images, and then change the source file of the **image** object each time the user clicks the Forward or Back button.

Similarly, you could create a portfolio gallery where users could click a thumbnail image to see a larger version of the same image. Changing the event handler associated with the change to the **image** object allows a developer to automatically change one image when the user rolls over a different image— which is called a ***disjointed rollover***.

Using loops, you can use JavaScript to create animations. You can create a ***keyframe animation,*** which is a series of still images played in rapid succession. For instance, if you want to create an animation of a circular logo rolling across a surface, you might create the seven images shown below.

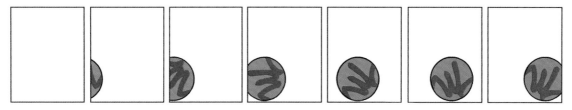

FIGURE 4.15

When using multiple images in a sequence, such as in a slideshow or animation, it is usually best to use a consistent naming scheme or a numbered sequence, such as pic1.jpg, pic2.jpg, and so forth.

Showing these images at short intervals in the same place on the screen creates the illusion of movement. At this point in your JavaScript studies, you have the requisite skills to create an animated sequence. Let's start the sequence by assigning a name to each image — a name easily manipulated in a JavaScript loop. The images in the sample code were created using a naming scheme that uses the word "ball" as the base, and then inserting the image number. For instance, the first image is named ball0001.gif, the second image is ball0002.gif, and the last image shown is ball0007.gif.

Next, you create the code to preload the images. An array provides a simple way to work with the images in JavaScript.

```
//setup array to hold and preload images
ballImage = new Array(7)
ballImage[1] = new Image();
ballImage[1].src="ball0001.gif";


ballImage[2] = new Image();
ballImage[2].src="ball0002.gif";


ballImage[3] = new Image();
ballImage[3].src="ball0003.gif";


ballImage[4] = new Image();
ballImage[4].src="ball0004.gif";


ballImage[5] = new Image();
ballImage[5].src="ball0005.gif";


ballImage[6] = new Image();
ballImage[6].src="ball0006.gif";


ballImage[7] = new Image();
ballImage[7].src="ball0007.gif";
```

A loop could be used to preload the objects, but that would add a little more complexity to the script. You can use an HTML **<img>** tag to name the image and place the first image on the page, as shown below:

```
<img name="slide" src="ball0001.gif" border="0" width="160"
height="200">
```

After you preload the images and display the first image, you can create a loop to display each image at a specified interval. You need a counter to keep track of which image is being displayed.

```
function changeSlide(){
        if (counter<7)
                counter++;
        else
                counter=1;
        document.slide.src=ballImage[counter].src;
        timerID = setTimeout("changeSlide()", 200);
} // end function
```

Consider the intent of this code. When the function invokes, it displays each image for 200 milliseconds. The function invokes repeatedly, and each time, 1 is added to the variable named **counter**, and the image is switched to display the image represented by this variable. If the **counter** is already at 7, the last image has already been displayed and the **counter** is reset to 1, causing the animation to loop.

A complete version of this code is shown in the file named animation.html, located in the WIP_04>animation folder. This file includes buttons designed to start and stop the animation.

A script designed to animate a sequence of images is one example of a complex image script. You can use similar techniques to create disjointed rollover effects, gallery pages, click-through slideshows, and other interesting effects. You explore these types of scripts in the following exercises.

Create Disjointed Rollovers

1 **In your text editor, open disjointed.html from the WIP_04>disjointed folder.**

2 **Examine the following code.**

```
// preload the images
var pic1 = new Image(720,121);
pic1.src = "pic1.jpg";
var pic2 = new Image(720,121);
pic2.src = "pic2.jpg";
var pic3 = new Image(720,121);
pic3.src = "pic3.jpg";
```

This code preloads the large images used in the page.

3 Find the following code that triggers the rollover effect for the first image.

```
<a href="#" onmouseover="changePic1()">
```

Code to trigger the rollover event was included within the **<a>** tag of each thumbnail image. By examining the **<a>** tag of each thumbnail, you can see that the page uses three functions — one for each image that displays. The names of these functions are **changePic1()**, **changePic2()**, and **changePic3()**.

4 Insert the following code in head of the document.

```
...
var pic3 = new Image(720,121);
pic3.src = "pic3.jpg";
// change the main picture
function changePic1 () {
        document.mainPic.src = pic1.src;
}


function changePic2 () {
        document.mainPic.src = pic2.src;
}


function changePic3 () {
document.mainPic.src = pic3.src;
}
</script>
</head>
<body>
    ...
```

5   Save the file in your text editor and open it in your browser.

FIGURE 4.16

6   Roll your mouse pointer over each thumbnail image.

The larger picture changes accordingly.

FIGURE 4.17

7   Close the file in your browser and text editor.

Create a Click-Through Slideshow

| 1 | In your Web browser, open slideshow.html from the WIP_04>disjointed folder. |

This is the finished version of the file that you create in this exercise.

| 2 | Click the Back and Next buttons to move through the available images. |

Notice that the slides go back to the beginning when you reach the end.

FIGURE 4.18

| 3 | Close the file in your Web browser. |

| 4 | In your Web browser and text editor, open slideshowstart.html from the WIP_04>disjointed folder. |

| 5 | Add the following code after the comment in your source code. |

```
...

<title>slideshowstart.html-creates a slideshow using
JavaScript</title>

<script language="JavaScript">

// start by initializing the variables

imageNumber = 1;

totalImages = 3;

// change the slide

</script>

...
```

This code initializes the variables in the slideshow script.

6　**Insert the function to allows users to click through the slides.**

```
...
imageNumber = 1;
totalImages = 3;
// change the slide
function changeSlide(direction) {
        imageNumber = imageNumber + direction;
        if (imageNumber < 1) {
                imageNumber = totalImages;
        }
        if (imageNumber > totalImages) {
                imageNumber = 1;
        }
        document.mainImage.src = "pic" + imageNumber + ".jpg";
} // end function
</script>
</head>
<body bgcolor="#FFFFFF">
...
```

Notice that the function allows the user to move forward or backward in the list of photos. The file name of the image is written dynamically whenever a user clicks the Back or Next button. The condition (**imageNumber>totalImages**) evaluates whether you have reached the end of the list and, if so, returns to the first image. The condition (**imageNumber < 1**) evaluates whether you have reached the beginning of the list if you are moving backward.

To Extend Your Knowledge...

ANIMATION IN JAVASCRIPT

It is possible to create animation in JavaScript by showing a sequence of images with a short delay between each, but this is impractical in most situations. Animation packages (such as Macromedia Flash) offer more efficient methods of animating sequences.

IMAGE ROLLOVER SCRIPTS

Image rollover scripts usually use functions to change the image from one state to another.

7   **Insert the following code to create the buttons.**

```
...
<body bgcolor="#FFFFFF">
<img name="mainImage" src="pic1.jpg" width="720" height="121"
border="0"><br>
<!-- buttons for changing slides, -->
<!--   -1 means go backward -->
<!--   1 means go forward -->
<a href="javascript:changeSlide(-1)">back</a> |
<a href="javascript:changeSlide(1)">next</a>
</body

</html>
```

The direction determines whether you go to the previous slide or to the next slide.

8   **Save your changes in the text editor and refresh your browser.**

9   **Click through the Back and Next buttons several times to ensure your page works correctly.**

If you receive an error, check your code against the finished file and search for typing errors.

10   **Close the file in your Web browser and text editor.**

CAREERS IN DESIGN

COMMUNITY SERVICE PROJECTS ENHANCE PORTFOLIOS

Many successful Web designers started their careers by building Web sites for community service organizations such as churches, homeless shelters, animal rescue agencies, or other non-profit agencies. Designers often build these sites for free; others charge only for the cost of stock photography or incidental expenses. Students are often surprised to learn that employers are very interested in hiring individuals who have completed community service projects. These projects show a student's dedication to helping others and willingness to give back to the community. Employers often favor an individual with a balance of good grades, work experience, and community service over another candidate who may excel in only one area.

Many times, non-profit or community-based projects offer opportunities to create unique design solutions. For example, a site for an animal shelter would have very different requirements than a typical e-commerce site. Building community-based sites will broaden your design skills and attract the praise and attention of others, as well as offer you the satisfaction of performing a service that benefits your community.

SUMMARY

In Project 4, you learned that interacting with forms and validating form information are two of the most popular uses of JavaScript. Whenever you add a `<form>` tag to an HTML page, JavaScript creates an entry in the `forms[]` array. For every `form` element created, JavaScript adds an entry in an `elements[]` array for that particular form.

You learned that the `form` object in JavaScript has several properties that are useful in a variety of situations: for check boxes and radio buttons, you can use the `checked` property to determine if a specific element has been checked; the `value` property of the element contains the information submitted by the user; and the `name` property contains any name assigned to the form or element in HTML.

You learned that the methods of the `form` object include `submit()` and `reset()` — not to be confused with the `onsubmit` or `onreset` event handlers — which allow you to manually submit or reset a form. You can use these methods whenever you wish within JavaScript, but they are often used after form validation.

In this project, you discovered that in general, most form validation scripts exist in functions that are triggered by the `onsubmit` event handler. Many of these scripts cancel the `onsubmit` method by returning negative values when the information entered doesn't meet your specifications.

You learned that JavaScript creates an `image` object for every `<img>` tag created in HTML, which allows you to manipulate images in ways not possible in HTML, including creating rollover effects and click-through slideshows. You also discovered how to create `image` objects in JavaScript. When you assign a `src` attribute to an `image` object, the image preloads before it needs to display. You found that when you change the `src` attribute of an image shown on the screen, you can change to a different image without loading a new page. Finally, you learned how to combine various JavaScript techniques to create advanced scripts to generate animated sequences and portfolio gallery pages.

KEY TERMS

Disjointed rollover	Normal state	State
Down state	Over state	Validate
Keyframe animation	Preload	

CHECKING CONCEPTS AND TERMS

MULTIPLE CHOICE

Circle the letter that matches the correct answer for each of the following questions.

1. The first form in an HTML document can be referred to as _____ in JavaScript code.

   a. `form[0]`
   b. `form[1]`
   c. `form1`
   d. `forms[0]`
   e. `forms[1]`

2. The first image in an HTML Web page can be referred to as _____ in JavaScript code.

   a. `image[0]`
   b. `image[1]`
   c. `image1`
   d. `images[0]`
   e. `images[1]`

3. What does the **elements[]** array represent in JavaScript?
   a. The attributes of an image
   b. Each element or form in an HTML document
   c. Each part of a form in an HTML document
   d. None of the above

4. When using radio buttons or check boxes, what does the keyword **checked** represent in JavaScript?
   a. Data entered into a text field
   b. A Boolean value indicating whether an element was selected
   c. Whether users have read text in a scrolling text field
   d. Whether a borderline appears around a form element

5. What is the purpose of using code such as **onsubmit="return validate()"** in a **<form>** tag?
   a. You can use the **post** protocol method to send the information from the form.
   b. The server can return information from a form-processing script.
   c. A function can be triggered to check information when the form is submitted.
   d. The content of the form can be encrypted on the client's browser.

6. What does the **method** property of the **form** object represent in JavaScript?
   a. The name of the form
   b. The file name of the server-side script where the form information is sent
   c. Whether the form will be submitted by the **post** or **get** method
   d. The type of operating system the user is currently using

7. What does the **action** property of the **form** object represent in JavaScript?
   a. The name of the form
   b. The file name of the server-side script where the form information is sent
   c. Whether the form will be submitted by the **post** or **get** method
   d. The type of operating system the user is currently using

8. To use JavaScript to preload an image, a user must _____.
   a. create an **image** object and assign a file name to the **src** attribute
   b. use the **preload()** method
   c. put the images into the JavaScript source folder on the server
   d. load each pixel using a **for** loop

9. What happens to an image created by an **<img>** tag when a developer changes the **src** attribute of the matching **image** object to a different image file?
   a. The image shown on screen changes to a different image.
   b. The browser generates an error.
   c. A green box appears over the image.
   d. The **image** object is deleted from memory.

10. Why is JavaScript usually used for form validation?
    a. Because most server-side processing scripts also use JavaScript
    b. Because no other language contains similar tools for validation
    c. Because JavaScript is primarily a client-side language and the processing can be done before the form is submitted to the server
    d. JavaScript is not usually used for form validation

DISCUSSION QUESTIONS

1. Why is the **form** object useful in JavaScript? How can you use this object to enhance HTML Web pages?

2. Why is the **image** object useful in JavaScript? How could you use the **image** object in JavaScript to improve the usability of an HTML Web page?

3. Describe two different situations where it might be useful to validate data submitted in an HTML form.

4. A portfolio Web site could use a sequence of identical pages to show a thumbnail gallery with links to pages that show larger versions of the thumbnail images. Why do you think it would be useful for a developer to build a single page using JavaScript to change the main image when a user clicks a thumbnail image?

SKILL DRILL

Skill Drill exercises reinforce project skills. Each skill reinforced is the same, or nearly the same, as a skill presented in the project. Detailed instructions are provided in a step-by-step format. You should work through the exercises in order.

1. Trigger a Form Validation Script

Creating scripts to validate form data is one of the primary uses of JavaScript. In this exercise, you use the **onsubmit** event handler to trigger a form validation. This page allows the user to enter a password to set up a new account.

1. In your text editor, open skilllength.html from your WIP_04 folder.

2. Find the following line of code, which creates the form.

    ```
    <form action="">
    ```

3. Insert the following code to trigger a function before the form is submitted.

    ```
    <form action="" onsubmit="return checkLength()">
    ```

4. In the head of the document, create a function named **checkLength()**.

    The function will not accept any values.

5. Inside the function you created in Step 4, insert the following lines of code.

    ```
    var passLength=document.forms[0].password.value.length;
    alert(passLength);
    ```

6. Open the file in your browser.

7. Type three letters into the Password field and click Send.

   An alert box should appear with the number "3."

8. Click OK to acknowledge the tracing alert.

9. Keep the file open for the next exercise.

2. Check for Field Length

When creating new user accounts, it is common practice to require users to enter a password and to ensure that the password is of minimum length. In this exercise, you check the length of a new user password.

1. In the open skilllength.html, find the beginning of the **checkLength()** function, which is shown in the following code.

   ```
   function checkLength() {
           var passLength=document.forms[0].password.value.length;
           alert(passLength);
   ```

2. After the last line of code in Step 1 and before the end of the function, create an **if** statement to evaluate whether the password length is less than six characters. If so, the following lines of code should execute.

   ```
   alert("Password must be at least 6 characters. Please resubmit.");
   // stop form submission
   return false;
   ```

3. Add an **else** statement to the **if** statement you created in Step 2. When the **if** statement evaluates to **false**, the following statement should execute.

   ```
   // continue form submission
   return true;
   ```

4. Save your changes in the text editor and refresh your browser. Test the file in your browser.

   An alert box should tell you the number of characters that were submitted. If you enter less than six characters, a second alert box should display a warning message and the form submission should stop. If you enter six characters, the Password field should clear to indicate the form was successfully submitted.

5. Remove the tracing alert that reveals the number of characters submitted.

6. Save and close the file in your browser and text editor.

3. Create a Gallery Page

1. In your browser, open skillgallery.html from your WIP_04>disjointed folder.

   This is the beginning of a portfolio gallery page.

2. Open the file in your text editor and find the following code, which, when triggered, changes the main image to the first picture.

```
// change the main picture
function changePic1 () {
        document.mainPic.src = pic1.src;
}
```

3. Find the following code, which is the function that changes the main image to the second picture.

   This function is incomplete.

```
function changePic2 () {
}
```

4. Insert code into the **changePic2()** function to change the source of the **mainPic** image object to the file named **pic2.src**.

   Hint: use the **changePic1()** function as your guide.

5. Insert code into the **changePic3()** function to change the source of the **mainPic** image object to the file named **pic3.src**.

6. Save your changes in the text editor.

7. Refresh in the browser and test the file by moving your mouse over each image.

   The main picture should change.

8. Keep the file open in your browser and text editor for the next exercise.

4. Use Onclick Events to Change Image Sources

1. In the open skillgallery.html, find the following line of code, which triggers the **changePic1()** function when the mouse moves over the thumbnail image.

   ```
   <p align="center"><a href="#" onmouseover="changePic1()">
   <img src="smallpic1.jpg" width="90" height="90" border="0"></a>
   ```

2. Change the code in Step 1 to use the **onclick** event to trigger the function, instead of using the **onmouseover** function.

3. Insert code to trigger the **changePic2()** function when the second thumbnail is clicked.

4. Insert code to trigger the **changePic3()** function when the third thumbnail is clicked.

5. Save your changes in the text editor.

6. Test the file in your browser.

   As you click each thumbnail, the main image should change.

7. Close the file in your browser and text editor.

CHALLENGE

Challenge exercises expand on, or are somewhat related to, skills presented in the lessons. Each exercise provides a brief introduction, followed by instructions presented in a numbered-step format that are not as detailed as those in the Skill Drill exercises. You should work through these exercise in order.

1. Validate Multiple Fields

Many corporate Web sites collect significant amounts of data through HTML forms. For example, a car repair shop may want to allow customers to schedule service appointments online, which means that scheduling can take place after business hours. This practice saves the company money, since the appointments can be scheduled even though the receptionist has already gone home for the day. Gathering correct information is extremely important in a situation such as this; it contributes significantly to a positive customer experience. In this exercise, you validate the information submitted by the user.

1. In your text editor, open checkblank.js from the WIP_04>external folder.

   This file contains a simple script that checks to see if a form field is blank. If the field is blank, the function returns **false**. If the field contains information, the function returns **true**.

2. Close the file in your text editor.

3. In your Web browser and text editor, open serviceform.html from the WIP_04>external folder.

   This is essentially the same form you used in the examples throughout this project.

4. In the head of the HTML document, create a **<script>** tag that has the **src** attribute set to an external file named **checkblank.js**.

5. Add the following code in the head of the document to create a function to validate two fields from the form.

```
<title>Service Department Form</title>

<script language="JavaScript" src="checkblank.js">

</script>

<script language="JavaScript">

function validate() {

        check1=checkBlank(serviceForm.Name);

        check2=checkBlank(serviceForm.Model);

        check3=checkBlank(serviceForm.Email);

}// end function

</script>

</head>
```

6. Add another line of code to create a variable named **check4**. Using code from the previous step as your example, assign the result of a **checkBlank()** function performed on the Description field of the form.

    The code you just added creates four Boolean variables by validating each of the form elements where users are required to type text into a field. You also need to cancel the form submission if any of the fields returns a **false** value from the **checkBlank()** function. You need to add a flow-of-control statement using logical AND operators to ensure every value is **true**.

7. Add the following lines of code to the function you created in Step 5, below the lines you entered in Step 6.

```
if (check1&&check2&&check3&&check4) {

    return true; }

    else

    return false;
```

8. Find the **<form>** tag in the HTML document and change the line to the following.

```
<form name="serviceForm" method="post" action="" onsubmit="return
validate()">
```

9.   Save your changes in the text editor and refresh your browser.

10. Click Send without filling out any values on the form.

11. Click OK to close the alert box.

12. Enter various values in the form and leave one or two of the text fields blank to test the validation script.

13. Close the file in your browser and text editor.

2. Incorporate External Rollover Scripts into a Web Page

Rollover scripts are one of the most common and useful ways to use JavaScript. When designing a Web page, it is useful to use these scripts on every page to create a consistent, easy-to-use navigation structure. In this Challenge, you incorporate an external rollover script into a Webpage. By repeating this process, you could share the script among all the pages on the site.

1.   In your text editor, open rollover.js from the WIP_04>externalrollover folder. Examine this script carefully.

Two functions are defined: one for when you want to change the image of the button (when the user rolls over the button), and one for when you want to return the button to normal (when the user rolls off the button).

2.   In your text editor and Web browser, open start.html from the WIP_04>externalrollover folder. Examine the source code.

The page consists of a simple table that displays three images.

3.   Insert the following code into the head section of the HTML document.

```
<html>

<head>

<title>start.html</title>

<script language="JavaScript">

</script>

</head>

<body>

<table width="23%" border="0" cellpadding="0" cellspacing="0"
bordercolor="#336666">
```

4.   Modify the code from Step 3 to set the **src** attribute of the **<script>** tag to rollover.js, which gives you access to the functions enclosed.

5.   Save your changes and keep the file open in your browser and text editor for the next exercise.

3. Add a Rollover Function

In this exercise, you insert the code to create a rollover effect when the user moves the mouse pointer over the first button.

1. Find the following code in the open HTML document.

   ```
   <a href="#"><img src="images/homenormal.gif" name="home" width="44"
   height="20" border="0" id="home"></a>
   ```

2. Change the code to the following to create the rollover effect.

   ```
   <a href="#"><img src="images/homenormal.gif" name="home" width="44"
   height="20" border="0" id="home"
   onmouseover="buttonOn('home','images/homeover.gif')"></a>
   ```

   Don't forget to use matching pairs of both single and double quotes.

3. Save your changes in the text editor and refresh your browser.

4. Roll your mouse over the home button.

   The image should change to the rollover image. At this point, the image doesn't change back when you move the mouse off the image.

5. Find the following code, which creates the About Us button.

   ```
   <a href="#"><img src="images/aboutusnormal.gif" name="aboutus"
   width="63" height="20" border="0" id="aboutus"></a>
   ```

6. Modify the code for the About Us button to use the **buttonOn** function when the user triggers the **onmouseover** event. The event should send two text strings to the function: "aboutus" and "images/aboutusover.gif" to capture the id and location of the image.

   Hint: Use Step 2 as a guide.

7. Modify the **<img>** tag for the Contact Us button to use the **onmouseover** event to trigger the **buttonOn** function. The event should send two text strings to the function: "contactus" and "images/contactusover.gif" to capture the id and location of the image.

8. Save and test your file.

   Each image should change as you move your mouse pointer over it.

9. Leave the file open for the next exercise.

4. Apply a Rolloff Effect

In this exercise, you modify the page to change the images back to the original images when the user rolls off the rollover images.

1. In the open file in your text editor, find the following code.

```
<a href="#"><img src="images/homenormal.gif" name="home"
width="44" height="20" border="0" id="home"
onmouseover="buttonOn('home','images/homeover.gif')"></a>
```

2. Modify this code to create a rolloff effect.

```
<a href="#"><img src="images/homenormal.gif" name="home"
width="44" height="20" border="0" id="home"
onmouseover="buttonOn('home','images/homeover.gif')"
onmouseout="buttonOff('home','images/homenormal.gif')"></a>
```

3. Save your changes in the text editor and refresh you browser.

   When you move the mouse off the home button, the button changes back to the normal image.

4. Find the code for the About Us button, which is shown below.

```
<a href="#"><img src="images/aboutusnormal.gif"

name="aboutus" width="63" height="20" border="0" id="aboutus"
onmouseover="buttonOn('aboutus','images/aboutusover.gif')"> </a>
```

5. Using Step 2 as your guide, change the code for the About Us button to use the **onmouseout** event handler to trigger the **buttonOff** function. The event handler should send two text strings to the function: "aboutus" and "images/aboutusover.gif" to capture the id and location of the image.

6. Modify the code for the Contact Us button to change the button back to the normal image when a user moves the mouse off the button.

7. Save your change in the text editor and refresh your browser.

   You should be able to move your mouse over any button and see the rollover and rolloff effects for each.

8. Close the file in your Web browser and text editor.

P O R T F O L I O   B U I L D E R

Create Image-Swap Effects

In Project 4, you learned how to create rollover effects with images, as well as how to create disjointed rollover effects. The true skill of a successful developer is combining multiple effects to create an effect greater than any of the individual parts. If the user sees the combination of effects as seamless, the illusion is complete.

■ Open swapimages.html from your Work_In_Progress>WIP_04 fodler in your browser. You see five images. Four are obvious because they are colored and numbered; the fifth image appears as text. Currently, the images have no effects applied to them. Your job is to create the image-swap effects for the numbered images, as well as a disjointed rollover for the "text" image. There are corresponding text images for each numbered image.

■ Use the following pseudo-code to create a function to swap images on mouse over:

```
swap image 1 for overstate image1 and swap text image for
text image over 1

swap image 2 for overstate image2 and swap text image for
text image over 2

swap image 3 for overstate image3 and swap text image for
text image over 3

swap image 4 for overstate image4 and swap text image for
text image over 4
```

P O R T F O L I O   B U I L D E R

Create Image-Swap Effects (continued)

■   Use the following pseudo-code to create a function to restore original images on mouse out:

```
swap overstate image 1 for image1 and swap text image over 1
for text image

swap overstate image 2 for image2 and swap text image over 2
for text image

swap overstate image 3 for image3 and swap text image over 3
for text image

swap overstate image 4 for image4 and swap text image over 4
for text image
```

■   Use the following example to combine the event handlers for both swap-image functions:

```
onMouseOver="swapImage(),swapTextImage()"
onMouseOut="restoreImage(),restoreTextImage()"
```

■   After you create and apply the functions, two images should swap at the same time: a numbered image and the text image. (Consider that users with slow Internet connections will have to wait for the swap image to download.)

■   Create a function to preload the images. You may not notice a difference because the files are local, but users with slow Internet connections will certainly appreciate that you added this feature to the page.

Customizing User Content

OBJECTIVES

In this project, you learn how to

- Create and access cookies

- Manipulate cookies

- Produce dynamically generated code

- Use escape characters and escape sequences

- Generate dynamic tables and pages

- Utilize bookmarklets

WHY WOULD I DO THIS?

HTML creates *static documents*, which means the pages do not change with user choices or changing conditions. An example of a static document is a word-processing file; it displays in the same way to any user who views it. A *dynamic document*, on the other hand, changes according to user choices or changing conditions. Programming and scripting languages are dynamic technologies; they react to user choices.

JavaScript was created to enhance HTML. JavaScript can also be used to create HTML code when a page is viewed. In *Essentials for Design: JavaScript Level 1* and earlier projects in this book, you used JavaScript to create HTML when you wrote statements such as:

```
document.write("A line of text.<br>");
```

This statement contains a **
** tag within the JavaScript statement. When you use the **document.write()** method, the results are sent to the HTML parser before they are output to the user. In other words, the JavaScript statement shown above would have the exact same effect as typing the following line of HTML:

```
A line of text.<br>
```

In either case, the HTML interpreter sees the strings as streams of characters it needs to parse. HTML code written by another computer program or script is referred to as *dynamically generated HTML*. Consider the following lines of code that mix JavaScript and HTML:

```
<script language="JavaScript">
document.write("<p>This is a paragraph.");
</script>
</p>
```

It is important to note that the HTML interpreter simply interprets the information passed to it, whether the information comes from HTML code or JavaScript code. Let's consider a simple table created in HTML.

FIGURE 5.1

Assuming you want JavaScript to dynamically create the table, you would write the following:

```
document.write('<table border="2">');

document.write('<tr>');

document.write('<td>apples</td>');

document.write('</tr>');

document.write('<tr>');

document.write('<td>oranges</td>');

document.write('</tr>');

document.write('<tr>');

document.write('<td>bananas</td>');

document.write('</tr>');

document.write('<tr>');

document.write('<td>pears</td>');

document.write('</tr>');

document.write('<tr>');

document.write('<td>carrots</td>');

document.write('</tr>');

document.write('</table>');
```

In the example code above, you placed each line of HTML code within a **document.write()** statement, which passes the string back to the HTML interpreter. Doing so made the code longer without any particular advantage, but the ability to contain the code within JavaScript raises interesting possibilities.

First of all, much of the table code is basically the same; you repeat the same code in each table row, changing only the value of the table data. Astute readers may wonder if it would be more efficient to use a function to create each table row and simply use a variable to pass the values for the table data. It is not only possible, it is often desirable to use JavaScript in this manner.

The ability to create code dynamically in JavaScript allows you to customize page content based on user choices or changing conditions, but it does not address another fundamental limitation of HTML. Specifically, if you visit a Web page and make preference choices, these changes are lost when the page unloads from the browser — such as when you go to another page or close the browser window. The solution to this problem is to add cookies to pages and sites. **Cookies** (small chunks of data stored in text files on computers) allow browsers (and Web sites) to remember user preferences or other information.

In this project, you explore a number of technologies that allow you to customize the content shown to users, including cookies, dynamically generated code, escape characters and sequences, dynamic tables and pages, and bookmarklets.

V I S U A L   S U M M A R Y

Bookmarklets are small chunks of JavaScript code used in places normally reserved for URLs. You can enter a line of JavaScript directly into the Address bar of your browser by using the **javascript** keyword and a colon. For example, if you enter **javascript:alert("hi");** into the URL field of the browser's Address bar, you receive the following result.

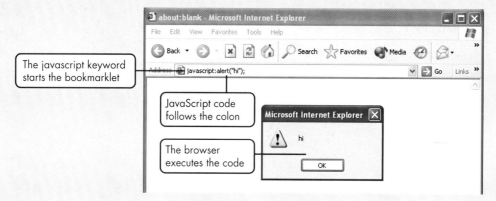

FIGURE 5.2

Bookmarklets are often used to store JavaScript code that the user can select from the Favorites menu in the browser. Consider the following illustration as an example, where a bookmarklet changes the size of the browser window to a specific resolution.

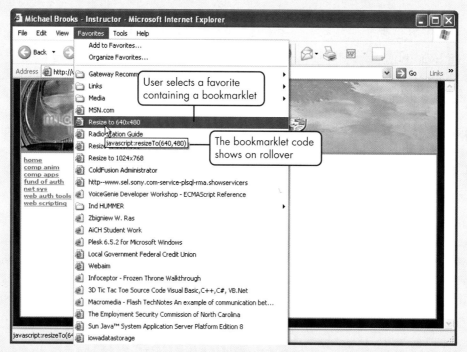

FIGURE 5.3

In this situation, the screen resizes to 640 by 480 pixels when the user chooses this option, regardless of the page that was opened in the browser. This is a useful option for designers who test pages at specific resolutions.

Cookies allow browsers to store user data, and then access the information whenever necessary. Many users fear cookies, feeling that they may invoke privacy violations; however, good developers can minimize these fears by taking proper security precautions. Most users know that they can delete cookies in Internet Explorer by choosing Tools>Internet Options>Delete Cookies.

FIGURE 5.4

LESSON 1   Creating and Accessing Cookies

Cookies are generated in many ways. When a user clicks the "Remember Me" check box on a Web page and presses Enter, a cookie is created. A username can be stored in a cookie and automatically entered into a Web form, allowing the page to "recognize" the user the next time he logs in. The size of the cookie varies by browser and Web site, but usually weighs around 4 k.

HTML is limited in its capacity to remember a particular state. A *state* is the current condition or situation — such as the up, over, and down states of buttons. By nature, HTML does not contain a mechanism to remember information while browsing from page to page. The communication between a user and Web site is considered *stateless*, meaning that HTML does not collect (or remember) the actions you perform while browsing the Web.

By creating a means of interaction, JavaScript and cookies allow the communication between a user and a Web site to enter a persistent state. A *persistent state* means the browser can record and retrieve information, even when the user leaves a page and subsequently returns to that page.

When a browser requests a page, the Web server:

- Receives the request from the browser

- Looks through a list of available cookies on the server

- Decides which cookie(s) to send, based upon the request

- Returns the selected cookie after evaluation

- Returns the requested document

The Web server returns both the cookie and the document to the browser. The cookie is sent to the browser as a header before the HTML content. A **header** is a small amount of text containing specific instructions for the Web browser. Headers are common in various types of files (not only Web pages), and they are often used in transmitted information, including email messages and digital phone calls.

Some common headers sent by Web servers to browsers ask, "When was the page last modified," "How should the browser handle page-caching," and "How should the content display using content-encoding." The term **caching** means placing the information in the browser's memory. The browser must decide whether to always reload the most current version of the document from the Web server, or if it can simply reload the document from the locally stored version. **Content-encoding** refers to the type of files being compressed and sent to the browser (such as JPEG or HTML).

As the browser reads the cookie header, the value is parsed and becomes part of the object model for the HTML document. After the browser reads all of the headers, the content (the HTML document) loads in the browser window. The content of the cookie is treated as a property of the **document** object; the cookie is assigned a string value, the same way a property or variable receives a value. Using pseudo-code, a cookie receives its value in the following fashion:

```
cookie = string value
```

The string value can contain a single attribute or multiple cookie attributes. Consider these cookies in pseudo-code:

```
cookie = "name=sub-value"
cookie = "name=Eva Kinney; userName=Evalyne"
```

The first cookie contains a single cookie attribute, **name=cookie attribute**, while the second contains two cookie attributes, **name=Eva Kinney** and **userName=Evalyne**. Both cookies contain a single string value. The only difference is in the cookie attributes.

To write a cookie, you must assign a value to the **cookie** property. To create a cookie that stores the username "Evalyne," you would write:

```
document.cookie = "userName=Evalyne";
```

or

```
userName = "Evalyne"
document.cookie = "userName=" + userName ;
```

The value of this cookie is:

```
userName = Evalyne
```

Both examples yield the same result; both assign a name-value pair to a single string value. The value contained in the cookie must consist of a name-value pair.

Reading a Cookie

Cookies are only valuable if the Web browser reads them. To ensure a browser reads a cookie, you can assign its content to a variable.

```
var theCookie = document.cookie;
```

When the browser reads **document.cookie**, it collects the value and makes the value available to the page while it loads. While the page processes, the cookie's string value is assigned (in this case) to the variable **theCookie**. The variable could be written to the page as:

```
var theCookie = document.cookie;
document.write(theCookie);
```

Create a Cookie

In this exercise, you create a cookie and assign a value. Every time the page loads, the cookie file is recreated on your computer.

1   **Copy the contents of the RF_JavaScript_L2>Project_05 folder into your Work_In_Progress>WIP_05 folder.**

You use these files throughout this project.

2   **In your text editor, open createcookie.html from your WIP_05 folder.**

A script was started for you.

3   Insert the following lines of code.

```
...

function createCookie() {

// insert cookie contents here

        userName = "userName=Evalyne";

        document.cookie = userName;

}

</script>

...
```

This code creates the variable **userName** and assigns the value of **Evalyne**. The code **document.cookie** creates the cookie and the variable **username** is assigned as its value.

4   Save the file in your text editor and open the file in your browser.

5   Click the Create Cookie button.

6   Open Explorer (the file browser, not the Web browser). Navigate to C:\Documents and Settings and choose your username from the list on the right.

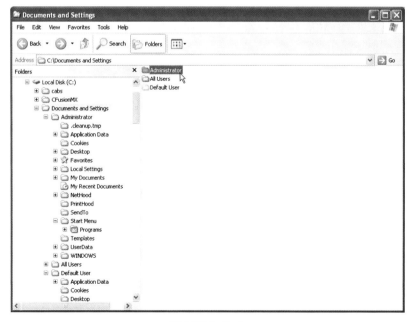

FIGURE 5.5

This exercise assumes that you are using Windows 2000 or Windows XP with sufficient privileges to see the contents of this folder. If you do not require a username or password to log on, you may be able to choose Default User.

7   **Open the Cookies folder.**

You should see a list of the available cookies on your computer, including the one you just created.

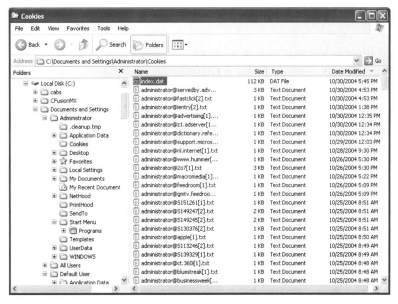

FIGURE 5.6

8   **Close the file-browsing window, but leave the file open in your text editor and browser for the next exercise.**

Read a Cookie

1   **In the open createcookie.html, find the following line of code.**

```
document.cookie = userName;
```

2   **Insert the following line of code.**

```
...
function createCookie() {
// insert cookie contents here
userName = "userName=Evalyne"
document.cookie = userName;
    alert("The value of your cookie is " + document.cookie);
  }
// -->
...
```

You can read the cookie by writing its value to a string — in this case, to an alert box.

| 3 | Save the file in your text editor and refresh your browser. |

| 4 | Click the Create Cookie button. |

An alert box appears with the value of the cookie as `userName=Evalyne.`

| 5 | Close the file in your browser and text editor. |

To Extend Your Knowledge...

SECURE COOKIES

You can use the HTTPS protocol to encrypt the information stored in cookies. Using the secure attribute (described in the next lesson), the information in the cookie can only be transmitted using encryption.

A *security certificate* is a license to use digital encryption. Security certificates can be purchased for individual Web sites through companies such as Verisign and Thawte. To obtain a security certificate for a Web site, clients must produce copies of various legal documents.

LESSON 2   Manipulating Cookies

Individual name-value pairs contained in a cookie are referred to as the attributes of the cookie. In the previous lesson, you created a cookie attribute named `userName` with the value set to `Evalyne`. Cookies may contain user-defined attributes or one of the four pre-defined optional attributes of the `cookie` property: `expires`, `domain`, `path`, or `secure`. Each attribute has a specific purpose.

Expires

The `expires` attribute allows a cookie to be stored and reused for a set amount of time. Once the expiration date has passed, a cookie can no longer be used. Most Web browsers delete expired cookie text files from their caches, while others do not. Using pseudo-code, you can create a cookie that expires in six months:

```
expires = 6 months from now
```

In JavaScript, you can create an `expirationDate` variable and assign an expiration date six months ahead by writing:

```
expirationDate = new Date();

expiration.setMonth(expirationDate.getMonth()+6);
```

Then, you could write this value to a cookie:

```
document.cookie = "expires=" + expirationDate.toGMTString() ;
```

Path

The **path** attribute allows a cookie to be read in a relative path from the page creating the cookie. By default, a cookie is available to other pages in the same folder. For example, a cookie created by viewing www.domain.com/tutorials/index.html would also be accessible to www.domain.com/tuorials/functions.html. The same cookie would not be accessible to www.domain.com/operators/index.html because the cookie and the operators folder reside in different directories. To overcome this limitation, you can set a **path** attribute in the cookie, as shown below:

```
path = /

path = /directory

path = /directory/subDirectory
```

The first value of "/" allows any page in the domain to access the cookie. The second value of "/" limits access to a specific directory, including all sub-directories. The third value of "/" further limits access to a specific sub-directory.

Specifying **path** ="" allows any page in the current directory to use (access) the cookie, which produces the same result as not specifying the **path** attribute at all. Specifying the **path** attribute with no value simply adds file size to the cookie. Leaving the **path** attribute at its default also allows it to be read by any file in the current directory without increasing the size of the cookie.

Domain

The third attribute is **domain**, which sets the visited domain as the only domain allowed to read the cookie. Setting this property restricts other Web sites from accessing the information and protects the visitor's privacy. For example:

```
domain = www.domain.com
```

This cookie is available to this domain, as well as to all canonical domain names. *Canonical domain names* are domain names that can be accessed through the main domain name, such as domain.com, mail.domain.com, and store.domain.com.

It is possible to set a domain equal to ".com" so that all ".com" pages can read the cookie. This practice is not recommended because it would allow any commerce (.com) Web page to read the content of any cookie created by any another ".com" site. Newer Web browsers prohibit this type of action because of the serious security risks involved. For example, if one Web site stored your credit card information in a cookie (although this is highly unlikely), another Web site would have access to the content of that cookie.

Secure

The third optional attribute is **secure**. This attribute determines whether the cookie should only be available during a secure session (HTTPS). *HTTPS* stands for Secure HyperText Transport Protocol; it ensures that all information transmitted between Web browsers and Web servers is encrypted. For example, during a credit card transaction, information often passes through multiple machines as it travels to its final destination (a Web browser or Web server). Using HTTPS, no other computer except the destination system has access to the information, so your credit card number remains safe. You set the **secure** value by writing:

```
secure
```

Secure is a value and does not allow assignment; it simply sets the value to **true** if the keyword is present or **false** if it is not included. To use the **secure** attribute, the Web server must have a security certificate installed.

Split()

Since the value of a cookie can contain one or more name-value pairs, you must perform a function to separate the attributes. You can use the **split()** method to separate the cookie's single-string value into multiple sub-values (attributes), according to the placement of a specified delimiter. The separated sub-values become elements of an array. This method allows you to work with the associated elements in the array. Let's reconsider the following cookie:

```
var theCookie = document.cookie;

document.cookie = "userName=Evalyne";
```

To output the username created in this cookie, you would write:

```
username = document.cookie.split('=')[1];
```

Using the **split('=')** attribute allows you to call either the **userName** string value or the **Evalyne** string value simply by calling the appropriate numeric value in the array. Because **userName** is encountered first, it becomes the first element of the array, and Evalyne becomes the second element. Using **split('=')[1]** allows you to specify the first element in the array, thereby singling out one chunk of cookie attribute data (**userName**). This method is not limited to a single split. Consider the following cookie that contains multiple attributes:

```
var theCookie = document.cookie;

document.cookie = "name=Eva Kinney;userName=Evalyne";
```

To output the username created in this cookie, you would write:

```
retrievedName = document.cookie.split(';')[1];

userName = retrievedName.split('=')[1];

document.write("userName = " + userName);
```

This script would output:

```
userName = Evalyne
```

Create a Cookie with an Expiration Date

1   In your text editor, open expirecookie.html from your WIP_05 folder.

2   Insert the following lines of code.

```
...
function createCookie() {
// insert cookie contents here
userName = "userName=Evalyne";
expiration = new Date();
expiration.setMonth(expiration.getMonth()+6);
document.cookie = userName;
}
</script>
...
```

Adding these two lines of code creates a new **date** object, assigns a date, and then adds six months to the date. This code creates a value of six months from the time the **date** object was created.

3   Find the following line of code.

```
document.cookie = userName;
```

4   Change the code to the following.

```
document.cookie = userName + ";expires=" + expiration.toGMTString() ;
```

This code concatenates the two attributes (**userName** and **expires**) into a single string that can be stored in the cookie. GMT (Greenwich Mean Time) attributes are often used as the standard method of noting time.

5   Save your changes in the text editor and open the file in your browser.

6   Click the Create Cookie button.

7   Close the file in your browser and text editor.

6   Enter a product name, description, and price for a second item.

7   When you receive the prompt to enter another item, click Cancel. Depending on the information you entered, you should see a table similar to the following.

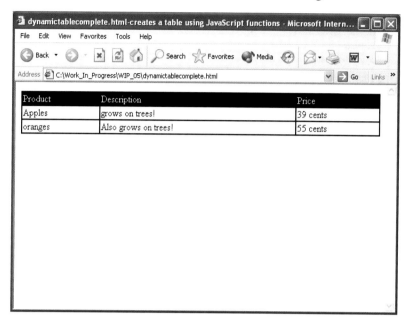

FIGURE 5.10

8   Close the file in your Web browser.

In the next exercise, you finish the necessary scripting to build the page you just tested.

To Extend Your Knowledge...

USING ARRAYS TO CREATE DYNAMIC CODE

The *for* loop dynamically populates the cells of an an array. You can use the `length` property of the array to determine how many times the loop should execute.

LESSON 4 Generating Dynamic Tables and Pages

In the previous lesson, you created a page that outputs a table of product information, including the product names, descriptions, and prices. In this lesson, you consider a more complex example of a page that creates HTML code dynamically. The code allows a user to enter the product information before the content of the page displays. This example is designed to mimic a page created from external data.

Generating HTML dynamically is often used hand-in-hand with server-side scripting technology. In many cases, the server-side script gathers information from a database, which is then placed within JavaScript variables to use in the dynamically created HTML. A complete discussion of server-side scripting is beyond the scope of this book, but the principles of creating dynamically generated HTML using a client-side language such as JavaScript are exactly the same.

Let's return to an example you first saw in the beginning of the project to experiment with the creation of dynamically generated HTML. You already noted that similar code is repeated multiple times with statements such as:

```
document.write('<tr>');
document.write('<td>oranges</td>');
document.write('</tr>');
```

Since JavaScript allows you to reuse code, you can write a function to replace the lines of code that construct each table.

```
function makeRow(item) {
        document.write('<tr>');
        document.write('<td>'+item+'</td>');
        document.write('</tr>');
} //end function
```

To move the table data information into an array for temporary storage, you can write:

```
var list=new Array("apples","oranges","bananas","pears","carrots");
```

Next, you can use the following code to create the table:

```
document.write('<table border="2">');
makeRow(list[0]);
makeRow(list[1]);
makeRow(list[2]);
makeRow(list[3]);
makeRow(list[4]);
document.write('</table>');
```

Using a function reduces the repetitive code, and the array allows you to hold the information. To demonstrate a point, let's assume that you are pulling information from an external source and placing it into the array, instead of assigning the array's content in the code. In such a situation, you have no way of knowing how many pieces of information you will have. Luckily, you can use the **length** property of the array to find out how many items have been stored. You can also use a **for** statement to create the table rows. Using these techniques, you could write the following code to create the table:

```
document.write('<table border="2">');

var list=new Array("apples","oranges","bananas","pears","carrots");

for (x=0; x<list.length; x++) {

        makeRow(list[x]);

} // end for

document.write('</table>');
```

If you use this script, you can add or subtract items from the array without changing the script. The script dynamically compensates for changes to the array whenever the page is viewed in the browser. Assuming you are creating a page based on a varying number of items (such as an online auction), you don't need to manually make changes whenever the number of items increases or decreases.

Create a Dynamically Generated Page

1   **In your text editor, open dynamictable.html from the WIP_05 folder.**

This is an unfinished version of the file you used in the previous exercise.

2   **Examine the code.**

A **do while** loop stores information in three arrays.

```
...

//populate array by asking for information

do {

    productName[x]=prompt("Enter a product name.","");

    productDesc[x]=prompt("Enter a description for the product.","");

    productPrice[x]=prompt("Enter a price for the product.","");

    anotherItem=confirm("Enter another item?");

    x++;

} while (anotherItem==true)

...
```

Remember that the **confirm()** method asks the user to confirm a question. If the user clicks OK, **true** returns. If the user clicks Cancel, **false** returns.

3   **Insert the following code.**

```
...
anotherItem=confirm("Enter another item?");
x++;
} while (anotherItem==true)
// start section to draw table
document.write('<table width="100%" border="1" bordercolor="#000033"
cellspacing="0">');
document.write('<tr bgcolor="#000033">');
document.write('<td><font color="#FFFFFF">Product</font></td>');
document.write('<td><font color="#FFFFFF">Description</font></td>');
document.write('<td><font color="#FFFFFF">Price</font></td>');
document.write('</tr>');
</script>
...
```

The code you inserted creates the first row of the table, which holds the column titles.

4   **Insert the following code to generate the rows of content.**

```
...
document.write('<td><font color="#FFFFFF">Description</font></td>');
document.write('<td><font color="#FFFFFF">Price</font></td>');
document.write('</tr>');
// start section to draw table rows
for (v=0; v<x; v++) {
document.write('<tr>');
document.write('<td>'+productName[v]+'</td>');
document.write('<td>'+productDesc[v]+'</td>');
document.write('<td>'+productPrice[v]+'</td>');
document.write('</tr>');
} // end for
</script>
...
```

In the code used to enter the information into the arrays, you used a variable named "**x**" to represent the element number. The **for** loop that creates the rows also references the "**x**" variable to determine how many rows to create. You could have used the **length** property of one of the arrays to determine how many times to perform the loop.

5   **Insert the following code to end the table.**

```
...

document.write('</tr>');

} // end for

</script>

</table>

</body>

</html>
```

6   **Save the file in your text editor and open it in your Web browser.**

7   **Experiment with the script by entering a varying number of products and inspecting the results.**

If you experience errors or other problems, compare the code in the file you created with the code in the example file (dynamictablecomplete.html).

8   **Close the file in your Web browser and text editor.**

To Extend Your Knowledge...

ENDING A DYNAMIC TABLE

In the previous exercise, you placed the `</table>` command outside the script to end the table. You can also use this command within the script with a command such as `document.write ("</table>");` by placing this code before the `</script>` tag.

LESSON 5   Using Escape Characters and Sequences

In Lessons 3 and 4, you learned that JavaScript can write dynamically generated HTML code. JavaScript can also write dynamic JavaScript code. The principle behind producing dynamic JavaScript code is essentially the same as generating dynamic HTML. You can use the **document.write()** statement to create JavaScript code, or you can use a combination of JavaScript and HTML code, which is then passed to the interpreter.

Imagine that you want to generate an alert when the user clicks a link on a page. Earlier in the book, you constructed inline JavaScript statements for this purpose, as shown in the following statement:

```
<a href="#" onclick="alert('hi')">hi</a>
```

You could try to write JavaScript statements to store the statement in a variable and output it to the interpreter, but doing so would create unique challenges. Consider the following statements:

```
command1='<a href="#" onclick="alert('hi')">hi</a>';

document.write(command1);
```

As you probably noticed, the first statement violates JavaScript syntax rules. You have a string for the variable with a nested string for the **onclick** event handler. The event handler also has a nested string for the **alert()** method. Since you only have two types of quotes, you cannot complete the statement without ending a prior string and confusing the interpreter.

To complete this statement (without violating any syntax rules), you need to use quote characters without *actually* using quote characters. Escape sequences are designed for this purpose. *Escape sequences* are codes you can use within JavaScript to represent characters that would normally create syntax errors. For instance, you know that JavaScript syntax rules restrict you from using the following code statement:

```
document.write('Jack O'Malley went home.');
```

The single quote in the middle of the string would confuse the interpreter because it would assume that you meant to close the string. In previous examples, you solved this problem by using combinations of single and double quotes. Consider the following statement, which is perfectly legal JavaScript syntax.

```
document.write("Jack O'Malley went home.");
```

Using an escape sequence to represent the single quote in O'Malley allows you to write the first statement as:

```
document.write('Jack O\'Malley went home.');
```

In this example, the backslash and single quote (\') tell the JavaScript interpreter to insert a single quote in this location. The backslash (\) is an escape character. An *escape character* simply marks the beginning of an escape sequence.

Returning to the previous example, you can use escape characters to create perfectly valid JavaScript:

```
command1='<a href="#" onclick="alert(\'hi\')">hi</a>';

document.write(command1);
```

The following list shows you the most common escape sequences.

Sequence	Character
\t	Tab character
\n	Newline character
\r	Carriage return
\'	Single quote
\"	Double quote
\\	Backslash character

It is important to note the escape sequence for the backslash character. Writing links to files requires that you use the backslash character. This can create problems, since the backslash character used in a file name can be mistaken for another escape sequence. You consider the implications of this issue in the following exercise.

Use Escape Sequence Characters to Correct Errors

1   **In your text editor, open escapebackslash.html from your WIP_05 folder.**

2   **Find the following lines of code.**

```
fileName="c:\newSite\JavaScriptBook\index.html";

command1='<a href="'+fileName+'">Link to File</a>';

document.write(command1);
```

This code writes a file name as dynamically generated HTML. In this exercise, you assign a local file name (and path) to the variable named **fileName**.

3   **Open the file in your browser and move your mouse over the hyperlink.**

Viewing this code in a browser with the status bar turned on reveals the problems with the code as currently written. Notice that when you move over the link, the status bar shows the link as the HTML interpreter sees it:

```
c:ewSiteJavaScriptBookindex.html
```

The interpreter misinterprets the file name because it assumes the **/n** in **c:/newSite** is part of the escape sequence for a newline character.

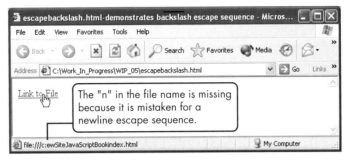

FIGURE 5.11

4 | Correct this error by using the escape sequence for a backslash character and entering a second slash in front of the first "n" character.

```
. . .

fileName="c:\\newSite\JavaScriptBook\index.html";

command1='<a href="'+fileName+'">Link to File</a>';

document.write(command1);

. . .
```

5 | Save your changes in the text editor and refresh the file in your browser.

6 | Move your mouse over the hyperlink.

This change in the code allows the HTML interpreter to see the file name as intended.

```
c:\newSite\JavaScriptBook\index.html
```

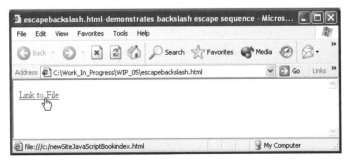

FIGURE 5.12

7 | Close the file in your browser and text editor.

To Extend Your Knowledge...

ESCAPE CHARACTERS

Programmers often use the escape sequences for single quotes (\ ') and double quotes (\ ") in text strings without the interpreter mistaking them for the ends of the strings. In these situations, the interpreter also understands that you don't intend to end the strings.

LESSON 6   Utilizing Bookmarklets

Bookmarklets are small chunks of JavaScript code that you can use in place of URLs in a variety of circumstances. You create a bookmarklet with the **javascript** keyword, followed by a colon, followed by a JavaScript command or commands. For example, consider the following JavaScript command:

```
window.resizeTo(640,480);
```

To create a bookmarklet, simply modify the command as follows:

```
javascript: window.resizeTo(640,480);
```

Bookmarklets are placed into URL fields and are normally activated in situations where files are loaded. For example, bookmarklets are often written as hyperlinks by placing the bookmarklet code into the **href** property of an **<a>** tag:

```
<a href="javascript: window.resizeTo(640,480);">resize screen to 640
by 480</a>
```

In this situation, you simply click the hyperlink to activate the code in the bookmarklet.

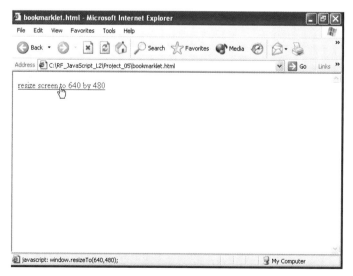

FIGURE 5.13

Since the code appears in the place normally reserved for a URL, the bookmarklet code appears in the browser's status bar. You can add the bookmarklet code to the Favorites menu in the same way that you would add a hyperlink. For example, if you right-click the link shown above, you can choose to add the link to the Favorites menu.

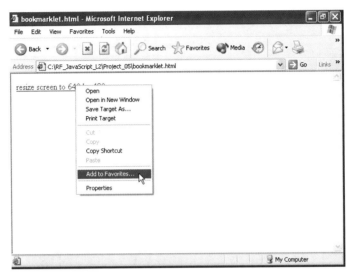

FIGURE 5.14

Security precautions may trigger warnings about doing so, however.

FIGURE 5.15

When you click Yes in the Security Alert dialog box, the bookmarklet is added to the Favorites menu.

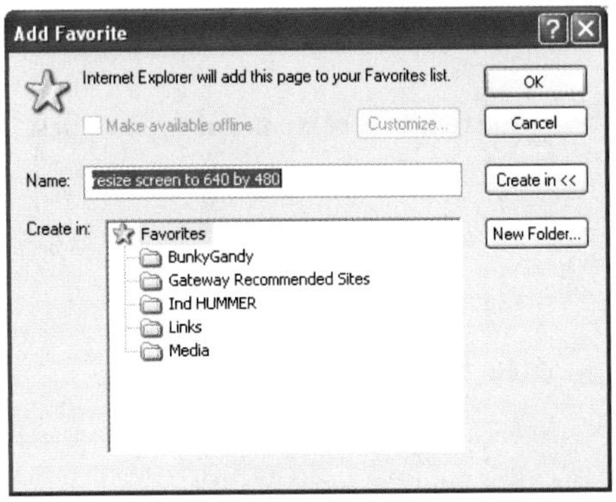

FIGURE 5.16

When you want to apply the code to a Web page or Web site, simply choose the bookmarklet from the Favorites list.

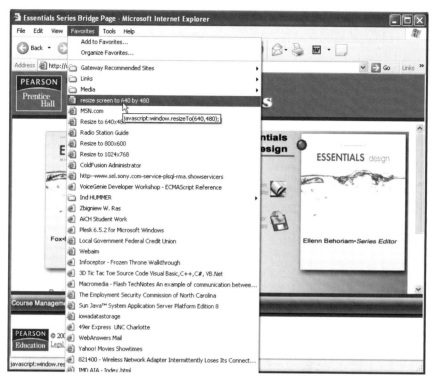

FIGURE 5.17

Bookmarklets can be used for a variety of purposes, since many scripts can be adapted for use as bookmarklets. Many Web sites, such as www.bookmarklets.com, offer free bookmarklets that you can download and install on your computer. In the following exercise, you create a bookmarklet to detect the last time a Web page was modified.

Create a Bookmarklet

1   In your text editor, open bookmarkletexercise.html from your WIP_05 folder.

2   Insert the following code.

```
...

<title>bookmarkletexercise.html</title>

</head>

<body>

<a href="javascript:alert(document.lastModified);">check last
modification date</a>

</body>

</html>
```

3   Save the file in your text editor and open the file in your browser.

4   Click the hyperlink.

FIGURE 5.18

5   Click OK.

The last modification date returns to the user.

6   Keep the file open in your browser and text editor for the next exercise.

Install and Use a Bookmarklet

1   In the open bookmarkletexercise.html in your browser, right-click the hyperlink.

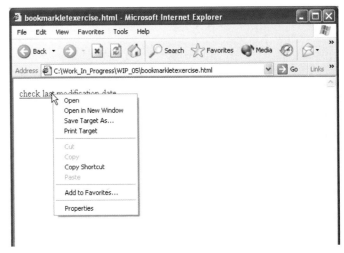

FIGURE 5.19

2   Choose Add to Favorites from the shortcut menu.

3   If you receive a security warning, click Yes.

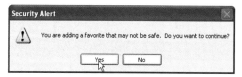

FIGURE 5.20

4   Name the bookmarklet "check last modification date" and click OK to add the bookmarklet to your Favorites menu.

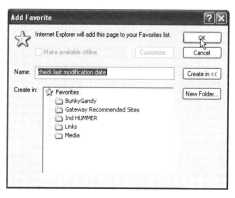

FIGURE 5.21

5   Change the URL field in your browser's Address bar to go to the Against The Clock Web site (http://www.againsttheclock.com).

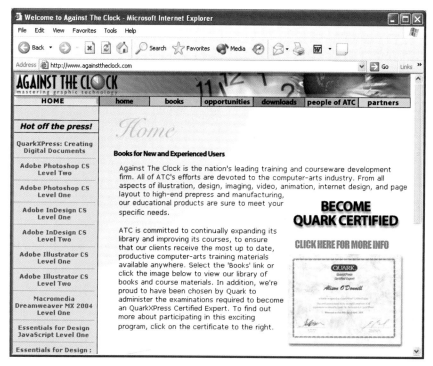

FIGURE 5.22

6   From the Favorites menu, choose the favorite named "check last modification date."

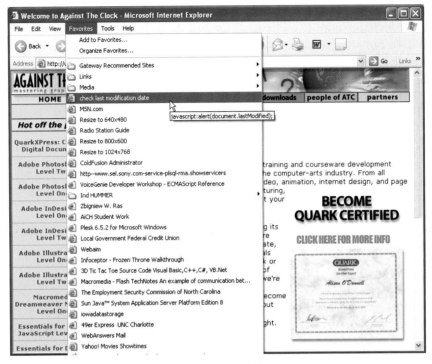

FIGURE 5.23

7   Click OK.

FIGURE 5.24

8   Close the file in your browser and text editor.

To Extend Your Knowledge...

BOOKMARKLETS

Bookmarklets can contain multiple lines of code. You can write JavaScript without newline characters since only semicolons are needed to mark the end of a line of code. The exact number of characters that you can use in a bookmarklet varies by browser, but most browsers can accommodate approximately five or six lines of code in the URL field.

SUMMARY

In Project 5, you considered a number of methods for customizing content. Cookies address a fundamental limitation of HTML by providing a way for the Web server and Web browser to remember users and to record information that they can retrieve later. Using cookies, you can record user preferences, such as the information stored in the shopping cart of an e-commerce Web site.

You also learned how to use JavaScript to dynamically create HTML code when a page is viewed. This method of using code to create code is an important tool that allows your pages to react to varying amounts of information and respond to end-user choices. Dynamically generated HTML code is usually created by outputting HTML code from **document.write()** statements. In the example of the e-commerce shopping cart, data could be retrieved from cookies and used to dynamically generate the shopping cart page whenever the page loads in the browser.

You learned that when using JavaScript to create HTML code dynamically, it often becomes necessary to use escape sequences to represent various characters. Escape sequences are codes that represent characters that would otherwise create syntax errors. Escape sequences always begin with the escape character, which is represented by a backslash (\) in JavaScript.

In the final lesson of the project, you learned that bookmarklets are small chunks of JavaScript code that are often stored in the browser's Favorites menu. Bookmarklets are usually created in the **href** property of an **<a>** tag, and then added to the Favorites menu. Once installed in the Favorites menu, you can apply your bookmarklets to any Web page.

KEY TERMS

Alias	Cookie	HTTPS
Bookmarklet	DHTML (Dynamic HTML)	Persistent state
Caching	Dynamic document	Security certificate
Canonical domain name	Escape character	State
CNAME record	Escape sequence	Stateless
Content-encoding	Header	Static document

CHECKING CONCEPTS AND TERMS

MULTIPLE CHOICE

Circle the letter that matches the correct answer for each of the following questions.

1. How is the **split()** method often used with cookies?

    a. To specify the names of files that can read the cookie

    b. To set the expiration date of the cookie

    c. To output the **path**, **secure**, and **domain** attributes of the cookie

    d. To split the name-value pairs stored in a cookie into the elements of an array

2. How is the **domain** attribute used in cookies?

    a. To set the type of data that can be stored in the cookie

    b. To allow any page from a specific domain to read the content of the cookie

    c. To set the size of the cookie file

    d. To specify that cookie contents must be transmitted using encryption

3. Individual name-value pairs stored in a cookie are referred to as _____ of the cookie.

    a. methods

    b. properties

    c. attributes

    d. objects

4. What does the acronym DHTML represent?

    a. Dynamically Generated HTML

    b. A combination of HTML, CSS, and JavaScript

    c. A new version of HTML that is only available in Netscape browsers

    d. The HTML code within a specific domain, such as a Web site

5. Why is it often useful to add the "\\" escape sequence when dynamically constructing file names in JavaScript?

    a. Because this sequence specifies the document content-encoding for a cookie property

    b. Because this sequence specifies colons (**:**) in file names

    c. To specify the proper protocol

    d. Because file name locations often contain forward slashes, which can be mistaken for other escape sequences

6. How can the **secure** attribute of a **cookie** object be used to improve security?

    a. By ensuring the cookie is deleted when the page unloads from the browser

    b. By requiring the user to enter a security code to read the cookie content

    c. By requiring a password and username to read the cookie content

    d. By requiring the HTTPS protocol to read the cookie content

7. If the **path** attribute of a cookie is not specified, what pages can access the cookie?

    a. Any page in any Web site

    b. Pages in the same folder

    c. Any page in the entire Web site domain

    d. Any page on the user's hard drive

8. Which cookie properties ensure a user's privacy is not violated?

    a. The **domain** property

    b. The **expires** property

    c. The **secure** property

    d. All of the above

    e. None of the above

9. What does the escape sequence \n represent in JavaScript?

a. The newline character

b. The URL character

c. A backslash (\)

d. A forward slash (/)

10. How can you use bookmarklets?

a. In the **href** property of an **<a>** tag

b. In the URL field of a browser's Address bar

c. As a favorite in the Favorites menu

d. All of the above

e. None of the above

DISCUSSION QUESTIONS

1. Why are cookies useful? How do cookies address inherent limitations in HTML?

2. Why do you think privacy advocates fear the use of cookies? What safeguards are built into cookies to keep Web sites from abusing this technology?

3. How could the ability to write HTML code dynamically be used to improve a Web site designed to sell goods or services? Assume you are able to access basic information about the user's shopping preferences.

4. Assume you can write a bookmarklet to accomplish any task that is possible in JavaScript. Without using the examples presented in this project, name two possible uses for bookmarklets that are accessible from the Favorites menu.

SKILL DRILL

Skill Drill exercises reinforce project skills. Each skill reinforced is the same, or nearly the same, as a skill presented in the project. Detailed instructions are provided in a step-by-step format. You should work through these exercises in order.

1. Create a Cookie with User Input

In this exercise, you create a cookie and assign a user's input as the cookie's value.

1. Open WIP_05>createusernamecookie.html in your text editor.

2. Find the following line of code.

   ```
   userName = "username = Evalyne";
   ```

   This script creates a variable named **userName** and sets its value equal to **Evalyne**. You need to modify this line of code to accept a user's entry.

3. Change the code to the following.

   ```
   userName = document.form.userName.value;
   ```

   When the user submits the form, the entry in the text field will be used as the **userName** value for the cookie. After collecting the form data, you need to concatenate the cookie attribute **userName** with its value.

4. Find the following line of code.

    ```
    document.cookie = userName;
    ```

5. Change the code to the following.

    ```
    document.cookie = "userName="+userName;
    ```

6. Save the file in your text editor and open it in your browser.

7. Enter a username.

8. Type a name in the text box.

9. Click the Create Cookie button.

    An alert box appears with the cookie value set to the user's input.

10. Leave the file open for the next exercise.

2. Conditional Cookies

1. Save the open file as "conditionalcookie.html" in your WIP_05 folder.

2. In your text editor, find the following script.

    ```
    ...
    <script language="Javascript">
    <!--
    function createCookie() {
    userName = document.form.userName.value;
    document.cookie = "userName="+userName;
    alert("The value of your cookie is " + document.cookie);
    }
    // -->
    </script>
    ...
    ```

    If the user enters a name in the form field on the page, the cookie is accurate. If a user neglects to type an entry, the cookie is written with no value for **userName**. By adding conditions, you can assure that your cookie has a proper **userName** value.

3. Insert the following **if** statement.

    Checking to see if the form field is not null allows you to stop a user-input error from becoming a cookie error later.

    ```
    ...
    <script language="Javascript">
    <!--
    function createCookie() {
    userName = document.form.userName.value;

    if (userName != ""){
            document.cookie = "userName="+userName;
            alert("The value of your cookie is " + document.cookie);

    }
    }
    // -->
    </script>
    ...
    ```

4. Create an **else** statement that will generate an alert box if the user does not enter a username. The alert should say, "Please enter a username and resubmit."

5. Save the file in your text editor.

6. Clear the cookies from your browser.

7. View the page in your Web browser.

8. Leave the Username field blank and click the Create Cookie button.

9. Reload the page and click the Create Cookie button.

    By entering a value in the text field, you create the cookie and store the user's input. When a user doesn't fill in the form, she receives an alert message that asks her to enter a username. The cookie is not created without a username value.

10. Close the file in your browser and text editor.

3. Use Escape Characters in an Alert Box

1. In your browser, open skillbookmarklet.html from the WIP_05 folder.

    This simple file contains two email hyperlinks and a script that can extract and display any email address stored in the Web page. The script currently has a minor problem: the email addresses appear on the same line.

2. Click OK to acknowledge the alert box.

3. Open the file in your text editor.

4. Find the following code.

```
...

emailAddress="";

for (x=0; x < document.links.length; x++) {

        if (document.links[x].protocol == "mailto:") {

                theEmail = document.links[x].toString();

                theEmail = theEmail.substring(7,theEmail.length);

                emailAddress += theEmail;

        }

}

alert(emailAddress);

...
```

    This code extracts all email addresses in the current page and displays them in an alert box. Notice how the \n escape sequence separates multiple addresses.

5. Find the following line of code.

```
emailAddress += theEmail;
```

    This code adds a found email address to a variable that records any found addresses. The code works well when a single address is found, but it does not work well when multiple addresses are found.

6. In the line of code you found in Step 5, add the \n escape sequence to the string of text stored in the **theEmail** variable.

7. Save the file in your text editor and refresh your browser.

   The email addresses should appear on separate lines.

FIGURE 5.25

8. Click OK to acknowledge the alert box.

9. Keep the file open in your browser and text editor for the next exercise.

4. Convert a Script to a Bookmarklet

1. In the open skillbookmarklet.html, find the following code.

```
...

emailAddress="";

for (x=0; x < document.links.length; x++) {

        if (document.links[x].protocol == "mailto:") {

                theEmail = document.links[x].toString();

                theEmail = theEmail.substring(7,theEmail.length);

                emailAddress += theEmail+ "\n";

        }

}

alert(emailAddress);

...
```

2. Remove all line separations and blank spaces from the code you found in Step 1 to create a single string of text.

```
emailAddress="";for(x=0;x<document.links.length;x++){if(document.lin
ks[x].protocol=="mailto:"){theEmail=document.links[x].toString();the
Email=theEmail.substring(7,theEmail.length);emailAddress+=theEmail+"
\n";}}alert(emailAddress);
```

3. Enclose the string you created in Step 2 within a pair of single quotes.

```
'emailAddress="";for(x=0;x<document.links.length;x++){if(document.li
nks[x].protocol=="mailto:"){theEmail=document.links[x].toString();th
eEmail=theEmail.substring(7,theEmail.length);emailAddress+=theEmail+
"\n";}}alert(emailAddress);'
```

4. Create a hyperlink, setting the **href** property equal to the string you created in the previous step.

5. Turn the **<a>** tag into a bookmarklet by inserting **javascript:** into the **href** property of the tag.

6. Remove the following line of code.

```
<script language="JavaScript">
```

7. Remove the following line of code.

```
</script>
```

8. Save the file in your text editor and refresh your browser. Your page should resemble the following.

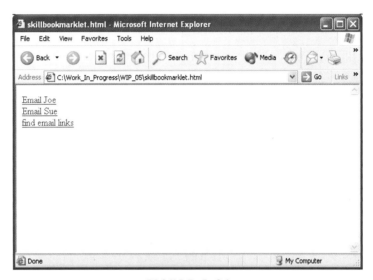

FIGURE 5.26

9. Test the file by clicking the hyperlink to activate the bookmarklet.

10. Keep the file open in your browser and text editor for the next exercise.

5. Install a Bookmarklet as a Favorite

1. In the open bookmarklet.html in your browser, add the bookmarklet in your page to the Favorites menu.

2. In your browser, go to http://www.scenicinteractive.com/ai.

3. Click the bookmarklet from your Favorites menu that you created in Step 1.

    An alert box should appear with an email address.

4. Click OK to acknowledge the alert box.

5. Close the file in your browser and text editor.

CHALLENGE

Challenge exercises expand on, or are somewhat related to, skills presented in the lessons. Each exercise provides a brief introduction, followed by instructions presented in a numbered-step format that are not as detailed as those in the Skill Drill exercises. You should work through these exercises in order.

1. Create HTML Code Dynamically

In this exercise, you create HTML code dynamically. A script was started for you; it extracts hyperlinks from a Web page and outputs the links to a pop-up window. Your job is to modify the existing script to create new hyperlinks by writing HTML code dynamically in the pop-up window.

1. In your browser, open challengedynamic.html from your WIP_05 folder.

   A script in this file extracts hyperlinks and outputs the **href** property of each link to a pop-up window.

FIGURE 5.27

2. Close the pop-up window.

3. Open the file in your text editor and find the following line of code.

   ```
   myWin.document.write(anAddress+"<br>");
   ```

4. Modify the line of code you found in the Step 3 to output the value as a hyperlink rather than plain text, as shown in the following illustration.

   Hint: surround the **href** property with single quotes and use the value of the **anAddress** variable for the **href** property and the link text.

FIGURE 5.28

5. Save and test your file.

6. Close the pop-up window.

7. Keep the file open in your browser and text editor for the next exercise.

2. Convert a Script to a Bookmarklet

The script you created in the previous exercise creates hyperlinks in a new window by searching through the currently open page and writing HTML dynamically. This script would be very useful if it allowed you to extract hyperlinks from any open Web page. In this exercise, you convert the script to a bookmarklet to accomplish this task.

1. In the open challengedynamic.html, convert the script to a bookmarklet in an **<a>** tag.

2. Save and test your file.

    The script should activate when you click the hyperlink.

3. Install the bookmarklet in your browser's Favorites menu.

4. Test your bookmarklet by navigating to various pages and using the bookmarklet.

5. Close the file in your browser and text editor.

3. Split Cookie Values

In this exercise, you utilize user input to create a cookie. After the cookie is created, you output the cookie value and its sub-values.

1. In your text editor, open splitcookievalue.html from your WIP_05 folder.

2. Insert the following code.

```
...
if (userName != ""){
document.cookie = "userName=" + userName;
// split cookie value and asign array elements to variables below
attribute = document.cookie.split('=')[0]
attributeValue = document.cookie.split('=')[1]
// assign variables to complete the following alert dialogs
alert("The value of your cookie is " + document.cookie);
alert("The attribute stored in the cookie is ");
...
```

Using the **split** method, you can break the cookie value into meaningful pieces. Here, you are splitting the attribute **userName** from its value. The attribute **userName** is the first item written into the array.

3. Modify the following lines of code to output cookie contents.

```
...
alert("The value of your cookie is " + document.cookie);
alert("The attribute stored in the cookie is " + attribute);
alert("The username value is " + attributeValue);
...
```

4. Save the file in your text editor and open it in your browser.

5. Enter a username.

6. Type a name in the text box.

7. Click the Create Cookie button.

    A series of alert boxes appears with the following values: cookie value, attribute, and attribute value.

8. Close the file in your browser and text editor.

4. Split Multiple Cookie Values

In this exercise, you extract the sub-values of a cookie string value by splitting the string into associative arrays. Then, you further split the string into **username** and **value**, and **expires** and **date** values.

1. In your text editor, open multiplesplitcookie.html from your WIP_05 folder.

2. Insert the following code.

```
...
if (userName != ""){
document.cookie = "userName=" + userName + ";expires=" + expires;
// split cookie value into individual strings
attribute = document.cookie.split(';')[0];
// assign variables to complete the following alert dialogs
alert("The value of your cookie is " + document.cookie);
alert("The username attribute is " + attributeName);
...
```

With the **split()** method, you use the "**;**" delimiter to divide the cookie string value in half.

3. Insert the following code.

```
...
document.cookie = "userName=" + userName + ";expires=" + expires;
// split cookie value into individual strings
attribute = document.cookie.split(';')[0];
attributeName = this.attribute.split("=")[0];
attributeValue = this.attribute.split("=")[1];
// assign variables to complete the following alert dialogs
alert("The value of your cookie is " + document.cookie);
alert("The username attribute is " + attributeName);
...
```

You can take one of the elements of the **attribute** array you created in the previous step and further divide it; you can extract the attribute's name and value as separate string values contained around the "=" delimiter.

4. Save the file in your text editor and open it in your browser.

5. Enter a username and type a name in the text box.

6. Click the Create Cookie button.

    A series of alert boxes appears with the following values: cookie value, attribute, and attribute value.

7. Find the following line of code.

```
attribute = document.cookie.split(';')[0];
```

8. Modify the line of code as follows.

```
attribute = document.cookie.split(';')[1];
```

9. Change the alert box messages to correspond with the change in attribute and value.

10. Save your changes in the text editor and refresh your browser.

11. Enter a username and type a name in the text box.

12. Click the Create Cookie button.

    A series of alert boxes should appear with the following values: cookie value, attribute, and attribute value.

13. Close the file in your browser and text editor.

PORTFOLIO BUILDER

Complete a Script to Create a Cookie

When you add interactive elements to your Web sites, you can use JavaScript to customize, personalize, and enrich the user's Web-browsing experience. When a user returns to a site and finds his personal information already in the fields of a form, he feels a sense of familiarity. This may be a small token of personalization, but users certainly appreciate and enjoy the gesture.

Open rememberusers.html in your text editor. Find the **fillForm():** function shown below:

```
function fillForm() {

// if  the cookie exists split into subvalues and write the
username value to the text field

}
```

Your task is to fill in the gaps in the script. The goal of this script is to fill in the Username field on a form with a username contained in the cookie value (if a cookie exists). To complete the task, you need to do the following:

1.   Write a condition for the **if** statement to verify that the cookie exists.

2.   If the cookie exists, read the cookie value.

3.   Split the cookie value around the "**;**" delimiter.

4.   Extract the value for **userName** from the **cookie** array.

5.   Write the **userName** value to the text field on page load.

6.   After you complete these steps, test the page in your Web browser. When the page loads, enter a username and click the Create Cookie button.

7.   Check the browser and verify that the cookie exists. Close the browser window.

8.   Reload the page and check that the username is still there. Clear cookies from the browser, and then close and reload the page. The username field should be blank.

Using Cascading Style Sheets

OBJECTIVES

In this project, you learn how to

- Use inline style sheets

- Redefine HTML tags

- Apply custom classes and ID selectors

- Add pseudo-classes

- Link to external CSS files

- Apply "the box" analogy and positioning

- Control visibility and layering

WHY WOULD I DO THIS?

In earlier projects, you discovered that HTML is not well suited for adding interactivity to a Web page, nor is it a suitable tool for controlling the formatting of a Web page. The solutions to these limitations are JavaScript for adding interactivity and Cascading Style Sheets (CSS) for controlling formatting.

Cascading Style Sheets were designed to separate the style of a Web page from its content. When you use CSS, HTML still describes the content, so the context of the data remains intact. With the content in place, the Cascading Style Sheets allow you to define the appearance of page elements in a single block of code. For instance, you can define the font for an entire document in one style sheet, without placing multiple **<font>** tags throughout the document. This method ensures greater consistency using simpler code that downloads faster.

CSS has capabilities that go beyond the scope of this book. The projects concerning CSS are meant to serve as an introduction for aspiring Web designers. After completing this book, you may want to consult a reference manual that offers a more in-depth exploration of CSS.

Similar to JavaScript, CSS was originally implemented inconsistently in different Web browsers. This led to compatibility problems when developing Web pages, which stopped many Web designers and developers from using the technology. As CSS has grown more standardized over the last few years, it has become a mainstream technology designated to play an important role in the future of Web design.

CSS offers several advantages over traditional HTML:

- A single style sheet can control the appearance of an entire Web site. By changing a single style sheet, you can change the appearance of the entire site.

- CSS allows greater control over the positioning of elements. Items can be precisely positioned on the page, even overlapped. Anyone who has used HTML tables to lay out a complex Web page understands the need for enhanced precision when positioning items.

- CSS allows greater control over formatting. For instance, you can specify the exact number of pixels or points to use for your font sizes, instead of choosing generic sizes in HTML.

- CSS allows designers to customize HTML for a Web page. For instance, you can modify the **<p>** tag to always display text in 10-point Arial.

- HTML will eventually be replaced by XHTML and XML, which are newer (enhanced) versions of HTML. Web designers and developers will be required to use CSS for both of those scripting technologies. Additionally, many HTML presentation tags (such as the **<font>** tag) will be eliminated from the standard.

- You can combine CSS, HTML, and JavaScript to create striking effects.

CSS and JavaScript were designed to work together as a virtual unit. As you may remember from Project 5, DHTML (Dynamic HTML) is a term used to describe the combination of CSS, JavaScript, and HTML. DHTML allows designers to create animations and other special effects. Designers and developers are expected to increase their understanding of DHTML and discover the advantages of using CSS, JavaScript, and HTML in unison.

This project and the one that follows offer an introductory guide to CSS. In this project, you consider the basics of CSS. In the next project, you explore DHTML in greater detail.

V I S U A L   S U M M A R Y

You can use CSS to enhance and improve Web sites in several different ways. For example, the EyeCareCenter.com site (shown below) uses CSS to position a background image in the upper-right corner of the browser window. No matter how the screen is resized, the image always remains in position in this area.

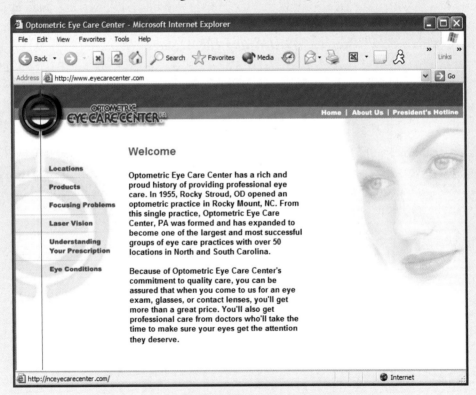

FIGURE 6.1

This is very different than a background image in HTML, which tiles at high resolutions and can't be placed in a specific area of the screen. Using the CSS code in the following illustration, you can position the background image in the top-right corner of the page and know that it will remain there regardless of whether the user scrolls downward or resizes the browser window.

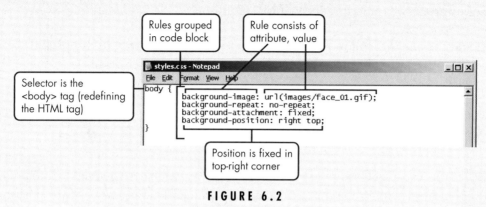

FIGURE 6.2

CSS code consists of *declarations*, which are chunks of CSS that consist of selectors and rules. The *selector* is the class to which the rule is applied. The selector can be an HTML tag, such as all **<table>** tags. When HTML tag names are used as selectors, the rule you apply overwrites the default display styles of the tag. This process is known as *redefining HTML tags*.

Let's use pseudo-code to explain the structure of CSS statements, which always follow this syntax:

```
selector { property: value; }
```

CSS commands establish rules for selectors. A *rule* is a guideline for how the selector will display on the page. A rule consists of a *property*, such as **background-color** or **font**, followed by a colon, and then the *value* assigned to the property. Depending on the property, the value can take on a number of attributes, such as **hidden**, **visible**, or **blue**.

Similar to JavaScript, a CSS statement ends with a semicolon, and multiple CSS statements can be grouped together using brackets (**{}**). You can establish more than one rule within brackets in the same way that multiple statements can be included in JavaScript. Take a moment to examine the following CSS statement:

```
body {

        background-color: red;

        font-family: Arial, Helvetica, sans-serif;

        font-size: 10px;

}
```

You can incorporate the CSS shown above into a Web page in three ways:

- As an *inline style sheet*, which works as an attribute within an HTML tag.

- As an *embedded style sheet*. Using this method, CSS rules are defined in the HTML document using the `<style>` tag.

- As a *linked (external) style sheet*. Using this method, the style sheets are saved as external documents, using the ".css" extension. The `<link>` tag links the HTML document to the external file. This is the most powerful way to use style sheets because a single file can control the appearance of an entire Web site or even multiple Web sites.

Selectors can also be custom classes that you can apply to any tag in the document. A class has much the same meaning in CSS as it does in JavaScript. A *custom class* is a rule (or rules) that tells the browser how to display any item to which the selector is applied. In other words, any member assigned to the class takes on the characteristics of the class.

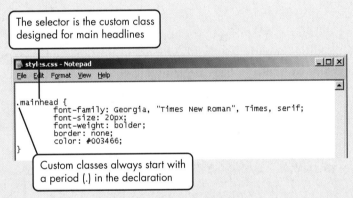

FIGURE 6.3

Inline styles are created with the **style** attribute of HTML tags. The **style** attribute is an extension to HTML that allows you to directly apply styles to a single HTML tag. You create inline styles as follows:

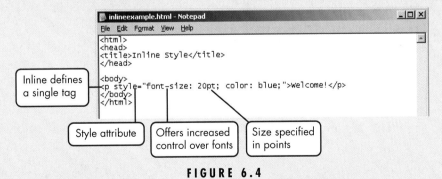

FIGURE 6.4

You can also create CSS styles to accommodate special situations. These styles are known as ***pseudo-classes*** because they represent situations that do not exist in HTML. Consider the following code that creates a rollover effect when the user moves the mouse pointer over a hyperlink.

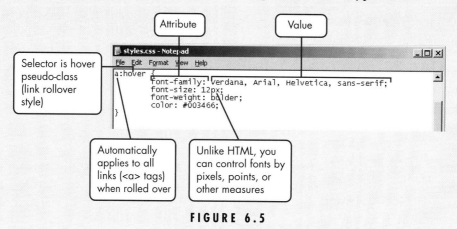

FIGURE 6.5

One of the most interesting aspects of CSS is its ability to control the placement of an object. In HTML, most positioning is static, meaning items appear in a position according to when they appear in the HTML code. CSS allows greater control over positioning in a number of ways. For instance, you can specify an ***absolute position***, which means that you specify the exact pixel position of an object on the page.

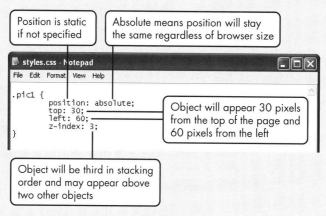

FIGURE 6.6

LESSON 1   Using Inline Style Sheets and Redefining HTML Tags

Inline style sheets are very similar to using inline JavaScript because the commands appear within HTML tags. Using this method, CSS rules are established using the **style** attribute of an HTML element, as shown in the following example:

```
<p style="font-size: 12pt; color: blue;">This sentence will display
in 12-point blue text.</p>
```

Notice how the rules stated in the **style** attribute are enclosed within quotes. This statement establishes multiple rules that are separated by semicolons (**;**). The rules established in the inline style sheet are written exactly the same as other rules.

Using inline style sheets isn't very different than using tags (such as **<font>**) because you are setting the formatting for each individual tag. This method allows you to use the powerful formatting control of CSS. For instance, you can set the font size to exactly 12 point, as shown in the previous example. This level of control cannot be accomplished with traditional HTML.

Inline style sheets are probably the least powerful way to use CSS because they do not allow you to set the styles for an entire Web page or Web site — which is, as you know, one of the primary benefits of using CSS. When you use CSS to apply styles globally, you reduce file size and ensure a consistent visual representation from section to section and from page to page. In addition, this method makes updating the page/site much simpler. Using inline styles doesn't take advantage of these benefits; for this reason, most developers rarely use inline styles.

Redefining HTML Tags

One of the most interesting aspects of CSS is its ability to customize existing HTML commands. This is also one of the easiest facets of CSS to use and understand. In this context, HTML commands are "redefined" to override the default style of the tag. When you redefine HTML tags, the default display of the tag is overridden and replaced by the new rules you create with CSS. For example, consider the following HTML page:

```
<html>
<head>
<title>style1.html-demonstrates basic CSS</title>
<!-- define a CSS rule for the body tag -->
<style type="text/css">
body {background-color: red;}
</style>
</head>
<body>
My Web page.
</body>
</html>
```

Notice the syntax of the CSS code. The **type="text/css"** tells the browser that you are using a CSS style in the same way **"language=JavaScript"** tells the browser that you are using JavaScript. The term **background-color** represents the **bgcolor** property of the **<body>** tag, which is also represented in JavaScript as **bgcolor**. In CSS, properties with more than one word are always hyphenated, such as **background-color** instead of **background color**.

The **<style>** tag creates a style sheet in the same way a **<script>** tag creates a script. You are creating a rule that states that the **<body>** tag will always have a red background. You established the rule in the **<head>** section of the document. (This isn't absolutely necessary, but seems reasonable because you want the rule applied to the entire page.)

You can also change the **<body>** tag in other ways. For example, consider the EyeCareCenter.com Web site shown in the Visual Summary. No matter how the window is resized, the image always appears in the top-right corner. As another type of example, consider that you can also use this type of command to redefine the **<table>** tag. Assume that you created a basic HTML page, and you are using the following code to insert a table:

```
<table width="500" height="277" border="3" cellpadding="0"
cellspacing="0">

</table>

table {

        background-image: url(images/face_01.gif);

        background-repeat: no-repeat;

        background-attachment: fixed;

        background-position: right top

}
```

The statements shown above place the image in a fixed position relative to the element that contains it. In the first example, the placement of the image is relative to the body (entire document) that contains it. In the second example, the placement of the image is relative to the table that contains it.

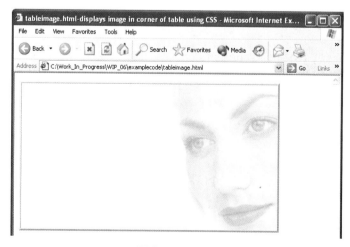

FIGURE 6.7

Redefining HTML tags often involves the use of specific fonts. For instance, the following command eliminates the need of the **<font>** tag in the document:

```
body {  font-family: Arial, Helvetica, sans-serif; font-size: 9px}
```

Because most text appears within the **<p>** tag, you can arrive at the same result by redefining the **<p>** tag:

```
p {  font-family: Arial, Helvetica, sans-serif; font-size: 9px}
```

Lastly, you can define rules for special situations that involve multiple HTML tags. For instance, you could define a rule that sets bold items in a list to the color blue. To do so, you must define a rule that says, "the content between the **** and **** tags should be blue if these tags are contained within the **<li>** and **</li>** tags." You establish this type of rule as follows:

```
li b {color: blue;}
```

Remember, this rule only affects bold type that appears within a list item.

Redefine HTML Tags

1   **Copy the content of the RF_JavaScript_L2>Project_06 folder into your Work_In_Progress>WIP_06 folder.**

2   **In your Web browser, open finish.html from the WIP_06>eyecare folder.**

This is the finished version of the file you work on throughout this project.

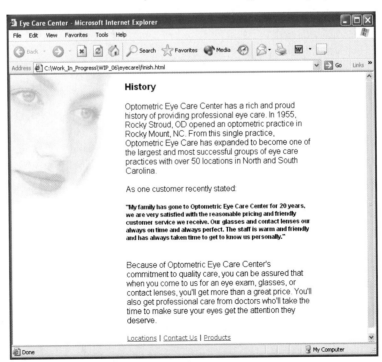

FIGURE 6.8

3   **After you inspect the file, close it in your Web browser.**

4   **In your Web browser and text editor, open start.html from the WIP_06>eyecare folder.**

This is your starting point for the page.

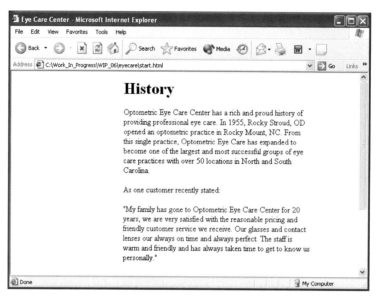

FIGURE 6.9

5   **Insert the following code directly before the </head> tag.**

```
<html>
<head>
<title>Eye Care Center</title>
<style type="text/css">
h1 {
        font-family: Arial, Helvetica, sans-serif;
        font-size: 18px;
        color: #333333;
        font-weight: bold;
}
</style>
</head>
<body>
...
```

This code creates a style for the main headline by redefining the **<h1>** tag.

6 | **Save the file in your text editor and refresh your browser.**

The text of the headline changes.

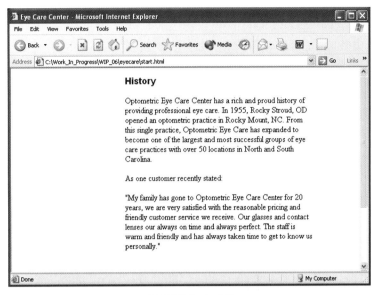

FIGURE 6.10

7 | **Insert the following commands directly before the </style> tag you just created.**

```
...
        color: #333333;
        font-weight: bold;
}
body {
        font-family: Arial, Helvetica, sans-serif;
        font-size: 10pt;
}
</style>
</head>
<body>
...
```

This code creates the style for the content text on the page. Since you want to use this style for most of the text, you define it as part of the **<body>** tag.

8 Save the file in your text editor and refresh your browser.

The text style changes.

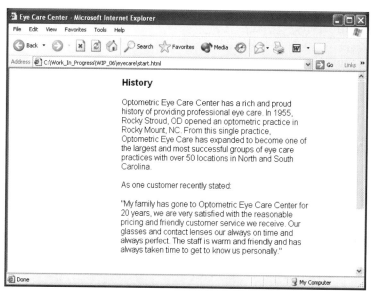

FIGURE 6.11

9 Close the file in your browser and text editor.

To Extend Your Knowledge...

RULE INHERITANCE

The term "cascading" refers to the rules of applying style sheets. For instance, a rule that establishes a text style for the **<body>** tag automatically applies to any **<p>** tags unless you override a specific **<p>** tag with a different rule.

DEFAULT STYLES

When defining a rule that you want to serve as a default style throughout a document (such as the style of your content text), it is usually best to redefine the **<body>** tag.

LESSON 2   Using Custom Classes and ID Selectors

Classes can be defined and shared among multiple tags. Instead of assigning a CSS rule to an HTML tag, you can create a custom class and assign the rule to the class. A class name always starts with a period. Consider the following style that turns certain text bold and red:

```
.boldred { font-weight: bold; color: red; }
```

You can assign the **.boldred** class to text by including it in the HTML tag using the **class** attribute.

```
<p class="boldred">This text will display bold and red.</p>
```

The **<span>** tag allows you to apply a style to text that exists within another tag, as shown in the following example:

```
<p>To get your refund <span class="boldred">you must mail in the
enclosed card</span> with the proper information.</p>
```

The **<span>** or **<div>** tag is often used to apply a style to elements that may not otherwise be logically grouped within a single tag. As an example, to create a span or div that contains an explanatory picture and quote, you could apply a border and change the background color and text to set this section apart from the rest of the page.

ID Selectors

ID selectors are very similar to custom classes. Since ID selectors are so similar to custom classes, you may wonder why they are used at all. The reason is that **_ID selectors_** are designed for one-time usage; you create an ID selector for a single element. The primary reason for ID selectors is to create a single element that can be referenced in JavaScript or other scripting languages.

A period starts the name of a class, but a hash symbol (**#**) marks the beginning of an ID selector. For instance, to create an ID selector named **blue**, you would write:

```
#blue {color:blue}
```

To define a table that will be used as a quote, you would write:

```
table#quote { font-size: 10 pt }
```

The previous statement requires you to use the **ID** attribute in the HTML tag that represents this selector, as shown below:

```
<table ID="quote">
```

Create and Use a Custom Class

1   **In your text editor and browser, open customclasses.html from your WIP_06>eyecare folder.**

This is essentially the same file you used in the previous lesson.

2   **In your text editor, insert the following code directly before the `</style>` tag.**

```
...
        font-family: Arial, Helvetica, sans-serif;
        font-size: 10pt;
}

.quote {
        font-family: Arial, Helvetica, sans-serif;
        font-size: 9pt;
        font-weight: bold;
}
</style>
</head>
<body>
...
```

This code creates a custom class for quotes. In CSS code, a period is always the first character in the name of a custom class.

3   **Find the following code in your document.**

```
<p>&quot;My family has gone to Optometric Eye Care Center
```

This marks the beginning of the quote.

4   **Change the statement to the following.**

```
<p class="quote">&quot;My family has gone to Optometric Eye Care
Center
```

This code applies the custom class to the quote in the document.

5 **Save the file in your text editor and refresh your browser.**

The quote text becomes slightly smaller and bold.

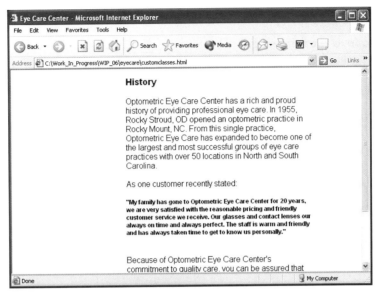

FIGURE 6.12

6 **Keep the file open in your text editor and browser for the next exercise.**

Create and Use an ID Selector

1 **In the open customclasses.html, insert the following code directly before </style> tag.**

```
...
    font-size: 9pt;
        font-weight: bold;
}
#menu {
        font-family: Verdana, Arial, Helvetica, sans-serif;
        font-size: 12px;
}
</style>
</head>
<body>
...
```

This code creates an ID selector for the menu of hyperlinks at the bottom of the page.

2 Scroll to the bottom of the page and find the following code.

```
<p><a href="locations.html">Locations</a>
```

3 Change the code to the following.

```
<p id="menu"><a href="locations.html">Locations</a>
```

This code applies the ID selector to the **<a>** tag.

4 Save the file in your text editor and refresh your browser.

5 Scroll to the bottom of the page to see the text style applied to the links.

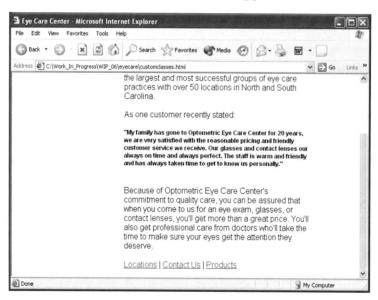

FIGURE 6.13

6 Close the file in your browser and text editor.

To Extend Your Knowledge...

INHERITANCE

In the previous exercise, you applied an ID selector to the **<p>** tag that enclosed the hyperlinks. In this instance, the text in the **<a>** tags inherits the properties of the parent **<p>** tag. You can override the parent properties by assigning properties to the **<a>** tag.

LESSON 3 Using Pseudo-Classes

The word "pseudo" means fake, pretend, or artificial. The term pseudo-class represents situations that don't actually occur in HTML. For instance, the **a:hover** class doesn't exist in HTML, but allows you to create a rollover effect for hyperlinks—without using images.

Pseudo-classes were designed to cover special situations. For instance, the **<a>** tag in HTML establishes a hyperlink. You can set up HTML code to change the color of a hyperlink, change the color of a selected link, or change the color of a previously visited link. Consider the following example, where the link color is set to a dark gray (**#666666**), the visited link color to a light gray (**#CCCCCC**), and the active link color to white (**#FFFFFF**).

```
<a href="#" link="#666666" vlink="#CCCCCC" alink="#FFFFFF">Link</a>
```

In JavaScript, you can control these properties with the **alinkColor**, **vlinkColor**, and **linkColor** properties of the **document** object. Using CSS, you can set the same properties in the following fashion:

```
a:link {
        color: #666666;
}
a:visited {
        color: #CCCCCC;
}
a:active {
        color: #FFFFFF;
}
```

The most useful pseudo-class in CSS is probably the **a:hover** class, which allows you to define a rule that specifies what happens when a user rolls the mouse over a hyperlink. Consider the following CSS statement, which changes a link color to green when a user moves the mouse over the link:

```
a:hover {
        color: #009966;
}
```

As an alternative, you could have used **onmouseover** events in the **<a>** tags, but the **a:hover** pseudo-class provides the added advantage of allowing you to set up one simple rollover that affects all of the links on the page.

Use Pseudo-Classes in an HTML Document

1   **In your text editor and browser, open pseudoclasses.html from your WIP_06 folder.**

This is essentially the same file you used in the previous lesson.

2   **Insert the following code directly before the `</style>` tag in the head section of the document.**

```
...
        font-family: Verdana, Arial, Helvetica, sans-serif;
            font-size: 12px;
    }
    a:link {
            color: #330066;
    }
    a:visited {
            color: #CCCCCC;
    }
    a:active {
            color: #666666;
    }
    a:hover {
            color: #993333;
    }
    </style>
    </head>
    <body>
    ...
```

To Extend Your Knowledge...

WHEN TO USE ID SELECTORS

Use ID selectors when you want to apply a style to a single element on the page and when you want to access the element in JavaScript or another scripting language.

3 Save the file in your text editor and refresh your browser.

Links now display in dark blue, visited links display in light gray, and active links display in dark gray. The links should change to burgundy when you move the mouse over them.

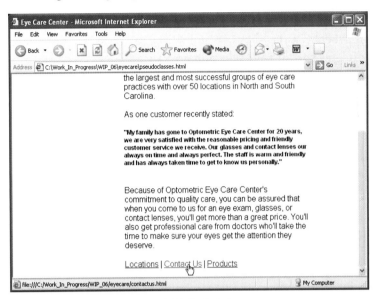

FIGURE 6.14

4 Close the file in your text editor and browser.

LESSON 4 Linking to External CSS Files

Similar to JavaScript, you can place CSS code in a separate (external) file. This is the most powerful way to use CSS since a single text file can control the formatting of an entire site. As a matter of convention, an external CSS file is a text file saved with a ".css" extension.

The text file contains only the CSS code you need in the site. For instance, let's assume that you want to create three CSS rules. One rule is for the primary headline of each page, which is used with the **\<h1\>** tag. Another rule is for the secondary headline of each page, which is used with the **\<h2\>** tag. A third rule is for the content text on each page, which displays between each **\<p\>** and **\</p\>** tag. Let's start by creating a text file with the following code:

```
p {font-family: sans-serif; font-size: small; color: gray}

h1 {font-family: serif; font-size: x-large; color: blue}

h2 {font-family: serif; font-size:large; color: blue}
```

To apply the external stylesheet to an HTML file, you use the **\<link\>** tag. For instance, if you name the file stylesheet.css, you can include the following code in the head section of the HTML document:

```
<link rel="stylesheet" href="stylesheet.css" type="text/css">
```

Link an External Style Sheet to an Existing File

1   In your text editor and browser, open external.html from your WIP_06>eyecare folder.

This is essentially the same file you used in the previous lesson.

2   Select all the text between the `<style>` and `</style>` tags. (Do not select the `<style>` tag or the `</style>` tag as part of your selection area.)

FIGURE 6.15

3   Choose Edit>Cut to remove the text from the document.

4   Save the file in your text editor.

5   Create a new text file. Choose Edit>Paste to paste the CSS code you cut in Step 3 into the new text file.

```
h1 {
        font-family: Arial, Helvetica, sans-serif;
        font-size: 18px;
        color: #333333;
        font-weight: bold;
}
body {
        font-family: Arial, Helvetica, sans-serif;
        font-size: 10pt;
}
.quote {
        font-family: Arial, Helvetica, sans-serif;
        font-size: 9pt;
        font-weight: bold;
}
#menu {
        font-family: Verdana, Arial, Helvetica, sans-serif;
        font-size: 12px;
}
a:link {
        color: #330066;
}
a:visited {
        color: #CCCCCC;
}
a:active {
        color: #666666;
}
a:hover {
        color: #993333;
}
```

FIGURE 6.16

6   Save the file as "mystyles.css" in the WIP_06>eyecenter folder.

7   If it is not already open, reopen external.html in your text editor from the WIP_06> eyecenter folder.

8   Find the following code in the head of the document.

```
<style type="text/css">


</style>
```

9   Delete the code you found in Step 8 and replace it with the following.

```
<html>
<head>
<title>Eye Care Center</title>
<link rel="stylesheet" href="mystyles.css" type="text/css">
</head>
<body>
<table width="599" border="0" cellspacing="0" cellpadding="0">
...
```

10   Save the file in your text editor and refresh your browser.

The styles are integrated from the external file you created.

11   Close the file in your text editor and browser.

To Extend Your Knowledge...

CUSTOM HOVER CLASSES

The **a:hover** pseudo-class allows you to create a uniform rollover effect for a page. You can also create custom classes, such as **a.top:hover** and **a.left:hover**, when you want to create different rollover effects for multiple navigation structures. You apply pseudo-classes to individual tags just as you apply other custom classes, such as **<a href="#" class="top">**.

LESSON 5 Understanding "The Box" Analogy and Positioning

CSS allows much greater control over the positioning of elements than allowed by traditional HTML. For the most part in HTML, the browser positions elements on the Web page in the order they appear in the source code, which is referred to as *static positioning*. Using CSS, you specify precise coordinates to position any element in an exact position on the screen, which is referred to as *absolute positioning*. Using absolute positioning, you can place elements in specific areas of the screen, such as the top, left, bottom, or right, or at an exact distance from the top, left, bottom, or right edges.

Relative positioning allows you to offset an element relative to where it would normally appear in the document. For example, you could specify that an image should appear 50 pixels to the left of where it would appear by default. When an element appears inside another element, such as when you use the **<span> </span>** tags within the **<p> </p>** tags, you can set the position of the element relative to the parent element. For instance, if an image resides within a table, you can specify that the image should appear on the right side of the table. If you prefer, you can place the image a specific number of pixels from the right side of the table.

Sometimes, images must remain unaffected when the page on which they reside scrolls up or down. To control an image in this way, you can place an image in a particular place on the screen, and then specify that the image should remain in that position when a user scrolls down the page; this is referred to as *fixed positioning*.

You can also specify whether an image should be visible or invisible. The **visibility** property determines whether you can see the element on the page. If you use the **visibility** property to make an element invisible (assign a value of **hidden**), space is still reserved for the element in the document's layout (in case you want to see the element later). As an alternative, you can use the **display** property to make an element invisible, but this property removes the element from the layout and does not reserve room for it.

The ability to specify the exact position of an element creates the possibility that elements might overlap one another. In this case, you can use the *z-index property* to specify the stacking order of positioned elements. You can stack elements above or below other elements. By default, elements are stacked from back to front in the order in which they appear in the HTML document.

The "Box" Analogy

CSS treats every element as if it were contained within an invisible box. The box contains (1) the element, (2) a padding area around the object, (3) a border around the padding area, and (4) an invisible margin around the border. You can control the padding, margin, and border through various CSS properties.

CSS was designed to give designers increased control over various aspects of each element. The "box" analogy is important because it affects the positioning of objects on the page. In addition, you can turn the visibility of the boxes on and off.

Positioning

With HTML, you have one positioning choice: the static model, which means the elements appear on the page in the order they appear in the code. CSS, on the other hand, supports many ways to position elements, including static positioning, absolute positioning, and relative positioning.

Absolute positioning allows you to move and position elements anywhere on the page. By specifying X,Y coordinates, you can place elements anywhere within the content area of the browser. The content area is where HTML pages display; in other words, the main part of the browser window, not including the title bar, location bar, status bar, and other browser controls. Absolute positioning also allows you to stack objects on top of one another.

Relative positioning starts with the place the element would normally appear if static positioning were applied and allows you to move the element relative to that position. In other words, you can move an element relative to the parent element that contains it (such as the browser window or a table).

You can use the **position** property to set the position of any element. The **position** property can be set to a value of **static**, **absolute**, **relative**, or **fixed**. The default value is **static**, which will be applied if no value is specified.

You can apply the **background-attachment** property to set the absolute position of an element with attributes such as **left**, **top**, **right**, or **bottom**. This property usually takes two attributes, such as **bottom** and **left** or **top** and **right**. The **background-attachment** property also has the added benefit of placing the element in the background so the element doesn't affect the placement of other elements on the page.

Use Absolute Positioning

In this exercise, you use absolute positioning and the **background-attachment** property to place an image.

1   **In your text editor, open mystyles.css from the WIP_06>eyecare folder.**

This is the external CSS file that you created in the previous exercise.

2   **Find the following CSS code that redefines the <body> tag.**

```
...
body {
        font-family: Arial, Helvetica, sans-serif;
        font-size: 10pt;
}
...
```

3   Insert the following code.

```
...
body {
        font-family: Arial, Helvetica, sans-serif;
        font-size: 10pt;
        background-image: url(images/face.jpg);
        background-repeat: no-repeat;
        background-position: left top;
}
.quote {
        font-family: Arial, Helvetica, sans-serif;
...
```

This code inserts the background image on the page.

4   Save the file in your text editor.

5   In your browser, open external.html from the WIP_06>eyecare folder.

This is the file that you modified in the previous lesson. Notice the background image in the top-left corner of the document.

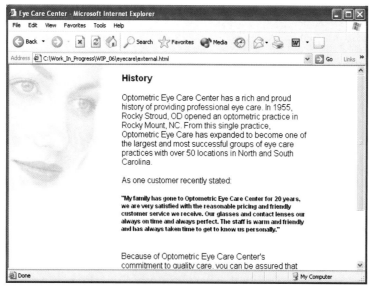

FIGURE 6.17

6   **Make sure your Web browser is sized small enough for the scroll bars to appear. Scroll to the bottom of the page.**

The image scrolls with the rest of the page because the default position is **static**.

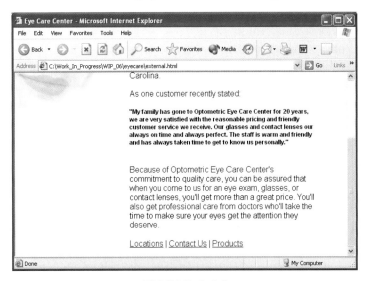

FIGURE 6.18

7   **Return to the mystyles.css file in your text editor. Find the code for the body selector and insert the following line.**

```
...
        background-image: url(images/face.jpg);

        background-repeat: no-repeat;

        background-position: left top;

        background-attachment: fixed;

}
.quote {

        font-family: Arial, Helvetica, sans-serif;

...
```

This code changes the background image to a fixed position.

8   **Save your changes to mystyles.css and refresh external.html in your Web browser.**

If you do not currently see a scroll bar, resize your window to force the scroll bars to appear. The image remains in a fixed position on the screen, even though the text scrolls.

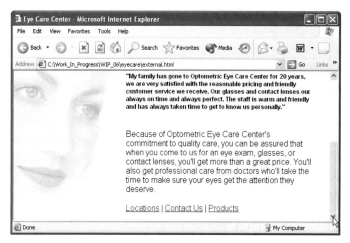

FIGURE 6.19

9   **Close the file in your browser and text editor.**

To Extend Your Knowledge...

PROPERTIES AS PERCENTAGES

The `left` and `top` properties may be expressed as percentages. Other properties, such as `right` or `bottom`, may not be expressed as percentages.

POSITIONING AND BROWSER COMPATILIBILITY

Use the `<div>` or `<span>` tags around elements that you want to position. Doing so helps to avoid compatibility issues in older browsers.

LESSON 6   Controlling Visibility and Layering

You can use the **visibility** or **display** properties to control the visibility of elements on a page. If you use the **visibility** property to make an element invisible, the page layout reserves space for the element, even though you can't see it. Using the **visibility** property, you can turn off the visibility of an element.

```
.hidden {
        visibility: hidden;
}
```

The **display** property is similar to the **visibility** property, but the **display** property removes the element from the layout, as well as removes the space the element occupied. To use the **display** property to remove an element, you would write:

```
display:none;
```

At this point, you may wonder about the usefulness of the **visibility** and **display** properties. To illustrate their importance, imagine that you want a menu to appear when a user rolls the mouse pointer over a button. When the user rolls off the button, you want the menu to disappear. When the user rolls over another button, you want the menu to change. Using the **visibility** and **display** properties with JavaScript allows you to create these (and other) advanced effects. You explore these effects in detail in the next project.

The Z-Index Property

As you learned earlier, the **z-index** property allows you to specify the stacking order for the elements on a page. This feature allows you to layer various elements, which can exist on top of or below other elements. You assign a number as the **z-index** property, which represents the element's position in the stack.

The **z-index** attribute can also be set to a value of **auto**. Elements with a value of **auto** take the default value that would normally be assigned by the browser. The **auto** attribute is only used in rare situations.

Elements with a low **z-index** value appear below elements with a higher **z-index** value. For example, if the highest-numbered element in a stack has a **z-index** of **9**, elements with **z-index 1–8** would appear below this element in the stack. To apply the **z-index** property to elements, you must first set their positioning.

A *layer* is a term many Web designers use to describe the use of CSS elements with absolute positioning and **z-index** values. When creating a layer (which can be any HTML element), designers typically add **<div>** and **</div>** or **** and **** tags around the items they want to move and stack, but doing so is not required. In the recent past, most designers avoided using layers due to compatibility issues with Netscape version 4 browsers. Most positioning incompatibilities have been resolved in current browsers, and the use of layers is quickly becoming commonplace.

Make Items Invisible

1   **In your text editor, open mystyles.css from the WIP_06>eyecare folder.**

This is the external CSS file you created earlier.

2   **Insert the following CSS code at the end of the document to create a new custom class.**

```
...
a:hover {
        color: #993333;
}
.hidden {
        visibility: hidden;
}
...
```

3   **Save your changes to the file.**

4   **In your text editor and browser, open invisible.html from the WIP_06>eyecare folder.**

This is essentially the same page you used in the previous lessons.

5   **Find the following code in the document.**

```
<p class="quote">&quot;My family
```

This **<p>** tag uses a custom class that you created earlier.

6   **Change the class by changing the code to read as the following.**

```
<p class="hidden">&quot;My family
```

7   **Save the file in your text editor and refresh your browser.**

The paragraph referenced by the custom class is now invisible. Notice that the browser still leaves room for the element even though it is no longer visible.

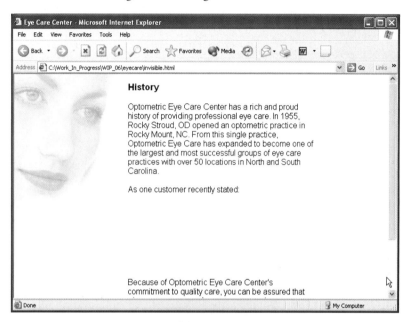

FIGURE 6.20

8   **Return to mystyles.css in your text editor. Find the following code at the bottom of the document.**

```
.hidden {
        visibility: hidden;
}
```

You created this code in Step 2.

9   **Change the code to the following.**

```
.hidden {
        display: none;
}
```

10 Save the file in your text editor and refresh your Web browser.

The **display** property removes the area reserved for the invisible element.

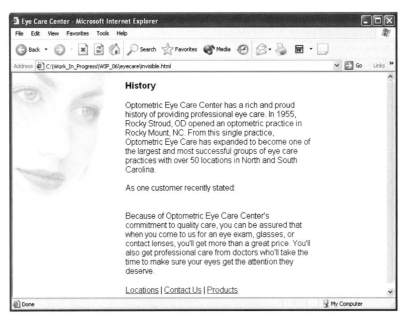

FIGURE 6.21

11 Close the file in your Web browser and text editor.

Use Absolute Positioning

1 In your Web browser and text editor, open absolute.html from the WIP_06>absolute folder.

This simple HTML file includes three **<img>** tags and displays three pictures.

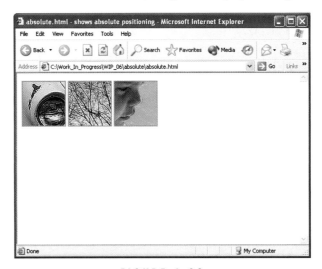

FIGURE 6.22

2   In your text editor, insert the following code directly before the </**head**> tag.

```
<html>
<head>
<title>absolute.html - shows absolute positioning</title>
<style type="text/css">
.pic1 { position: absolute;
     top: 50;
     left: 60;
}
</style>
</head>
<body>
<img src="smallpic1.jpg" width="90" height="90">
...
```

3   Find the following code that establishes the first image.

```
<img src="smallpic1.jpg" width="90" height="90">
```

4   Change the statement to apply the class you created in Step 2.

```
<img src="smallpic1.jpg" width="90" height="90" class="pic1">
```

5   Save the page in your text editor and refresh your browser.

The position of the image changes from its original static location to the absolute position you specified in the code.

FIGURE 6.23

6   **Return to your text editor and add the following code directly before the `</style>` tag to create a second custom class.**

```
. . .
        top: 50;
        left: 60;
}
.pic2 { position: absolute;
        top: 50;
        right: 60;
}
</style>
</head>
<body>
. . .
```

This code specifies a location of 50 pixels from the top margin and 60 pixels from the right margin.

7   **Find the second `<img>` tag in your document and change the code to apply the second custom class.**

```
. . .
</head>
<body>
<img src="smallpic1.jpg" width="90" height="90" class="pic1">
<img src="smallpic2.jpg" width="90" height="90" class="pic2">
<img src="smallpic3.jpg" width="90" height="90">
</body>
</html>
```

8   Save the file in your text editor and refresh your browser.

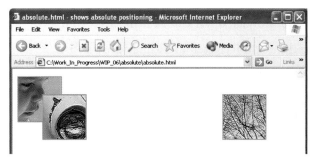

FIGURE 6.24

9   Change the size of the browser window.

The image should remain 60 pixels from the left margin no matter how you resize the window.

10   Return to your text editor and find the custom class for the second image, as shown in the following code.

```
...
.pic2 { position: absolute;
      top: 50;
      right: 60;
}
...
```

11   Change the code to replace the word "top" with the word "bottom".

```
...
.pic2 { position: absolute;
      bottom: 50;
      right: 60;
}
...
```

12   Save the file in your text editor and refresh your browser.

13   Change the size of the browser window.

The image should stay 50 pixels from the bottom of the window no matter how you resize the window.

14   Close the file in your text editor and browser.

Use the Z-Index Property to Layer Elements

1   **In your text editor and browser, open zindex.html from your WIP_06>absolute folder.**

This file is similar to the one you created in the previous exercise.

FIGURE 6.25

The page uses absolute positioning to "layer" each image on top of the others. The images are layered according to the order in which they appear in the HTML document — the first image appears on the bottom because it appears first in the code.

2   **Find the following code in the head of the document. It establishes the position of the first image.**

```
...
.pic1 { position: absolute;
      top: 30;
      left: 60;
}
...
```

3   **Change this code to the following to establish a z-index of 3.**

```
...
.pic1 { position: absolute;
      top: 30;
      left: 60;
      z-index: 3;
}
.pic2 { position: absolute;
      top: 50;
      left: 80;
...
```

4   **Save the file in your text editor and refresh your browser.**

The first picture moves to the top of the stacking order.

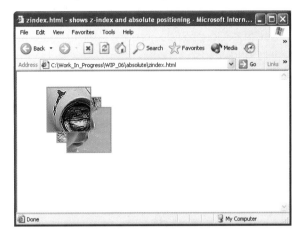

FIGURE 6.26

The images always appear with the lowest **z-index** value on the bottom and the highest on the top of the stacking order.

5   **Close the file in your text editor and browser.**

To Extend Your Knowledge...

USING CUSTOM CLASSES

Remember, custom classes use a period in the selector when the rule is created. The period is not used in the HTML. For example, the rule `.quote { color:blue; }` could be applied by a statement such as `<p class="quote">`, but not `<p class=".quote">`. This is a common mistake when applying classes.

LAYERING

A `z-index` parameter is not required when elements overlap. The browser automatically assigns a stacking order based on where the elements appear in the code. If you want to change the default stacking order, you must use the `z-index` parameter.

C A R E E R S   I N   D E S I G N

BEWARE OF OPENING ANIMATIONS AND SPLASH SCREENS

Web sites are designed to provide information that is easy to understand and access. Animated openers and splash screens often work in opposition to these goals. As you design your professional portfolio Web site, keep this fact in mind.

Most professional designers believe that an animated opening sequence keeps the user from reaching the content of a site. Rather than wait for the opening file to download and then view the 15- or 30-second animation, many users will abandon the site altogether. Similar results occur when a user encounters a splash screen; if the user can't access a site until he clicks an "Enter Site" button, he may choose to leave the site in favor of one that is more readily accessible.

Opening animations and splash screens also create confusing navigation situations. For example, does the Home button link to the opening sequence or to a different screen, such as a home page that appears after the introduction? The safest option is to avoid opening animations and splash screens; instead, create engaging and useful home pages that any user can easily access and understand. For best results, incorporate elements of your portfolio pieces into this page. You can show your best artwork or display previews (thumbnails) of items in your gallery.

S U M M A R Y

In this project, you considered the basic uses of CSS. You received adequate background to use CSS as a formatting tool. Now, you are prepared to use JavaScript, CSS, and HTML to create animations and other effects no possible when using traditional HTML alone.

You discovered that CSS was created to separate the content (markup) of a Web page from its formatting. CSS allows designers to override the default styles used by the browser. It also allows developers to create custom styles that they can apply whenever necessary. CSS allows you to remove many formatting tags, including the **<font>** and **<b>** tags. Using CSS, you can write simpler, shorter code, accompanied by smaller file sizes.

You learned that you must use declarations to create CSS statements. A declaration consists of a selector and a rule. A selector is the object assigned to the rule, and a rule consists of an attribute and a value. A selector can be an HTML tag that you are redefining; it can also be a special situation, known as a pseudo-class, which is a name given to a rule that you can apply to specific HTML elements.

You discovered that the most powerful way to use CSS is through external style sheets, which can link to HTML documents through the **<link>** tag. Using an external style sheet allows a Web designer to control the formatting of an entire Web site from one external file.

As you completed the lessons in this project, you found that CSS allows much greater flexibility in positioning elements than can be accomplished using traditional HTML. You can position elements relative to where they would normally appear in the document, or you can use absolute positioning to specify exact coordinates for placing the element on the page. Finally, you learned that using the **z-index** attribute allows designers to control the stacking order of elements that may appear above or below other elements on the page.

KEY TERMS

Absolute positioning	ID selector	Relative positioning
Cascading Style Sheets (CSS)	Inline style sheet	Rule
Custom class	Layer	Selector
Declaration	Linked style sheet	Static positioning
Embedded style sheet	Property	Value
External style sheet	Pseudo-class	Z-index
Fixed positioning	Redefining HTML tags	

CHECKING CONCEPTS AND TERMS

MULTIPLE CHOICE

Circle the letter that matches the correct answer for each of the following questions.

1. How can you use CSS in Web pages?

  a. To override the default styles of HTML tags

  b. To create custom classes

  c. To create a style for a single tag by using its ID

  d. As an inline style placed in a single HTML tag

  e. All of the above

  f. None of the above

2. How are inline styles applied to HTML tags?

  a. By creating a custom class of objects

  b. By redefining the **<body>** tag

  c. By placing the style in an external file

  d. By using the **style** attribute in the tag

3. Why do developers often avoid using inline styles?

  a. Because they do not apply to the entire Web page

  b. Because they do not redefine the default style of an HTML tag

  c. Because they do not apply to the entire Web site

  d. All of the above

  e. None of the above

4. Why is an external CSS file the most powerful way to use CSS in a Web site?

  a. Custom classes are only allowed in external CSS files

  b. ID selectors are only allowed in external CSS files

  c. Flow-of-control loops in external files can be used to format multiple lines of text

  d. The appearance of the entire site can be controlled by a single file

5. What is the default value of the **position** property?

  a. **static**

  b. **absolute**

  c. **relative**

  d. **fixed**

6. You can use the _____ pseudo-class to create a text rollover effect when the user moves the mouse over a hyperlink.

  a. **a:mouseover**

  b. **a:rollover**

  c. **a:hover**

  d. **a:onclick**

7. Since ID selectors are similar to custom classes, why are they used?

   a. Because they allow glow properties

   b. To create an entire class of objects

   c. Because they allow the use of the Back button

   d. To create a single element that can be referenced in JavaScript or other scripting languages

8. If an image's **visibility** property is set to **hidden**, space is still reserved for the image in the layout of the page (even though it is invisible).

   a. True

   b. False

9. If an image's **display** property is set to **none**, space is still reserved for the image in the layout of the page (even though it is invisible).

   a. True

   b. False

10. What constitutes a CSS rule?

   a. Attributes and values

   b. Event handlers and element styles

   c. Layers, elements, and properties

   d. HTML and JavaScript

DISCUSSION QUESTIONS

1. When formatting a Web site, why is CSS a better alternative than HTML?

2. How can you position items in CSS?

3. How does CSS address shortcomings in JavaScript?

4. Why is the use of CSS in an external file the most powerful way to use JavaScript? How might this technique make Web site development and maintenance more profitable for a designer?

SKILL DRILL

Skill Drill exercises reinforce project skills. Each skill reinforced is the same, or nearly the same, as a skill presented in the project. Detailed instructions are provided in a step-by-step format. You should work through the exercises in order.

1. Redefine HTML Tags

In this exercise, you add a custom class to an existing HTML document. By adding a custom class, you can define new styles and redefine the default styles of the HTML tag created by the browser.

1. Open WIP_06>skillpopulation.html in your text editor and browser.

2.   In your text editor, insert the following lines of code.

```
...
<style type="text/css">
<!--
/* add body styles here */
body {
        font-family: Verdana, Arial, Helvetica, sans-serif;
        margin: 0px;
}
h1 {
        font-size: 18px;
        color: #FFFFFF;
...
```

3.   Insert the following lines of code.

```
...
        margin-left: 20px;
        border: thin solid #666666;
}
/* add th & td styles here */
th {font-size: 12px; background-color: #CCCCCC; padding: 2px;}
td {font-size: 11px; background-color: #FFFFCC; padding: 5px;}
.rank {
        text-align: center;
        border-right-width: thin;.population {text-align: right;
...
```

Notice how each declaration was written on a single line.

4.   Save the file in your text editor and refresh your browser.

5.   Leave file open for the next exercise

2. Add a Custom Class

In the previous exercise, you added three style rules to a page by redefining HTML tags. In this exercise, you further expand the use of CSS by creating custom classes.

1. In the open skillpopulation.html in your text editor, insert the following lines of code.

```
...
        text-align: right;
}
/* Add a custom class */
.country {
        border-right-width: thin;
        border-right-style: solid;
        border-right-color: #666666;
}
.rank {
        border-right-width: thin;
        border-right-style: solid;
        border-right-color: #666666;
}
-->
</style>
</head>
...
```

2. Save the file in your text editor and refresh your browser.

The custom class adds borders to the columns on the Population table.

3. Close the file in your text editor and browser.

3. Style Pseudo-Classes

In this exercise, you create pseudo-class rules for the **<a>** tag. You create the four states of a link (link, visited, hover, and active), as well as give the browser instructions to use these rules in place of HTML default link colors and styles. Now you can create rollover states without creating graphic images or writing JavaScript code.

1. Open WIP_06>skillcoolcompany.html in your text editor and browser.

   Some CSS style rules were already created.

2. In your text editor, insert the following lines of code.

   ```
   ...
           color: #333333;

           margin: 0px;

           text-align:center;}
   /* insert link pseudo-classes here */
   a:link { text-decoration: none;      color: #FFFFFF;}

   a:visited {text-decoration: none;     color: #CCCCCC;}

   a:hover {text-decoration: underline;  color: #FFFF99;}

   a:active {text-decoration: none;      color: #FFFF00;}

   /* html headings */
   h1 {font-size: 24px;     color: #99CCFF;     text-align: left;}

   h2 {font-size: 14px;     color: #000000;}

   ...
   ```

3. Save the file in your text editor and refresh your browser.

   The browser renders links to match the design of the page.

4. Leave the file open for the next exercise

4. Position Elements

In this exercise, you use **text-align**, **padding**, and **margin** values to position elements in the browser window. With careful planning, these rules allow designers to bypass the limitations of HTML styles and positioning so they can finely control page layout.

1. In the open skillcoolcompany.html in your text editor, insert the following code.

```
...
/* This style controls the div placement*/
#pageHeader {
background-color: #333366;
text-align: right;
width: 533px;
height: 400px;
background-image: url(images/blue_keys.jpg);
padding: 25px 0px 15px 25px;
margin: 0px;
}
/* This style controls the actual link placement*/
-->
...
```

2. Save the file in your text editor and refresh your browser.

    The rule you created is applied where the ID selector is used (**id="pageHeader"**). In this case, the **<div>** tag has specified **width**, **height**, **background-image**, **padding**, and **margin** values. The **padding** attribute forces text to move inward from the edges of the div. The **margin** value order is top, right, bottom, and left (the **margin** attribute adds space around a **<div>** tag). In this case, **0px** is specified, which ensures that all margins are equal.

3. Insert the following lines of code.

```
...
h3 {font-size: 10px; color: #999999;}
/* This style controls the actual link placement*/
.pageNavigation {
text-align: right;
padding-right: 330px;
}
-->
...
```

This rule aligns the link text to the right side of the div. The **padding** value holds the link 330 pixels from the right edge.

4. Find the following line of code.

```
h3 {font-size: 10px;  color: #999999;}
```

This is a partial style rule. The formatting of the code is compacted to remove white space. You need to reformat the rule to the default style that you have been using in this project, and then modify the code by adding an additional property.

5. Change the code you found in the previous step to the following.

```
...
h2 {font-size: 14px; color: #000000;}
h3 {font-size: 10px;
color: #999999;
margin-top: 200px;
margin-right: 15px;
}
/* This style controls the div placement*/
#pageHeader {
...
```

The **<h3>** tag moves 200 pixels down and 15 pixels in from the edge of the div.

6. Save the file in your text editor and test the file in your browser.

7. Close all files in your browser and text editor.

CHALLENGE

Challenge exercises expand on, or are somewhat related to, skills presented in the lessons. Each exercise provides a brief introduction, followed by instructions presented in a numbered-step format that are not as detailed as those in the Skill Drill exercises. You should work through these exercises in order.

1. Redefine Nested HTML Tags

In this exercise, you use nested tags as selectors to create style rules to format the U.S. Bill of Rights. Creating precise rules allows you to attain a level of visual control that was formerly reserved for print design. Consider the following lines of code that appear in the HTML document.

```
<p><strong>articles</strong>...</p>

<p><strong class="rights">Amendment I:</strong>...</p>
```

Both lines show the **<strong>** tag nested within a **<p>** tag. In this exercise, you create a CSS style rule to apply only to a **<strong>** tag nested within a **<p>** tag.

1. From your WIP_06 folder, open challengecustom.html and styles.css in your text editor.

2. Insert the following lines of code in styles.css.

```
...

/* custom selectors.*/

/* controls text when strong tag nested is inside paragraph tag

example: "<p><strong>TEXT</strong></p>"   */

p strong {

        font-size: 14px;

        text-transform: uppercase;

        color: #000000;

        margin-right: 5px;

        font-style: italic;

}

/* controls text when strong tag with a class of rights is nested
inside paragraph tag

example: "<p><strong class="rights">TEXT</strong></p>" */

...
```

3.   Save the file in your text editor and open the file in your browser.

All instances of the **<strong>** tag nested inside a **<p>** tag are styled. Next, you apply a different style to the amendment headings.

4.   Insert the following lines of code.

```
...

/* controls text when strong tag with a class of rights is nested
inside paragraph tag

example: "<p><strong class="rights">TEXT</strong></p>"  */

p strong.rights {

        font-size: 12px;

        text-transform: capitalize;

        color: #000066;

        margin-right: 5px;

        font-style: normal;

}

/* controls text when strong tag is nested inside paragraph tag

example: "<td class="header"><h1>TEXT</h1></td>"  */

...
```

5.   Save the file in your text editor and refresh your browser.

6.   Keep these files open for the next exercise.

2. Create Custom Pseudo-Classes

In the file you just created, main navigation links exist on the left, and named anchor links exist below each amendment. The way the pseudo-classes for the **<a>** tag are written, both links look the same. Combining the power of pseudo-classes and custom classes allows you to change the appearance of one of the navigation structures to improve the usability of the site.

1.   Review the open challengecustom.html in your browser.

2.   In your text editor, insert the following code in styles.css.

```
...
a:hover {text-decoration: underline;}
a:active {text-decoration: none;}
/* mainNav html links */
a.mainNav:link {text-decoration: none; color: #000033;}
a.mainNav:visited {text-decoration: none; color: #006699;}
a.mainNav:hover {text-decoration: underline; color: #990000; back-
ground-color: #FFFFFF;}
a.mainNav:active {text-decoration: none; color: #FF0000;}
/* custom classes */
.navigation {
        font-size: 12px;
...
```

3.   Save the file in your text editor and refresh challengecustom.html in your browser.

     Links in the main navigation structure and text anchor links display differently.

4.   Close the file in your text editor and browser.

3. Add a Temporary Style for Positioning

CSS displays an element using the box analogy to determine the boundaries of the element. Positioning is affected by the various properties used in the box analogy. This can make positioning difficult, since many of the boundaries of an object are invisible by default. In this exercise, you create a temporary style to resolve this problem.

1. In your browser, open challengeposition.html from your WIP_06 folder.

   You see two images of Mount Rushmore and the text "Mount Rushmore." With default settings and no styles applied, the document appears rather simplistic.

2. Open positionstyles.css and challengeposition.html in your text editor.

3. In challengeposition.html, use the **`<link>`** tag to attach the positionstyles.css file to the HTML page.

4. Refresh challengeposition.html in your browser.

   The document should now have styles applied. In the next step, you create a temporary style to better see **`<div>`** tags as you position elements.

5. Insert the temporary style into the head of the page.

   ```
   ...
   <!-- create link here -->
   <link href="positionStyles.css" rel="stylesheet" type="text/css">
   <style type="text/css">
   div {
   border: thin solid red;
   }
   </style>
   </head>
   <body>
   ...
   ```

6. Refresh challengeposition.html in your browser.

   All **`<div>`** tags display on screen with a thin red line around them. This aids in seeing the effect of the **`margin`** and **`padding`** values, as well as the effect positioning has on the **`<div>`** tag.

7. Leave both files open for the next exercise.

4. Use Absolute and Relative Positioning

In the previous exercise, you created a temporary style to make it easier to see the outer boundaries of elements placed on the page. In this exercise, you position the objects, and then remove the temporary style you created in the previous exercise.

1. In positionstyles.css, insert the following positioning properties.

```
...

}

#parent{

position:absolute;

width:800px;

height:600px;

z-index:1;

background-image: url(images/rushmore_bg.jpg);

border: medium solid #FFFFCC; left: 25px; top: 25px;

...
```

The position is set to **absolute** to make **<div id="parent">...</div>** inherit positioning from the browser window. The **width** and **height** properties are set to make the div the same size as the background image.

2. Insert the following rule for the **<div>** tag with the **child ID**.

```
...

}
/* Insert rule for child 1 here */

#child1{

        position: relative;

        width: 179px;

        height: 121px;

        z-index: 4;

        left: 25px;

        top: 38px;

}
/* Insert rule for child 2 here */

#child2{

...
```

The **position** is set to **relative** to make **<div id="child1">...</div>** inherit positioning from **<div id="parent">...</div>**. The **width** and **height** properties are set to make the div the same size as the nested image. Finally, the **z-index** is set to **4** to layer the image above the background.

3. Insert a rule for **<div id="child2">...<.div>**.

```
...
        top: 38px;

}
/* Insert rule for child 2 here */
#child2{
        position: relative;
        width: 121px;
        height: 179px;
        z-index: 4;
        top: 180px;
        left: 625px;
}
#text{
        position:absolute;
        width:100%;
...
```

4. Save positionstyles.css in your text editor and refresh challengeposition.html in your browser.

   The images reposition in the browser. The banner with "Mount Rushmore" is the last item to reposition.

5. Insert the following lines of code in the **#text** rule.

```
      ...
            left: 625px;
      }
      #text{
            position:absolute;
            width:100%;
            height:40px;
            z-index:2;
            left: 0px;
            top: 460px;
            background-color: #FFFFFF;
            border: 1px none #000000;
      }
      ...
```

6. Remove the temporary div rule you created in the previous challenge

7. Save positionstyles.css in your text editor and refresh challengeposition.html in your browser.

8. Close both files in your text editor and browser.

P O R T F O L I O   B U I L D E R

Create CSS Rules

In this project, you found that utilizing CSS allows you to achieve a level of visual sophistication unavailable with simple HTML. When you construct CSS rules (which are easy to write), you follow simple rules of syntax. How you apply style rules determines their success.

As you learned in the lessons, rules are inherited from parent rules and in turn inherit the styles of nested rules (children). By creating a style rule to apply a font to the **\<body\>** tag contents, (**\<body\>...\</body\>**), you force nested tags to inherit your choice of font. Any **\<h1\>...\</h1\>** content will appear in the same font face unless you create a rule that applies specifically to **\<h1\>** tags.

To complete this Portfolio Builder, follow these steps:

1. In your Web browser, open cssinheritance.html from your WIP_06 folder. The document contains default HTML heading, anchor, and paragraph styles.

2. Attach the inheritthestyle.css style sheet from your WIP_06 folder.

3. Preview cssinheritance.html again in your browser. The page shows which heading (**h1**, **h2**, **h3**, **h4**, **h5**, **h6**) controls which content. This structure creates "content hierarchy," which allows for easier data surfing by individuals with disabilities. Creating style rules for body pages and heading tags allows you to control the visual hierarchy of your content.

4. Modify the body style rule to add a **font-family** of **Verdana**, **Arial**, **Helvetica**, **sans-serif**, and a **font-size** of **11px**. This expanded rule allows you to control the use of font, as well as set a base font size of 11 pixels. Any tag in the body without a specific style rule will inherit these font values.

P O R T F O L I O   B U I L D E R

Create CSS Rules (continued)

5. Add heading styles to control the visual balance of elements. We recommend using the following values:

Redefine	Font size (pixels)	Color (hexadecimal)	Style
h1	36	#E8FDFF	bold
h2	22	#666666	bold
h3	14	#990000	bold
h4	14	#FFFFFF	bold
h5	10	#666666	bold
h6	10	#999999	bold

6. When creating the rules for headings, consider that each heading has a **style** value of **bold**. You could easily write each rule to contain the **bold** value. Remember, however, that you can combine CSS rules. To simplify your styles, you can create a companion style for your headings. Any heading rule will inherit this rule, as well as use its individual style rule. Any heading style could in turn ignore the **bold** value by specifying its own style. By specifying **normal**, you can ignore this inheritance.

```
h1, h2, h3, h4, h6, h6 {
        font-style: bold;
}
```

Exploring DHTML

OBJECTIVES

In this project, you learn how to

- Manipulate inline styles

- Interact with style sheets

- Control positioning dynamically

- Create a drop-down menu effect

- Use text style properties

- Incorporate background and display properties

WHY WOULD I DO THIS?

Dynamic HTML (DHTML) isn't a technology per se. More accurately, DHTML is a marketing term used by major browser companies to describe the integration of CSS, HTML, and JavaScript. In particular, DHTML refers to the way JavaScript interacts with CSS. With DHTML, you can use JavaScript to change the CSS rules created as inline styles or with **ID** selectors. For each CSS style defined, a matching **style** object is also created in JavaScript. The properties of the **style** object represent the same attributes that you can set or modify in CSS declarations.

As DHTML is a voluminous subject, we cannot cover all the aspects of the "technology" in the confines of this book. Instead, this project is meant to serve as a general introduction to DHTML and to illustrate how CSS and JavaScript work together. In this project, you discover how to change CSS styles dynamically through JavaScript. You also learn how to create animated sequences and drop-down menus. For more information on using DHTML, you may want to consult a comprehensive DHTML reference guide.

V I S U A L   S U M M A R Y

Remember that the Document Object Model (DOM) is a term that describes the hierarchy of the JavaScript language. The DOM provides a method for interacting with HTML elements (since JavaScript creates a matching object for every HTML tag found in a document). Employing various aspects of the DOM, you can use JavaScript to access or change the HTML code.

Newer versions of the DOM also create objects in JavaScript to reference CSS declarations and properties. This is the true strength of JavaScript: it allows users to access and manipulate the markup, styles, and properties of HTML and CSS with all of the power of a traditional programming language.

Consider an e-commerce Web site that displays a table of products. Visitors use the table to purchase products online. You can use CSS to set the colors of the table, as shown in the following example.

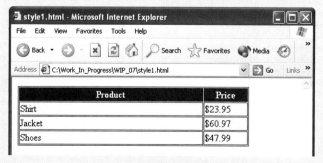

FIGURE 7.1

Whenever an HTML tag is encountered in the code, a corresponding object (otherwise known as an element or element object) is created in JavaScript. Likewise, a JavaScript **style** object is created for any element that has CSS styles attached. The **style** object has properties that represent CSS attributes. Using JavaScript to manipulate these CSS properties, you can change the corresponding CSS code in the same way you used JavaScript to manipulate HTML code.

DHTML provides exciting new options for improving usability. For example, you could change the color of the table row when the user moves the mouse pointer over one of the products.

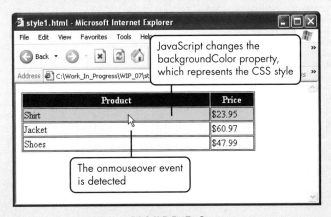

FIGURE 7.2

This code effectively creates a rollover effect by changing the background colors in the table. The code to accomplish this task is very simple.

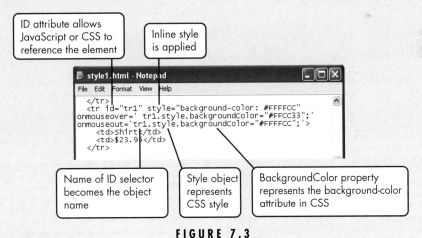

FIGURE 7.3

This method of changing styles works well for inline styles. When using style rules created in style sheets, however, you need to use the **getElementById()** method. The **getElementById()** method is a subordinate method of the **document** object.

LESSON 1   Manipulating Inline Styles

You can control CSS styles through JavaScript and the **document** object, which is similar to the way you manipulate HTML code through JavaScript. For example, to use JavaScript to access HTML tags, you can use the **name** or **id** attribute in the HTML tag. Either attribute is used to assign a unique name to the tag. The **name** attribute is being phased out, but is still required for forms because of compatibility issues with server-side scripts. The following tag creates a form:

```
<form name="theForm" id="theForm">
```

Assume that the form contains a field named **phone**. You can use the following statement to access the value stored in the **phone** field:

```
document.theForm.phone.value
```

In some cases, the **name** attribute is required to access the content of an HTML tag, such as with the **<form>** tag. DHTML, in contrast, requires developers to use the **ID** attribute to reference elements. Consider the following HTML tag:

```
<p id="content">This is a sentence.</p>
```

Assume that you want to access the text of the HTML tag. To do so, you could use the **innerHTML** property of the tag, as shown in the following statement:

```
content.innerHTML
```

The Style Object

The **style** object in JavaScript represents the **style** property of an HTML tag. Consider the following inline style as an example:

```
<p id="content" style="color: red"> This is a sentence.</p>
```

To change the CSS attributes set in the inline style, you could use the **style** object. For example, to change the text to blue, you would write the following line of code in JavaScript:

```
content.style.color="blue"
```

This technique raises interesting possibilities. For instance, you could change the color of the text when a user moves the mouse pointer over the content of the tag:

```
<p id="content" style="color: red" onmouseover='
content.style.color="blue"; '> This is a sentence.</p>
```

This technique works for most HTML tags, but it only works for inline styles. In other words, you cannot access styles created in style sheets, as shown in the following example:

```
<style type="text/css">
#myStyle {
        color: white;
}
</style>
```

The **style** object supports a wide variety of appearance changes, including background color, text spacing, font sizes, and visibility. Properties exist for other CSS categories, such as padding, margins, scroll bars, and cursor styles. You explore these and other style properties throughout this project.

Use Style Object Properties

1   **Copy the content of the RF_JavaScript_L2>Project_07 folder to your Work_In_Progress>WIP_07 folder.**

2   **In your text editor and browser, open style1.html from your WIP_07 folder.**

FIGURE 7.4

3   **Find the following lines of code.**

```
...
<tr>
    <td>Shirt</td>
    <td>$23.95</td>
  </tr>
...
```

These lines of code create the first product row, which currently shows the default background color.

4 | Modify the code as follows.

```
...

<tr id="tr1" style="background-color: #FFFFCC" >
    <td>Shirt</td>
    <td>$23.95</td>
  </tr>

...
```

This code creates an **ID** for the tag and applies an inline style.

5 | Insert the following code.

```
...

<tr id="tr1" style="background-color: #FFFFCC"
onmouseover=' tr1.style.backgroundColor="#FFCC33";'
onmouseout='tr1.style.backgroundColor="#FFFFCC";'>
    <td>Shirt</td>
    <td>$23.95</td>
  </tr>

...
```

Rollover effects now apply to the first table row.

6 | Save the file in your text editor and refresh your browser.

7 | Move your mouse over the first product.

The background of the table row changes color.

FIGURE 7.5

8 | Close the file in your browser and text editor.

To Extend Your Knowledge...

STYLE PROPERTIES

JavaScript element object properties don't always precisely match CSS properties. For instance, although they represent the same property, the **background-color** property in CSS is known as **backgroundColor** in JavaScript. This minor discrepancy is primarily related to different semantic rules. CSS properties that contain two words are written as all lowercase with a hyphen between the words. You don't use hyphens (or spaces) when you write JavaScript properties, and the second word in a two-word JavaScript property is usually capitalized, which is referred to as *camelback notation*.

LESSON 2 Interacting with Style Sheets

In the previous lesson, you learned how to directly interact with properties of the **style** object by using the same style of dot syntax notation that is always used in JavaScript. This method is useful for changing CSS properties dynamically, but only works for inline styles. Styles created in style sheets with the **<style>** tag or placed in external style sheet files require a different method of access.

The **getElementById()** method of the **document** object allows you to access information about a particular element. By passing the **ID** of an element to this method, you can access the matching object in JavaScript. Recall from the previous project that you use an **ID** selector to apply a style to a particular HTML element, and that the **ID** selector can also be referenced in JavaScript. For instance, you can use the following code to create an **ID** selector to place an object at an absolute position:

```
<style type="text/css">
#eddieImage {
        position: absolute;
        top: 80px;
        left: 10px;
        visibility: visible;
}
</style>
```

Next, you can apply the **ID** selector style by using an **ID** attribute within an HTML tag. For instance, the following code applies the style to an image:

```
<img src="eddie.jpg" ID="eddieImage">
```

By accessing the element object through the DOM using the **getElementById()** method, you can change any aspect of the element's styles using properties of the **style** object. For instance, to change the **left** CSS property of the element, you would write:

```
document.getElementById('eddieImage').style.left=130;
```

Any property that can be used in a style declaration can be accessed or changed with this method. The properties are named in a similar fashion to how they appear in the CSS code, in the same way that other object properties have matching HTML attributes. Bear in mind that the **getElementById()** method must be spelled correctly. It is a common mistake to spell this method as **getElementByID()** or **getElementbyId()**, both of which cause errors in many (but not all) browsers.

Reference Style Attributes in JavaScript

1   **In your text editor and browser, open colorchange.html from the WIP_07 folder.**

This page uses the **background-color** attribute in an **ID** selector to create a blue background behind a short sentence.

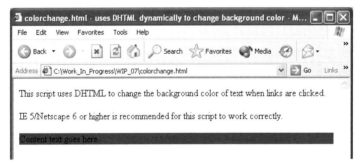

FIGURE 7.6

2   **Insert the following code to create links to change the background color of the text.**

Notice how an **onclick** event triggers the function, and that the color value passes to the function.

```
...
<p ID="content">Content text goes here</p>
<p>
<!-- ***color links go here*** -->
<a href="#" onclick="colorChange('red')"> Red </a><br>
<a href="#" onclick="colorChange('blue')"> Blue </a>
</p>
</a>
</body>
...
```

3   Insert the following code in the **<head>** section of the document.

```
...
<!-- ***color change script goes here*** -->
<script language="JavaScript">
function colorChange(color) {
        document.getElementById('content').style.backgroundColor=color;
} // end function
</script>
...
```

This code creates the color-change function.

4   **Save the file in your text editor and refresh your browser.**

5   **Click the links at the bottom of the page.**

The background color changes as the **background-color** property changes.

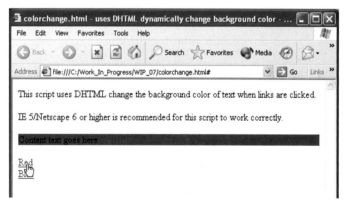

FIGURE 7.7

6   **Close the file in your browser and text editor.**

To Extend Your Knowledge...

PROPERTIES OF THE STYLE OBJECT

For a complete list of the properties of the **style** object, visit http://www.w3.org/TR/REC-CSS2, which is the official page for the newest CSS specification.

LESSON 3 Control Positioning Dynamically

In a previous project, you used JavaScript to create a simple animation by changing the source file of an **image** object at a short interval. In other words, you showed a slightly different image at short intervals in the same location on the screen, which resulted in a basic animation. This method is rather inefficient because you must load multiple images to create the animated sequence. As you know, multiple images lead to large file sizes and an intensive use of computer resources.

A more efficient method is to animate a single image. For instance, you could make the image larger, smaller, or move it across the screen. You already explored many of the building blocks necessary to accomplish all of these image changes. You can use HTML to create an image object, load the file, and display the image on the screen. Then, you can use CSS to control the placement of the image and move it to any absolute position. Next, you can use JavaScript to create a loop to animate the object.

To move an object from the left of the screen to the right, follow these three simple steps:

- Place the image in a CSS style.

- Use absolute positioning to place the image in a starting position.

- Use JavaScript to change the x,y coordinates of the image to create the illusion of movement.

This sequence creates simple results: the image seems to disappear from one position and appear elsewhere on the screen. You can create a more complex animation by including a loop that repeatedly moves the object across the screen. To ensure the animation is smooth, you could include a timer that controls the interval between each movement. For instance, you could create a JavaScript loop that moves the object 10 pixels to the right every 500 milliseconds.

Animate an Element

In this exercise, you create a simple animation by manipulating CSS positioning properties through JavaScript.

1 **In your browser and text editor, open move.html from the WIP_07>move folder.**

This file displays an image of a dog named Eddie. The file uses absolute positioning to initially place the image on the page.

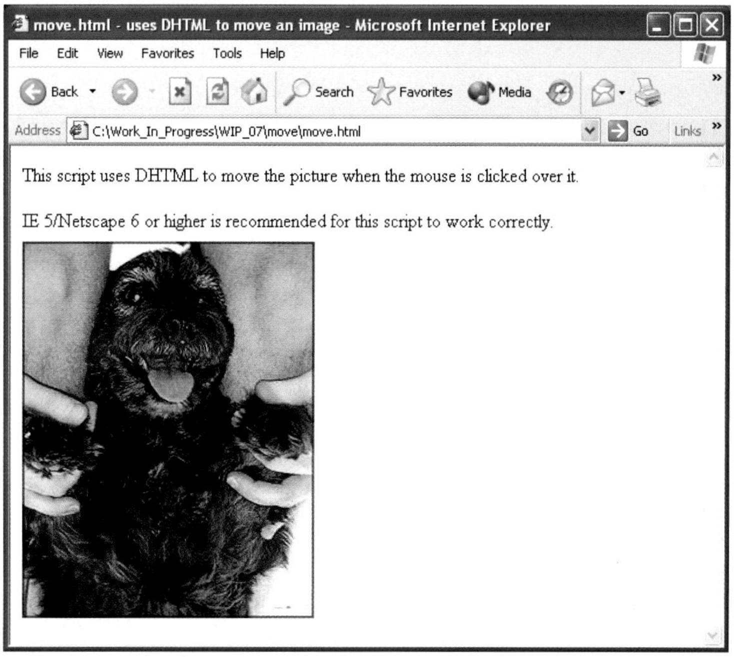

FIGURE 7.8

2   **In your text editor, find the following code.**

```
...
<a href="#" ID="eddieImage" width="250" height="315">
<img src="eddie.jpg" border="0">
</a>
...
```

Since the goal is to move the image to a new location when the user clicks the image, the **<img>** tag was placed between the **<a>** and **</a>** tags. An **ID** attribute applies the style to the content of the **<a>** tag. The style that positions the image is in the head of the document.

3   **Change the code to read as follows.**

```
...
<a href="#" ID="eddieImage" width="250" height="315"
onclick="moveObject()">
<img src="eddie.jpg" border="0">
</a>
...
```

This code adds the event handler to trigger the function that moves the image.

4 Insert the following code in the head of the document.

```
...
<title>move.html - uses DHTML to move an image</title>
<script language="JavaScript">
// *** insert function below ***
function moveObject() {
        document.getElementById('eddieImage').style.left=130;
        document.getElementById('eddieImage').style.top=100;
} // end function
</script>
<style type="text/css">
#eddieImage {
...
```

This function moves the element object when the user clicks the image.

5 Save the file in your text editor and refresh your browser.

6 Click the image.

The image moves to a different position on the screen.

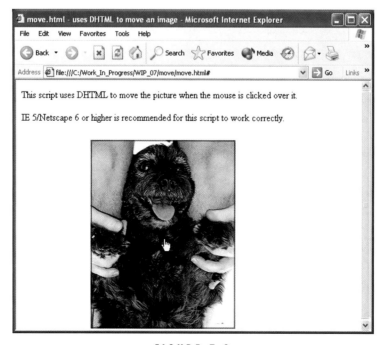

FIGURE 7.9

7   **Close the file in your text editor and browser.**

You now know how to access and change properties of an element through the **style** object. You also know how to move an element dynamically by changing the CSS properties through JavaScript. To animate the element, you would add a loop to move the object incrementally. You could also use a timer to control the smoothness and speed of the animation.

To Extend Your Knowledge...

INCORPORATING ANIMATION

Always remember that a small amount of animation goes a long way. Where a small amount of animation adds a bit of zest to a site, too much animation ruins a page by taking attention away from the branding and content.

LESSON 4   Creating a Drop-Down Menu Effect

Many modern Web sites involve the use of drop-down menus to create striking effects. These menus are similar to traditional modern software interfaces; they allow designers to place several links, organized by category, into an easy-to-understand navigation scheme. When the user rolls the mouse pointer over a category name, a list of links appears, as shown in the following example.

FIGURE 7.10

You cannot use HTML to create drop-down menus, but DHTML provides the necessary power to create this type of navigation structure. DHTML drop-down menus have recently begun to appear in various Web sites, but the adoption rate for this technology is rather slow.

DHTML drop-down menus have two primary disadvantages. First, incompatibility issues result in many browsers displaying drop-down menus incorrectly. This problem is partially mitigated by the forgiving nature of browsers — they tend to ignore code that they do not understand. Secondly, code for DHTML drop-down menus is complex and requires significant understanding of both CSS and JavaScript.

When creating DHTML drop-down menus, developers typically want to apply significant customization to the appearance and style of the menus for a particular project. Given this fact and the other disadvantages associated with using drop-down menus, it makes sense to follow certain guidelines when creating them:

- Use drop-down menus for informational sites where the information fits into easy-to-understand categories.

- The target audience should use newer browsers that can support the technology.

- Older browsers should be able to ignore the code, and the user should be able to navigate to all sections regardless of whether the drop-down menus appear on the screen.

For all of these reasons, it typically makes sense to use a Web-design program (such as Macromedia Dreamweaver or Fireworks) to create drop-down menus. Both of these programs contain easy-to-understand interfaces that allow users to create and customize drop-down menus that work well across most browser platforms.

To better understand the fundamental concepts of DHTML, you create a basic drop-down script in the following exercise. A basic drop-down menu script uses several concepts that you read about earlier. First, you use CSS properties to create and hide the drop-down menu. Then, you use JavaScript to detect when a user rolls over the menu's trigger area. Next, you use JavaScript to reveal the CSS layer and change the CSS properties. Finally, you use JavaScript to hide the CSS layer (after a certain interval) when the user moves the mouse off the trigger area.

Hide Navigation Menus

1 **In your text editor and browser, open dropdown.html from the WIP_07>dropdown folder.**

2 **Examine the file in your Web browser and try rolling over the links.**

The links generate errors because the files mentioned in the code aren't present.

FIGURE 7.11

3 **Examine the source code in your text editor.**

The file uses some simple CSS commands to create a gray box with a blue stroke. The box has three hyperlinks. The **a:hover** pseudo-class creates a rollover style for the links. Notice how the **<div>** tag separates the grey box in the HTML code, and that an **ID** selector named **menu** applies the styles, as shown below.

```
<div ID="menu">
```

4   Find the CSS declaration that creates the **menu** style, as shown below.

```
...
#menu {
        visibility=visible;
        z-index=100;
        background-color: #cccccc;
        width=75px;
        border: thin solid #330099;
        padding=5px;
}
...
```

5   Change the **visibility** attribute to "**hidden**", as shown in the following code.

```
...
#menu {
        visibility=hidden;
        z-index=100;
        background-color: #cccccc;
        width=75px;
...
```

This value renders the menu invisible when the page initially loads.

6   Save the file in your text editor and refresh your browser.

The box is now hidden from view.

FIGURE 7.12

7   Keep the file open in your browser and text editor for the next exercise.

Show and Hide Menus

1   In the open dropdown.html, find the line of code that displays the word "**products**," as shown below.

```
<p><font color="#000099">products</font>
```

2   Change this code to trigger functions when the mouse rolls over or off the text.

```
<p onmouseover="showMenu()"
onmouseout="timer=setTimeout('hideMenu()',2000)"><font


color="#000099">products</font>
```

This timer tells the box to remain visible for two seconds. Without the timer, users would find it difficult to click the drop-down options before they disappeared.

3   Insert the following function into the head of the document.

```
...

// showMenu function goes here

function showMenu() {

document.getElementById('menu').style.visibility="visible";

} // end function

// hideMenu function goes here


</script>
</head>
...
```

This function causes the menu to appear.

To Extend Your Knowledge...

DROP-DOWN MENUS

Drop-down menus work well for sites that have a significant amount of informational content, where the information is easily separated into categories that a user can understand.

4   **Insert the following function to hide the menu.**

```
...
        document.getElementById('menu').style.visibility="visible";
} // end function
// hideMenu function goes here
function hideMenu() {
        document.getElementById('menu').style.visibility="hidden";
        clearTimeout(timer)
} // end function
</script>
</head>


<body>
...
```

5   **Save the document in your text editor and refresh your browser.**

A drop-down menu appears when you move your mouse over the word "products" and disappears two seconds after you move off the word.

6   **Close the file in your browser and text editor.**

LESSON 5   Using Font and Text Properties

As a designer, you must use text and font styles appropriately to create engaging and interesting visual experiences for your Web visitors. Graphic designers who become Web designers are often frustrated by the lack of flexibility that HTML offers in regard to font styles and sizes. CSS alleviates these restrictions by providing designers with greatly increased control of fonts and the appearance of text elements on the page.

DHTML offers additional flexibility in this area by allowing JavaScript to control fonts as the page loads or as the user interacts with the page. For example, you can use JavaScript to determine the size of the screen, and then size the text appropriately to complement that particular resolution.

A number of CSS attributes and their matching JavaScript properties are listed in the following table.

CSS attribute	JavaScript property	Description
color	Color	Sets or retrieves the color of the text of the object.
font	font	Sets or retrieves a combination of separate font properties of the object. Alternatively, sets or retrieves one or more of six user-preference fonts.
font-family	fontFamily	Sets or retrieves the name of the font used for text in the object.
font-size	fontSize	Sets or retrieves a value that indicates the font size used for text in the object.
font-style	fontStyle	Sets or retrieves the font style of the object as italic, normal, or oblique.
font-variant	fontVariant	Sets or retrieves a value that states whether the text of the object is in small capital letters.
font-weight	fontWeight	Sets or retrieves the weight of the font of the object.
letter-spacing	letterSpacing	Sets or retrieves the amount of additional space between letters in the object.
line-height	lineHeight	Sets or retrieves the distance between lines in the object.
text-decoration	textDecoration	Sets or retrieves a value that indicates whether the text in the object has blink, line-through, overline, or underline decorations.
	textDecorationLineThrough	Sets or retrieves a Boolean value indicating whether the text in the object has a line drawn through it.
	textDecorationNone	Sets or retrieves the Boolean value indicating whether the textDecoration property for the object has been set to none.
	textDecorationOverline	Sets or retrieves a Boolean value indicating whether the text in the object has a line drawn over it.
	textDecorationUnderline	Sets or retrieves a Boolean value that indicates whether the text in the object is underlined.
text-indent	textIndent	Sets or retrieves the indentation of the first line of text in the object.
text-justify	textJustify	Sets or retrieves the type of alignment used to justify text in the object.
text-transform	textTransform	Can be set to capitalize, uppercase, or lowercase.
word-spacing	wordSpacing	Sets or retrieves the amount of additional space between words in the object.
word-wrap	wordWrap	Sets or retrieves a value that states whether to break words when the content exceeds the boundaries of its container.

Imagine how you might use these properties to enhance accessibility to a Web site. In the following exercise, you use DHTML to make text larger when the user clicks a button. This simple change makes the site much more accessible to those users who have vision problems.

Use Text Properties

1   **In your text editor and browser, open text.html from your WIP_07 folder.**

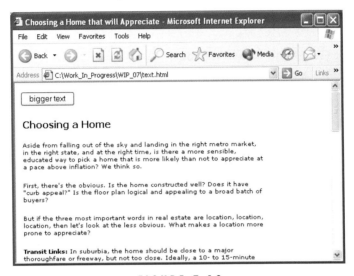

FIGURE 7.13

This page offers advice on buying a new home.

2   **Find the following CSS style in the head of the document.**

```
...

#myBody {
        font-family: Verdana, Arial, Helvetica, sans-serif;
        font-size: 10px;
}

...
```

This style sheet sets the page content to 10-pixel text. An **ID** attribute in the **\<table>** tag applies the style.

3   **Find the following line of code.**

```
<p>  <input type="button" name="bigger text" value="bigger text">
```

This code establishes the button at the top of the page.

4   Modify the button code as follows.

```
<p>  <input type="button" name="bigger text" value="bigger text"
onclick="getBigger()">
```

This code triggers the function when the user clicks the button.

5   Insert the following function in the head of the document.

```
...
<script language="JavaScript">
// insert makeBigger function
function getBigger() {
        document.getElementById("myBody").style.fontSize='20';
}
</script>
</head>
<body bgcolor="#FFFFFF" text="#000000">
...
```

6   Save the file in your text editor and refresh your browser.

7   Click the bigger text button.

The text size increases.

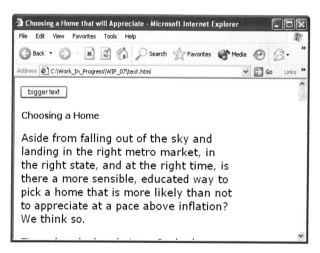

FIGURE 7.14

8   Close the file in your browser and text editor.

To Extend Your Knowledge...

FULL LIST OF STYLE OBJECT PROPERTIES

Microsoft provides a comprehensive list of `style` object properties supported by Internet Explorer at http://msdn.microsoft.com/library/default.asp?url=/workshop/author/dhtml/reference/objects/obj_style.asp.

LESSON 6   Incorporating Background and Display Properties

JavaScript contains several properties that allow you to use a style sheet to control the positioning and display of objects. As you may remember from Project 6, CSS offers excellent flexibility when you position items on the page. Using JavaScript properties to control matching CSS attributes, you can easily move an item from one position to another position.

A number of properties allow you to specify background images, as well as to position background images. For example, you can use the **background-image** attribute to specify a background image in CSS. The **backgroundImage** property in JavaScript allows you to change this property and effectively change the source of the background image.

CSS also allows you to layer objects. Using the **z-index** property in CSS, you can stack elements on the page however you prefer. JavaScript takes this feature one step further by allowing you to use the **zIndex** property to change the **z-index** setting, which means you can change the stacking order of objects on the page. For example, you could design a page that showed numerous manila folders stacked on a desk. When you click the tab on one of the file folders, that folder would move to the top of the stacking order because it would assume a higher **z-index** value.

CSS also allows you to hide objects by manipulating the **display** or **visibility** property. Again, JavaScript allows you to take this feature one step further: you can hide or unhide items as necessary while the user interacts with the page.

The following table includes a number of common CSS attributes and their matching JavaScript properties. You can use these attributes and properties to manipulate the visibility, background, and positioning of various items on the page.

CSS attribute	JavaScript property	Description
background-attachment	backgroundAttachment	Sets or retrieves how the background image is attached to the object within the document.
background-color	backgroundColor	Sets or retrieves the color behind the content of the object.
background-image	backgroundImage	Sets or retrieves the background image of the object.
background-position	backgroundPosition	Sets or retrieves the position of the background of the object.
background-position-x	backgroundPositionX	Sets or retrieves the x-coordinate of the backgroundPosition property.
background-position-y	backgroundPositionY	Sets or retrieves the y-coordinate of the backgroundPosition property.
background-repeat	backgroundRepeat	Sets or retrieves how the backgroundImage property of the object is tiled.
cursor	cursor	Sets or retrieves the type of cursor to display as the mouse pointer moves over the object.
display	display	Sets or retrieves whether the object is rendered (visible).
position	position	Sets or retrieves the type of positioning used for the object.
	posLeft	Sets or retrieves the left position of the object in the units specified by the left attribute.
	posRight	Sets or retrieves the right position of the object in the units specified by the right attribute.
	posTop	Sets or retrieves the top position of the object in the units specified by the top attribute.
	posWidth	Sets or retrieves the width of the object in the units specified by the width attribute.
visibility	visibility	Sets or retrieves the value that states whether the content of the object displays on screen.
width	width	Sets or retrieves the width of the object.
z-index	zIndex	Sets or retrieves the stacking order of positioned objects.

In the following exercise, you create a script that changes the stacking order of items on the page. Combining this technique with JavaScript event handlers allows an item to appear to move to the front of the stack or move farther back in a stack of objects. Developers often refer to the process of changing the stacking order of objects as *swapping depths* because one object appears to go behind another exposed object.

Swap Depths

1   **In your browser and text editor, open changedepth.html from your WIP_07>depth folder.**

This document uses CSS absolute positioning to display two images. The **z-index** property was used to overlap the objects.

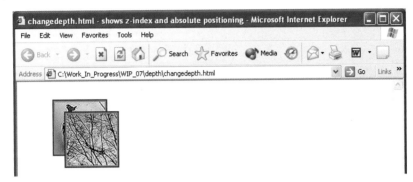

FIGURE 7.15

2   **Insert the following function.**

```
...
<script language="JavaScript">
// insert function here
function swapDepth(myLayer) {
        document.getElementById(myLayer).style.zIndex='20';
}
</script>
</head>
...
```

This function changes the depth of the **ID** selector to **20**, which forces the image to appear above the other image.

3   **Find the following code.**

```
<a href="javascript:void(0)"><img src="smallpic1.jpg" width="90"
height="90" id="pic1"></a>

<a href="javascript:void(0)"><img src="smallpic2.jpg" width="90"
height="90" id="pic2"></a>
```

This code creates the image and applies the style sheet properties. Notice that the images are enclosed within hyperlinks so that the users' mouse pointers will change to pointing fingers to indicate that they can click the images.

4 Insert the following code.

```
...

<a href="javascript:void(0)"><img src="smallpic1.jpg" width="90"
height="90" id="pic1" onclick="swapDepth('pic1');"></a>

<a href="javascript:void(0)"><img src="smallpic2.jpg" width="90"
height="90" id="pic2" onclick="swapDepth('pic2');"></a>

...
```

This code triggers the function when the user clicks either image.

5 Save the file in your text editor and refresh your browser.

6 Click the image located behind the top image.

The images change positions.

FIGURE 7.16

7 Close the file in your browser and text editor.

To Extend Your Knowledge...

OTHER PROPERTIES

A number of other properties allow you to control the color of the browser's scroll bars, padding, borders, margins, and more.

SUMMARY

In Project 7, you learned how to use DHTML to create interesting and complex visual effects. You found that the DHTML "technology" integrates JavaScript, CSS, and HTML to create striking effects that aren't otherwise possible. You learned that the **getElementById()** method allows JavaScript to access and change CSS styles dynamically. In addition, you found that the **style** object contains a number of JavaScript properties that represent CSS attributes.

You discovered that DHTML is often used to create simple animated sequences and effects, including dropdown menus. Most mainstream Web designers have been slow to adopt DHTML because of compatibility issues that exist between different browsers; but most of these issues have been corrected in newer browsers, which has led to wider adoption and use of DHTML. A number of large corporate Web sites have embraced DHTML, which suggests that it will soon become a mainstream technology.

KEY TERMS

Camelback notation

Swapping depths

CHECKING CONCEPTS AND TERMS

MULTIPLE CHOICE

Circle the letter that matches the correct answer for each of the following questions.

1. You need to use the **getElementById()** method to access _____.
   a. Netscape 3.0 styles
   b. styles created with **<style>** tags
   c. inline styles
   d. styles created with **<text=attribute>** tags
   e. None of the above

2. How are properties of the **style** object similar to CSS attributes?
   a. They both use all lowercase letters.
   b. They both use camelback notation.
   c. They both use dots to separate parts of names.
   d. None of the above.

3. The **getElementById()** method is a method of the _____ object in JavaScript.
   a. **document**
   b. **style**
   c. **CSS**
   d. **window**

4. _____ uses the **ID** parameter to reference a particular HTML tag.
   a. CSS
   b. JavaScript
   c. Both of the above
   d. None of the above

5. How can you use DHTML in Web pages?
   a. To create rollover effects in table rows
   b. To move an object across the screen
   c. To temporarily hide items, such as drop-down menus
   d. All of the above
   e. None of the above

6. Why should you use a timer when creating drop-down menus in DHTML?
   a. To allow users enough time to read menu choices
   b. To allow users enough time to make choices
   c. Both of the above
   d. None of the above

7. Which items use camelback notation?
   a. JavaScript style properties
   b. CSS attributes
   c. Both of the above
   d. None of the above

8. Which items use a hyphen to separate two-word names?
   a. JavaScript style properties
   b. CSS attributes
   c. Both of the above
   d. None of the above

9. Which CSS attribute and JavaScript property control the stacking order of objects?
   a. `position-number` and `positionNumber`
   b. `z-index` and `zIndex`
   c. `stack` and `stackingOrder`
   d. `vector-position` and `vectorPosition`

10. DHTML properties control the color and style of the browser's scroll bars.
    a. True
    b. False

DISCUSSION QUESTIONS

1. How are inline styles and styles defined in style sheets treated differently in DHTML?

2. What types of tasks can you accomplish with DHTML that you cannot accomplish using CSS or HTML alone?

3. How can you use DHTML to improve the accessibility of a Web page?

4. What are the major categories of CSS attributes that can be controlled by DHTML?

SKILL DRILL

Skill Drill exercises reinforce project skills. Each skill reinforced is the same, or nearly the same, as a skill presented in the project. Detailed instructions are provided in a step-by-step format. You should work through these exercises in order.

1. Create Smooth Animation

In this Skill Drill, you use JavaScript to control CSS positioning to create a smooth animation. Smooth animation requires at least 10 frames per second. Since a millisecond is 1/1000 of a second, intervals greater than 100 milliseconds usually result in jerky motion and poor animation.

1. In your text editor and browser, open skillanimation.html from your WIP_07>move folder.

    This is essentially the same file you used in a previous exercise.

2. Modify the following line of code, located near the bottom of the page.

    ```
    <a href="#" ID="eddieImage" width="250"
    height="315"onclick="moveObject(10,80)">
    ```

    This code passes starting x,y coordinates to the function.

3. Find the following function in the head of the document.

    ```
    ...
    // *** function will go here ***

    function moveObject() {

            document.getElementById('eddieImage').style.left=130;

            document.getElementById('eddieImage').style.top=100;

    } // end function

    ...
    ```

4.   Change the function code to the following.

This change adds a loop, timer, and statements to increment the x,y variables each time the function is called.

```
...

function moveObject(x,y) {

        if (x<300) {

                document.getElementById('eddieImage').style.left=x;

                document.getElementById('eddieImage').style.top=y;

                x=x+3;

                y++;

                setTimeout('moveObject('+x+','+y+')',20);

        } //end if

} // end function

...
```

5.   Save the file in your text editor and refresh your browser.

6.   Click the image.

The image should move smoothly to the lower-right area of the browser window. Notice that the image moves 3 pixels to the right for every 1 pixel it moves down.

7.   Return to your text editor and find the timer statement that sets the interval between movements. Change the number of milliseconds from **20** to a larger or smaller number and see how this change affects the speed and smoothness of the animation.

8.   Find the statements that increment the x,y variables. Change the numbers to make the animation faster, and then change the numbers to move the animation in a straight line from left to right with no downward movement.

9.   Close the file in your browser and text editor.

2. Add JavaScript Event Handlers to Change CSS Styles

JavaScript event handlers allow you to detect user events and respond accordingly. In this exercise, you create rollover style effects for tabular data to improve the usability of an e-commerce Web site.

1. In your text editor and browser, open skillstyle.html from the WIP_07 folder.

    This is essentially the same file you used earlier.

2. Move your mouse over the table row for the first product.

    The table row changes color as you move your mouse over or off the row.

3. In your text editor, find the inline JavaScript code that triggers the rollover effect for the Shirt row.

4. Add the same rollover effect to the other two product rows (Jacket and Shoes).

5. Save your changes in the text editor. Test the file in your browser.

    Each of the three rows should change color as your mouse moves on and off the row.

6. Close the file in your browser and text editor.

3. Manipulate Text Properties

CSS offers a number of new ways to work with text, and DHTML offers new ways to interact with users. In this exercise, you create a page that offers new accessibility options to users: you allow users to dynamically change the size of the content that displays on the screen.

1. In your browser and text editor, open skilltext.html from the WIP_07 folder.

    This is essentially the same file you used in a previous exercise, but a "smaller text" button was added to the page.

2. Create a function named **makeSmaller()** that changes the font size of the **myBody ID** selector to **10**.

    Hint: use the **getBigger()** function as a guide.

3. Create inline JavaScript to trigger the **makeSmaller()** function when the user clicks the smaller text button.

4. Save your changes and test the file in your browser.

    The text should become larger when you click the bigger text button, and then the text should shrink when you click the smaller text button.

5. Close the file in your browser and text editor.

4. Change Layering

In this exercise, you change the stacking order of layered objects, making some objects appear closer or farther away than other objects. To accomplish this task, you use the **zIndex** property to change **z-index** values created by CSS.

1. In your text editor and browser, open skilldepth.html from the WIP_07 folder.

   This file is similar to the file you created in a previous exercise, but a third image has been inserted onto the page. If you click one of the first two images, the image appears above the other images.

2. Create an **ID** selector named **pic3** in the existing **<style>** tag. Position the **pic3** object at a **top** setting of **70** and a **left** setting of **100**. Set the **pic3** object's initial **z-index** value to **3**.

   The **ID** attribute was already included in the **<img>** tag to link the tag to the style sheet.

3. Save the file in your text editor and refresh your browser.

   The image moves to a different position on the screen.

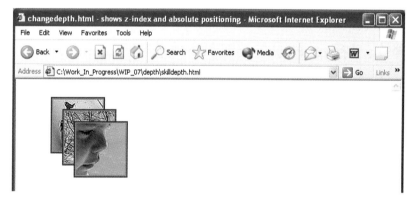

FIGURE 7.17

4. Find the following line of code.

   ```
   <a href="javascript:void(0)"><img src="smallpic3.jpg" width="90"
   height="90" id="pic3"></a>
   ```

5. Modify the code you found in Step 4 to trigger the **changeDepth()** function when the user clicks the image to change the position of this image.

6. Save and test your file.

7. Close the file in your browser and text editor.

5. Modify the Class Associated with an Object

In this project, you used DHTML properties to change the CSS attributes of an object to create a rollover effect. The **className** property offers a different way to change attributes. The **className** property allows you to change the entire class of styles associated with an object. You use the **className** property in this exercise.

1. In your browser and text editor, open skillswapclass.html from the WIP_07 folder.

2. Roll your mouse pointer over the menu items.

   You see no effect.

3. Insert the following code.

   ```
   ...
   </head>
   <body>
   <div id="menu" class="menu">
   <div class="navMenu"
   onmouseover="this.className='navMenuOver'">Home</div>
   <div class="navMenu" id="menuItem">Products</div>
   <div class="navMenu" id="menuItem">Services</div>
   <div class="navMenu" id="menuItem">Contact</div>
   ...
   ```

4. Refresh the page in your browser.

   When the mouse rolls over the Home menu item, the background and text colors change, and the text becomes underlined because the class changes.

5. Insert code to change the class of the same **<div>** so that it changes back to the **navMenu** class when the **onmouseout** event occurs.

   Hint: use the code in Step 3 as a guide, but change the event handler and class name.

6. Refresh the page in your browser and test the file to ensure that the rollover effect appears when the mouse pointer moves on or off the first menu item.

7. Save and close the file in your browser and text editor.

CHALLENGE

Challenge exercises expand on, or are somewhat related to, skills presented in the lessons. Each exercise provides a brief introduction, followed by instructions presented in a numbered-step format that are not as detailed as those in the Skill Drill exercises. You should work through these exercises in order.

1. Use DHTML to Create an Interactive Button

In Project 4, you used JavaScript to create image rollovers. You can accomplish the same effect with CSS and JavaScript by using background images.

1. In your text editor, open challengebutton.html from the WIP_07 folder.

2. Use the **onmouseover** event handler to change the class, as shown below.

```
...

</head>

<body>

<div class="button" onmouseover="this.className='buttonOver'"
></div>

</body>

</html>
```

3. Use the **onmouseout** event handler to change the class back to the **button** class.

4. Save and refresh the file in your browser.

   The image should change as you move over and off the button.

5. Close the file in your text editor and browser.

2. Open (Show) a Menu

In this Challenge, you use **<div>** tags to create menu effects: **button**, **menu**, and **closer**. The **button** effect adds an **onmouseover** effect to a navigation button. The **menu** effect opens or shows a div by changing visibility. The **closer** effect collapses the menu. Start the exercise by adding code to make the menu visible.

1. In your browser and text editor, open challengemenu.html from the WIP_07 folder.

2. Find the following code.

```
function showMenu() {
        document.getElementById('closer').style.visibility = "visible";
} // end function
```

The code currently changes the **closer** object to **visible**.

3. Modify the **showMenu** function to change the visibility of **menu**. Use the following pseudo-code as a guide.

```
change the visibility of the div with id=menu to visible
```

4. Find the following code.

```
<a href="#">
```

5. Modify the code you found in the Step 4 to use the **onmouseover** event handler to trigger the **showMenu()** function.

6. Save and refresh the file in your browser.

   The menu appears as you move the mouse pointer over the image.

7. Keep the file open for the next Challenge.

3. Collapse (Hide) a Visible Menu

In this Challenge, you write code to collapse a menu.

1. In the open challengemenu.html, find the following code.

```
// hideMenu function goes here
function hideMenu() {
        document.getElementById('closer').style.visibility="hidden";
} // end function
```

This function currently modifies the **closer** object.

2. Modify the **hideMenu()** function to change the visibility of **menu**. Use the following pseudo-code as a guide.

```
change the visibility of the div with id=menu to hidden
```

3. Find the following code.

```
<div id="closer" >
<img src="images/closer_trigger.gif" width="100%" height="100%">
</div>
```

4. Use the **onmouseover** event to trigger the **hideMenu()** function when the user moves the mouse pointer over the closer_trigger.gif image.

5. Save and refresh the file in your browser.

   The div's (**id="closer"**) **visibility** value changes from **hidden** to **visible** when the **onmouseover** event occurs. This div contains a single image set to 100% wide and 100% tall. When the mouse rolls over the image or off **menu**, the **menu** visibility changes. The **closer** object must be below the **menu** and the **button** in **z-index**, which assures that the **hideMenu()** function does not trigger while the mouse is over the **button** or **menu**.

6. Keep this file open for the next exercise

4. Style Menu Items

In this Challenge, you create a pull-down menu effect by changing the class of the div when the user moves the mouse pointer over a link.

1. In the open challengemenu.html, find the following code.

```
<div id="menu" class="menu">

        <div class="navMenu">Home</div>

        <div class="navMenu">Products</div>

        <div class="navMenu">Services</div>

        <div class="navMenu">Contact</div>

</div>
```

   This code creates a menu (of class **menu**) and four menu items in the **navMenu** class.

2. Add **onmouseover** events to the four menu items to change the class to "**navMenuOver**" when the user moves the mouse pointer over the contents of the **<div>** tags.

   Hint: use **this.className** in your code.

3. Add **onmouseout** events to the four menu items to change the class to "**navMenu**" when the user moves the mouse pointer off the contents of the **<div>** tags.

4. Save and refresh the file in your browser.

   The **button** image swaps, the menu appears and disappears, and menu items change when a user rolls the mouse pointer over them. Combining multiple effects allows you to create a dynamic menu system.

5. Close the file in your browser and text editor.

P O R T F O L I O   B U I L D E R

Create a Navigational System

Creating an effective navigational (menu) system is of critical importance because the menu system has a direct impact on the user. The most common navigational control element a user experiences is the horizontal menu bar located along the top of virtually every application's interface. Leveraging such well-known conventions allows designers to develop systems that users find familiar and comfortable, which results in freely browsing the content of the sites — rather than trying to figure out what to do and how to do it.

In this Portfolio Builder, your task is to complete a menu system for a Web site. To finish the job, follow these steps:

1. Open WIP_07>multiplemenus.html in your text editor and browser. The file is nearly complete.

2. Attach the multiplemenus.css style sheet (also in the WIP_07 folder) and refresh the Web page in your browser. Most of the styling is complete.

3. Move your mouse over the products link. The menu that appears is out of place. Look for the **ID** rule in the style sheet for the menu (**#productsMenu**). Adjust the positioning until the menu is centered below the products in the menu bar.

Create a Navigational System (continued)

4. Examine the **showMenu()** and **hideMenu()** functions in multiplemenus.html. The functions change the visibility of **productsMenu**. The **showMenu()** function is triggered by an **onmouseover** event that makes two layers visible. The layers are named **productsMenu** and **closer**. The **hideMenu()** function triggers when the mouse moves off the menu and over the layer named **closer**. The only purpose of the **closer** selector is to close menus.

5. Two additional menus have a **visibility** value of **hidden** in the multiplemenus.html file. You need to correct the positions of these menus. In addition, you must adapt the **showMenu()** and **hideMenu()** functions to accept values passed by the **onmouseover** and **onmouseout** events to tell the function which menu needs to be visible.

6. Once the menu system is working correctly, examine the CSS styles. Make additional adjustments to perfect the overall look and feel of your menu system.

Using JavaScript with Other Technologies

OBJECTIVES

In this project, you learn how to

- Determine OS and browser information

- Communicate with Java applets and CGI scripts

- Implement JavaScript from Flash

- Use JavaScript-to-Flash communications

- Incorporate Dreamweaver behaviors

- Write XHTML-compliant scripts

WHY WOULD I DO THIS?

JavaScript works well as a bridge between many different technologies. As an example, consider browser incompatibility issues, which, as you know, cause significant problems when you use JavaScript, DHTML, and CSS. In cases where you cannot avoid browser incompatibility issues, you may decide to use JavaScript to detect the browser type and version.

Many technical tasks require the use of CGI scripts or the Java programming language. You can use JavaScript to interact with these technologies, which allows you to arrive at a better result than when using JavaScript alone. For example, assume that you sell custom-made motorcycles from a Web site:

- If a user chooses a particular frame, he must also choose a certain type of gas tank.

- If a user chooses a particular gas tank, he must also choose certain types of hoses.

- If a user orders a specific quantity of motorcycles, the price per unit must be adjusted downward.

To control these complicated variables and tally these complex calculations, you need a computer program. You could use JavaScript for the job, but JavaScript may not be able to complete the calculations quickly enough to satisfy your customers. In addition, using JavaScript would allow your competitors to view the source code and discover your pricing structure — both of which are undesirable.

Instead, you could choose HTML or Flash to create an engaging, easy-to-use interface. Then, you could use JavaScript to pass the information to Java, which would complete the calculations quickly and securely. When the user finishes making his choices, you could use JavaScript to send the information to a CGI script that would send the user an email to confirm his order.

Many Web design professionals use Macromedia Dreamweaver and Macromedia Flash to create content for their Web pages and sites. Dreamweaver offers a powerful combination of visual layout tools, application-development features, and code-editing support that allows designers to build Web sites and applications. Its toolset contains extensive support for JavaScript, including built-in JavaScript code segments that you can easily customize. Flash allows designers and developers to integrate video, text, audio, and graphics into feature-rich experiences. In addition, Flash includes a built-in scripting language named ActionScript.

This project provides an overview of how to create Web pages that include JavaScript, ActionScript, and HTML. Many designers find that working with all three of these important technologies allows them to achieve far more effective results than if they used only one technology in isolation. Web developers quickly discover the benefits of integrating the best facets of each program in their Web pages. The lessons on Flash assume an intermediate knowledge of ActionScript; the lessons on Dreamweaver assume a basic familiarity with that program. If you do not have a basic understanding of these technologies and applications, you may want to skim the written material and avoid technology-specific exercises. Exercises, Skill Drills, and Challenges that require a specific technology are clearly labeled.

V I S U A L   S U M M A R Y

Early adopters of JavaScript found that it was virtually impossible to write one set of scripts that worked correctly in every browser. Most modern browsers support the ECMAScript standard, the newest version of CSS (CSS Level 2), and the most recent version of DHTML (DOM Level 2). However, certain browsers still contain bugs that cause problems. For instance, Macintosh versions of Internet Explorer are notoriously incompatible when it comes to JavaScript code.

One workaround to these ongoing compatibility issues is to use JavaScript to determine the user's browser type and operating system. Once JavaScript knows which browser and OS are in use, it can run advanced code that targets the specific configuration. JavaScript uses the **navigator** object to accomplish this task. The **navigator** object was originally named for the Netscape browser, but it is used in virtually all Web browsers. The **navigator** object contains a number of properties that determine the language being used, the operating system (platform), and the browser type and version.

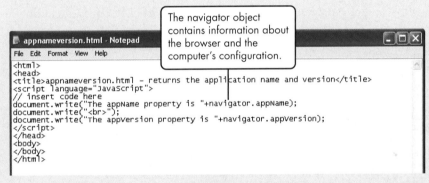

FIGURE 8.1

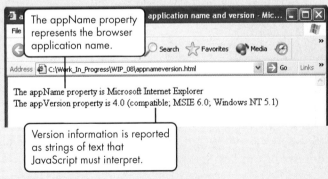

FIGURE 8.2

Interface designers must often use a variety of tools to accomplish a specific task. For example, to construct a large site, a designer may need to work with Macromedia Dreamweaver and/or Flash, as well as interact with other Web technologies and languages, including CGI, ActionScript, and/or Java. Dreamweaver allows users to create JavaScript code in a number of ways, such as using the Behaviors panel. The Behaviors panel includes a number of pre-written scripts that you can use as-is or customize however you choose.

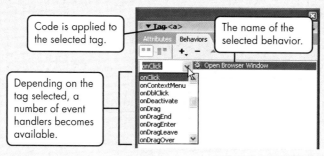

FIGURE 8.3

Using browser plug-ins, you can integrate many technologies into HTML pages, including Flash and Java. To add these items to a Web page, you use the **<object>** tag. Consider the following code, which inserts a Flash movie into an HTML page.

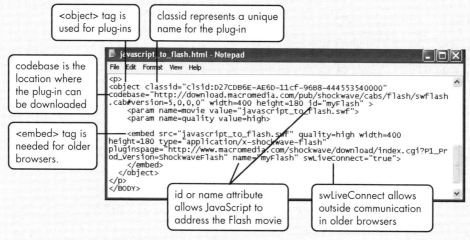

FIGURE 8.4

By including the **id** attribute in the **<object>** tag, the item shown by the plug-in — in this case, a Flash movie — can be addressed from JavaScript, as shown below:

```
document.myFlash
```

By addressing the Flash movie in JavaScript, you can control the movie in various ways, such as changing the value of variables in the Flash movie. Flash can also be used to trigger JavaScript code. Consider the following Flash movie, which consists of a button that, when clicked, opens a pop-up window.

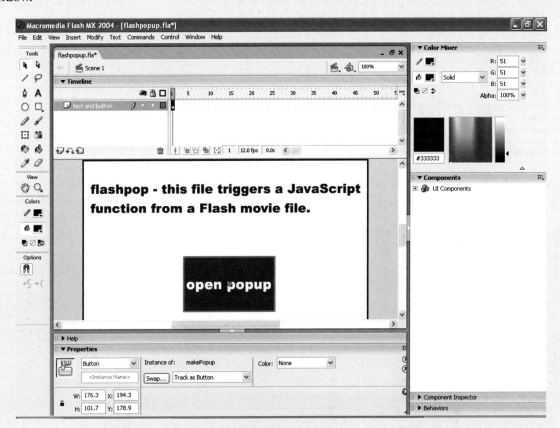

FIGURE 8.5

ActionScript, the scripting language built into Flash, allows you to use the **getURL()** method to send a URL to the browser and load the page in the browser window. You can modify the URL to use the keyword **javascript** to trigger JavaScript code in the HTML document. For example, you could create a button in Flash to trigger a JavaScript function in the HTML page called **makePopup()**, as shown below.

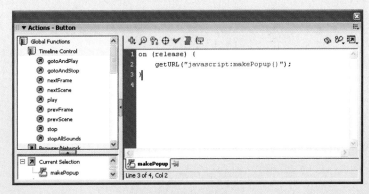

FIGURE 8.6

LESSON 1 Determining OS and Browser Information

Using JavaScript's **navigator** object, you can determine the browser (and version) currently being used. The **navigator** object is a subordinate object of the **window** object. You can refer to the **navigator** object as **window.navigator**. Even though the **navigator** object was named for the original Netscape Navigator browser, it works with all browsers.

The **navigator** object contains various properties that determine the browser brand and version. The most useful properties of the **navigator** object are those used by all browser manufacturers. Specific properties that exist for individual browsers can also be useful because they tell you that a certain browser was detected.

appName and appVersion

The **appName** property of the **navigator** object tells you the name of the company that made the browser being used and the type of browser. The value of the **appName** property is stored as a text string. For instance, Netscape browsers return "Netscape" and Microsoft browsers return "Microsoft Internet Explorer." The **appVersion** property, on the other hand, tells you the version number of the browser being used. The information returns as a string value, not as a number. For example, the following code statements return the browser's name and version number:

```
document.write("The appName property is "+navigator.appName+"<br>");

document.write("The appVersion property is "+navigator.appVersion);
```

When using the Netscape Navigator 7.0 browser, the following result appears.

FIGURE 8.7

There was never an official version 5 of the Netscape browser. Internally, Netscape refers to versions 6 and 7 as version 5. This explains why Netscape 7 reports "5.0" as the version number. The Mozilla Firefox 1.0 browser returns the same results as Netscape 7.0.

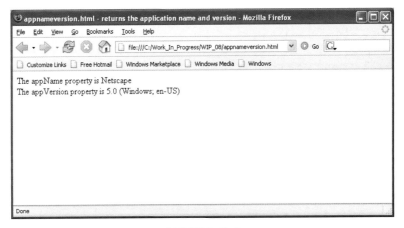

FIGURE 8.8

In each case, notice that the **appVersion** property returned a long text string that included not only the version number, but also some additional information. You should also notice that Internet Explorer reported the information in a different format than other browsers, which makes comparisons difficult. For example, consider that you want to write a script that performs an action if the user has any browser that is version 4.0 or higher. To do so, you must write a script that searches the text string provided by the **appVersion** property and extracts the number of the version.

Determining User Language

Internet Explorer and Netscape browsers (both Navigator and Communicator) contain properties that identify the language the browser is set up to display. The problem, however, is that each browser uses a different property to identify the language: Netscape uses the **language** property and Internet Explorer uses the **userLanguage** property. You can check for the existence of any language property by asking JavaScript if the property is not equal to **null**, since the property must otherwise exist. For instance, you could write the following simple script to generate an alert box that returns the language being used, regardless of which browser is being used.

```
if (navigator.language != null) {

    // must be Netscape

    alert(navigator.language)

}

if (navigator.userLanguage != null) {

    // must be Internet Explorer

    alert(navigator.userLanguage)

}
```

With the code shown above, using Mozilla Firefox 1.0 on an operating system set to United States English yields the following result.

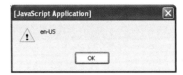

FIGURE 8.9

Platform Property

The **platform** property contains a text string that identifies the computer platform in use. For example, if you write a script that contains the **alert(navigator.platform);** statement, most Windows operating systems will return "Win32," which stands for the Microsoft Windows 32-bit operating system.

FIGURE 8.10

Determining Specific Browser Version and Properties

If you decide to use a new feature of CSS, JavaScript, or DHTML — or any other technology that is only found in newer browsers — you should ensure site visitors are using browsers that support the feature/technology. Those users who have older browsers can be redirected to a page that does not require the newer technology. This method ensures a positive experience for all of your site visitors, regardless of which page they view or which browser they use. This may sound like a great deal of trouble and, in truth, it is. Extracting the version number of the browser is relatively easy, but designing multiple sites for different browsers adds significantly to your workload.

As you know, redundant content in multiple sites can result in complicated maintenance procedures and create a breeding ground for inconsistencies between the two interfaces. To illustrate this situation, let's consider a soft drink company. The company wants its Web site to convey a cutting-edge, fun, and interesting atmosphere, with only a small amount of textual information presented to the viewer. The latest Web-design technologies are a perfect match for this type of project, but the company wants to ensure that all of its customer — including those who have older browsers — can access and view the site.

In a scenario such as this, it is quite usual for a design team to build two sites. The sites may look similar, but different technologies were used to create the two versions. It is also likely that developers may apply JavaScript code that writes HTML or CSS dynamically, depending on the browser and version number found. Either solution requires significant extra effort on the part of the development team.

Remember that browsers typically return **navigator** properties as text strings. Since browsers report information differently, it is difficult to extract version information. The solution requires code that extracts the browser name and version information from the string provided by the browser.

Determine Application Name and Version

1   Copy the content of the RF_JavaScript_L2>Project_08 folder into the Work_In_Progress>WIP_08 folder.

2   In your text editor, open appnameversion.html from the WIP_08 folder.

3   Insert the following code.

```
...

<title>appnameversion.html - returns the application name and ver-
sion</title>

<script language="JavaScript">

// insert code here

document.write("The appName property is "+navigator.appName);

document.write("<br>");

document.write("The appVersion property is "+navigator.appVersion);

</script>

</head>

<body>

...
```

4   Save the file in your text editor and open it in your browser.

A computer running Windows XP and Internet Explorer 6.0 would return the following result.

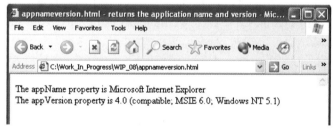

FIGURE 8.11

Windows XP is actually a version of the Windows NT operating system. Microsoft abandoned the NT marketing name with the release of version 5, which was named Windows 2000.

5   Close the file in your text editor and browser.

To Extend Your Knowledge...

APPLICATION CODE NAME PROPERTY

The **appCodeName** property was intended to return the code name that was used during the development of the browser (before the product was released to the public). The Netscape Navigator was based on a browser named Mozilla, and Navigator returns "Mozilla" as its **appCodeName** property. Interestingly enough, Microsoft browsers also return the Mozilla code name in an attempt to encourage compatibility between browsers. Since both browsers return the same code name, the **appCodeName** property is useless for any practical purpose.

USING INCLUDED BROWSER-DETECTION SCRIPTS

Anyone who purchases this textbook can freely use the file named browsercheck.js, located in your RF_JavaScript_L2>Project_08 folder. The file contains JavaScript functions that detect the browser being used by a site visitor. For your convenience, the file contains comments that explain the purpose of each function. You use this file in the Challenge exercises at the end of this project.

LESSON 2 Communicating with Java Applets and CGI Scripts

JavaScript is an excellent client-side scripting language, but it is not the best choice for database interaction and animation. To achieve the best possible results, you must often use JavaScript in conjunction with other technologies, ranging from client-side technologies (Macromedia Flash) to server-side technologies (CGI scripts).

One drawback of HTML and JavaScript is that these languages allow a site visitor to see the source code of a Web page. Any determined Web surfer can access JavaScript source code to discover how particular scripts were written, which, as you may imagine, is often undesirable. When building complex scripts that you want to protect, you may opt to use Java or Flash because these technologies can protect your source code from being seen or imported.

Java Applets

The Java programming language allows greater flexibility and provides powerful features not found in JavaScript. *Applets* are mini-applications created in Java that you add to HTML pages using the **<object>** tag. To integrate an applet on a page, you might write the following statements:

```
<object classid="clsid:CAFEEFAC-0014-0002-0000-ABCDEFFEDCBA"
width="600" height="450" align="baseline" id="gameApplet"
codebase="http://java.sun.com/products/plugin/autodl/
jinstall-1_4_2-windows-i586.cab#Version=1,4,2,0">
```

The **id** attribute contains the name that JavaScript uses to communicate with the applet. When the **id** attribute is included in an **<object>** tag, the object becomes part of the DOM and can be addressed by JavaScript.

Java allows you to create **public methods** and **public properties**. These objects are equivalent to global methods and variables in JavaScript, which means that they can be accessed from anywhere. For security reasons and to prevent programmer errors, other methods and properties have a very limited scope by default. If an applet defines a method or property as "public," JavaScript can access the method or property in the HTML document. For example, if you named an applet **calculations** in the **id** attribute of the **<object>** tag, you could use the following statement to access a public method named **figureInterest()**:

```
document.calculations.figureInterest();
```

Assuming the **calculations** applet had a public variable named **interestAmount**, you could access the variable in the following fashion:

```
document.calculations.interestAmount
```

CGI Scripts

Common Gateway Interface (**CGI**) is a server-side technology that allows programs of various languages to run on a Web server. CGI isn't a programming language. Instead, it is a protocol that allows a client-side script to exchange information with a server-side script or program. For example, consider a mailform script, which is a program that converts information from a Web page into an email message. Mailform scripts are often written in the Perl programming language. CGI is typically used to communicate between the HTML page and the mailform script.

The CGI protocol uses two techniques (known as methods) for communicating with a Web page. The methods are known as **post** and **get**. The **get** method transmits information by appending data to the end of the URL of the CGI application. The **post** method is better suited to transmitting large amounts of data because it hides the data within the HTTP protocol without appending it to the URL. Using the **post** method, the data remains hidden during transmission, whereas the **get** method displays the information during transferal. Regardless of whether you use the **get** or **post** method to send the data, it looks the same to the CGI application. The CGI script refers to the data it receives as a **search/query string**. The following statement is an example of a search/query string:

```
fName=Michael&lName=Brooks
```

To send information from one script to another script, you place a question mark after the file name. For example, the string **formmail.pl?lastName=Smith** sends the value of **Smith** for a **form** element named **lastName**. The information is sent to a file named **formmail.pl**.

A query string includes the variable name (or **form** element name), followed by an equal sign (=), followed by the value of the variable. The ampersand sign (**&**) separates various variables. To send the information to the CGI program, you enter the URL of the CGI script, followed by a question mark (**?**) and the search/query string.

To design forms that send data by either method, you can use the **method** attribute of the **<form>** tag, as shown in the following statements:

```
<form method="get">

<form method="post">
```

Regardless of the method used to send the information, the browser formats the information in the same fashion. For example, assume you have a form that is going to submit information to a CGI script. Assume the name of the CGI script is **formmail.pl**, which is located in a folder named **cgi-bin**. The **<form>** tag might resemble the following:

```
<form method="post" action="cgi-bin/formmail.pl">
```

If the form contains two **form** elements, one named **fName** (for first name) and one named **lName** (for last name), the information would be submitted to the Web browser as follows:

```
cgi-bin/formmail.pl?fName=Michael&lName=Brooks
```

In the statement, the URL of the CGI script comes first. The question mark shows the server where the search/query string begins. The **form** element (or variable name) is stated, followed by the equal sign (=). The ampersand sign (&) separates the variables. Obviously, the browser is completely capable of transmitting form data using either method. In some situations, it is necessary to send data directly from JavaScript. To do so, you can build the search/query string in JavaScript from scratch:

```
function buildString() {

        var passString="fName=Michael&lName=Brooks";

        return passString;

}
```

To submit the string, you use a statement such as:

```
location.href="cgi-bin/formmail.pl"+"?"+buildString();
```

In the following exercise, you use JavaScript to communicate with a Java applet that was inserted into a Web page. To view the applet file in your browser, you must install the Java 1.4.2 plug-in on your computer. Designers who are interested in the Java programming language can find the Java source files in the RF_JavaScript_L2>Project_08>java folder.

Communicate with a Java Applet

| 1 | **In your browser and text editor, open gameApplet.html from the WIP_08>java folder.**

This file includes a simple 3-D Tic-Tac-Toe game created by a Java applet.

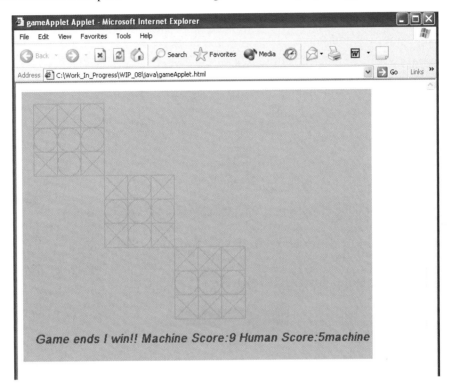

FIGURE 8.12

| 2 | **In your text editor, find the following code.**

```
<object classid="clsid:CAFEEFAC-0014-0002-0000-ABCDEFFEDCBA"
width="600" height="450" align="baseline" codebase=
"http://java.sun.com/products/plugin/autodl/jinstall-1_4_2-
windows-i586.cab#Version=1,4,2,0">
```

The **<object>** tag allows the browser to use the plug-in to display the applet.

| 3 | **Insert the id attribute into the <object> tag.**

```
<object classid="clsid:CAFEEFAC-0014-0002-0000-ABCDEFFEDCBA"
id="gameApplet" width="600" height="450" align="baseline"
codebase="http://java.sun.com/products/plugin/autodl/jinstall-
1_4_2-windows-i586.cab#Version=1,4,2,0">
```

The **id** attribute allows the object to become part of the DOM, allowing you to address it by name in JavaScript.

4   Insert the following code into the script near the bottom of the HTML page.

```
...
</object>
<script language="JavaScript">
// insert code here
myScore=document.gameApplet.getHumanScore();
alert("Your current score is "+myScore);
</script>
    </body>
</html>
```

This code invokes a public method in the applet named **getHumanScore()**.

5   **Save the file in your text editor and refresh your browser.**

An alert box appears. Your score is "0" when the game starts. To check your score during the progress of the game, you could invoke this method by clicking a button.

FIGURE 8.13

6   **Click OK to acknowledge the alert box.**

7   **Close the file in your browser and text editor.**

To Extend Your Knowledge...

DETECTING BROWSER PLUG-INS AND MIME-TYPES

The **plugins[]** and **mimeTypes[]** arrays contain information on installed browser plug-ins and the types of files used in a Web page. This information could be useful to Web developers, but the features aren't supported in many browsers, including many versions of Internet Explorer. As such, developers commonly avoid these features.

LESSON 3   Implementing JavaScript from Flash

With Flash, you can create elaborate vector-based graphics, which makes the program an excellent choice for cutting-edge interfaces. The Flash ActionScript language is based on ECMAScript and is very similar to JavaScript in its syntax and methods.

Even though ActionScript and JavaScript are similar languages, it is often desirable to combine certain elements of Flash with JavaScript's impressive ability to control the browser and interact with HTML. For example, consider that Flash has a built-in method for retrieving Web pages (the **getURL()** method). The following ActionScript code displays the Macromedia home page when a user clicks a button.

```
on (release) {

        getURL("http://www.macromedia.com");

}
```

This statement displays a Web page in much the same way as an HTML hyperlink. The **getURL()** method simply passes the URL to the browser, and then the page loads in the browser window. The **getURL()** method does not allow the same level of control over the size and characteristics of the window as JavaScript's **window.open()** method.

Recall from an earlier project that you can use bookmarklets in URL fields to trigger JavaScript commands. This technique also works when using URLs in ActionScript. To trigger a JavaScript command from within Flash, you use the keyword **javascript**, followed by a JavaScript command in the URL field of the **getURL()** method. For example, consider the following ActionScript code that triggers a JavaScript function from a Flash button:

```
on (release) {

        getURL("javascript:makePopup()");

}
```

The **getURL()** method of triggering a JavaScript function using ActionScript does not work correctly in Internet Explorer 3.0 on Windows, nor does it work properly on Internet Explorer 4.5 or earlier on a Macintosh because these browsers do not support bookmarklets or the **javascript** keyword. To be triggered from ActionScript, the JavaScript function must also be included within the HTML page or in a linked external file.

```
<script language="JavaScript">

        function makePopup() {

        popup=window.open("http://www.macromedia.com","popup",
"height=250, width=200");

}

</script>
```

To reuse the function to create multiple pop-up windows, simply add variables to the function and pass them from the function call from within Flash. For example, when placed in the **URL** attribute of the **getURL()** method in Flash, the following statement passes the information to the JavaScript function as variables:

```
javascript:makePopup('http://www.macromedia.com','thewin',
'height=400,width=400');
```

When you use this method, you must tweak your function so that it can accept and use the information being passed as variables.

```
<script language="JavaScript">
function makePopup(URL,windowName,properties) {
        popup=window.open(URL,windowName,properties);
}
</script>
```

Use ActionScript with JavaScript

This exercise includes a Flash movie. To view the Flash movie in a Web page, you must install the Flash Player 4.0 or higher plug-in. The page may prompt you to download the plug-in if it is not already loaded on your computer.

1   **In your browser, open flashpopupfinished.html from your WIP_08>flashpopup folder.**

FIGURE 8.14

This file shows a simple Flash movie embedded within a Web page.

2   **Click the "open popup" button.**

A pop-up window displays the Against The Clock home page.

| 3 | Close the pop-up window and the open file in your browser. |

| 4 | Open flashpopupfinished.html in your text editor. |

| 5 | Find the following code. |

```
function makePopup() {

        popup=window.open("http://www.againsttheclock.com","popup",
"height=250, width=200");

}
```

This is the JavaScript function that was triggered from the Flash movie.

| 6 | Close the file in your browser and text editor. |

Trigger a JavaScript Function from a Flash Movie

This exercise shows you how to trigger the JavaScript function from within the Flash movie. The exercise assumes that Flash MX (or MX 2004) is loaded on your system and that you have a basic understanding of how to use Flash.

| 1 | In the Flash editor, open flashpopup.fla from the WIP_08>flashpopup folder. |

This is the Flash source file for the movie you used in the previous exercise. The button has not yet been programmed to invoke the JavaScript function.

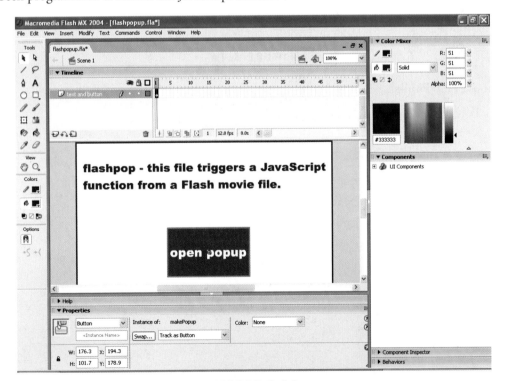

FIGURE 8.15

2 **Single-click the "open popup" button.**

This selects the button.

3 **Choose Window>Development Panels>Actions.**

The Actions panel opens on your screen. The words "Actions-Button" should display in the title bar of the Actions panel. If the words "Actions-Frame" appear in the title bar, you did not select the button.

4 **On the right side of the Actions panel, insert the following code to program the button to trigger the JavaScript function.**

```
on (release) {
    getURL("javascript:makePopup()");
}
```

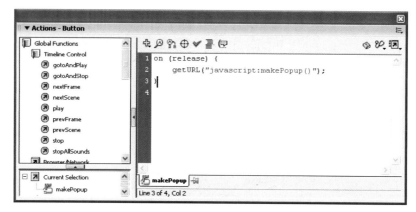

FIGURE 8.16

5 **Choose File>Publish Settings.**

The Publish Settings dialog appears.

6   **In the Publish Settings dialog, make sure Flash (.swf) is the only format selected.**

This step ensures that you do not create a new HTML file, which would overwrite the JavaScript code in the existing HTML file.

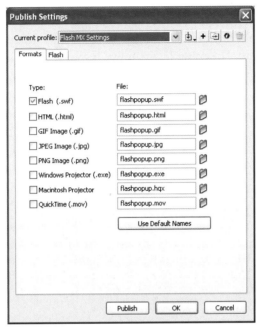

FIGURE 8.17

7   **Click the Publish button, and then click OK.**

8   **In your browser, open flashpopup.html from the WIP_08>flashpopup folder and test your file.**

The file should work exactly the same as in the previous exercise.

9   **Save your changes and close the Flash editor.**

10   **Close the open file in your browser.**

To Extend Your Knowledge...

USING JAVASCRIPT IN FLASH

The Publish Settings feature in Flash allows you to create an HTML page to display a Flash movie. If the HTML option is enabled in the movie's Publish Settings dialog box, the page is recreated every time the Flash file is published. A common mistake is to insert a JavaScript function into the HTML page, and then accidentally overwrite the existing code — including any JavaScript code — when the page is republished. To avoid this problem, uncheck the HTML option in Flash's Publish Settings dialog box.

LESSON 4 Using JavaScript-to-Flash Communications

To insert Flash files into HTML documents, you use the **<object>** tag. By specifying an **id** attribute within the **<object>** tag, you can also add a Flash movie to the DOM and communicate with the movie from JavaScript. Older browsers may require the **<embed>** tag to display the file. The **<embed>** tag also allows communication between JavaScript and Flash movies on older browsers by using a **name** attribute and setting the **swLiveConnect** attribute to **true**. For example, the following code embeds a Flash file into an HTML page that is visible in most browsers and can be accessed through JavaScript.

```
<object classid="clsid:D27CDB6E-AE6D-11cf-96B8-444553540000" code-
base="http://download.macromedia.com/pub/shockwave/cabs/flash/swflas
h.cab#version=5,0,0,0" WIDTH="400" HEIGHT="180" id="myFlash">

    <PARAM NAME=movie VALUE="flash_to_javascript.swf">

    <PARAM NAME=quality VALUE=high>

    <PARAM NAME=bgcolor VALUE=#CCCCCC>

    <EMBED src="flash_to_javascript.swf" quality=high bgcolor=
#CCCCCC  WIDTH="400" HEIGHT="180" NAME="myFlash" swLiveConnect=
"true" TYPE="application/x-shockwave-flash" PLUGINSPAGE=
"http://www.macromedia.com/go/getflashplayer"></EMBED>

</object>
```

Extracting Variable Information from Flash

Using the **fscommand()** method, you can send information from ActionScript. The **fscommand()** method allows a Flash movie to send commands to the media player that is currently playing the movie. The media player is usually the Flash plug-in used to display the Flash file in the browser. Assume you have a variable in Flash named **myVar**. Using the **send_var** parameter of the **fscommand()** method, you can use the following statement to send information from ActionScript to the browser:

```
fscommand ("send_var", myVar);
```

JavaScript has the ability to determine when information has been sent from the **fscommand()** method in ActionScript. Consider this function, which automatically detects the value sent from ActionScript and inserts the value into a variable known as **args**:

```
var InternetExplorer = navigator.appName.indexOf("Microsoft") != -1;

function myFlash_DoFSCommand(command, args)                  {

  var myFlashObj = InternetExplorer ? myFlash : document.myFlash;

}
```

Inserting Variables into Flash from JavaScript

Assume that you embedded a Flash file into an HTML document and used the **id** attribute and **name** attribute to name the Flash movie. You can use the **SetVariable()** method in JavaScript to dynamically change a variable in the Flash movie:

```
window.document.myFlash.SetVariable("myVar", sendText);
```

In this example, the value of the **sendText** variable, which exists in the JavaScript code, is being inserted into the **myVar** variable that exists within the Flash movie. The **SetVariable()** method is available for any Flash movie represented in JavaScript.

Use Flash-to-JavaScript Communications

In this exercise, you use a Flash file to pass information to JavaScript and create an alert box. To complete this exercise, you must install the Flash 4.0 or higher browser plug-in.

1   **In your text editor and browser, open flash_to_javascript.html from your WIP_08 folder.**

This file contains a simple Flash file embedded into an HTML document.

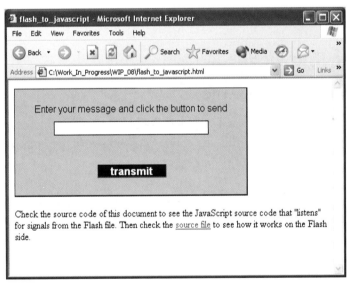

FIGURE 8.18

2   **Enter a message and click the "transmit" button.**

An alert box appears with your message.

FIGURE 8.19

| 3 | Click OK to acknowledge the alert message. |

| 4 | In your text editor, find the following lines of code. |

```
...
var InternetExplorer=navigator.appName.indexOf("Microsoft") != -1;
function myFlash_DoFSCommand(command, args)                    {
  var myFlashObj=InternetExplorer ? myFlash : document.myFlash;
  alert (args);
}
...
```

This code determines if Internet Explorer is being used and if the Flash file named **myFlash** is present. Additionally, if information is sent using the **fscommand()** method in Flash, an alert box is generated.

| 5 | Close the file in your browser and text editor. |

To Extend Your Knowledge...

FLASH-TO-JAVASCRIPT COMMUNICATIONS

Macromedia, the company that develops Flash and Dreamweaver, maintains an extensive technical support site at www.macromedia.com. This site contains a wide variety of information for developers, including tutorials on Flash-to-JavaScript communications.

LESSON 5 Incorporating Dreamweaver Behaviors

The Macromedia Dreamweaver application is the editing program of choice for many Web page designers. Dreamweaver contains a number of valuable features, including code hints and reference panels for CSS, JavaScript, and HTML code. The program also contains a number of pre-written JavaScript scripts that it refers to as **behaviors**. Behaviors have simple interfaces that allow you to customize the scripts to meet your specific needs. Behaviors are tied to specific HTML tags through JavaScript event handlers. Behaviors can be added quickly and easily to a Web page, and they are designed to ensure optimal browser compatibility.

This lesson focuses on the use of JavaScript behaviors in Dreamweaver. The lesson assumes a basic knowledge of Dreamweaver and is written specifically for Dreamweaver MX 2004 users.

Selecting an HTML Tag

Before selecting a behavior, you must first choose the HTML tag that will be bound to the behavior using inline JavaScript. You can choose a tag by selecting its content in the Design view portion of the screen. For example, you can select an **<img>** tag by selecting the associated image.

You can also select a tag by choosing the entire tag (including the ending portion) in the Code view window. The easiest way to select a tag is to use the tag selector, which is the gray bar near the bottom of the Design view section of the screen.

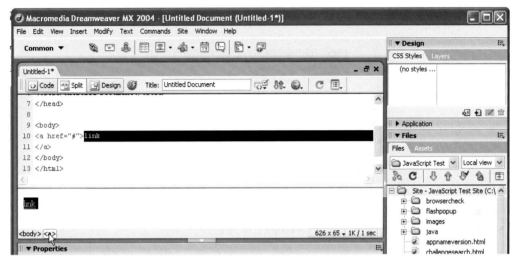

FIGURE 8.20

Targeting Specific Browsers

To select a behavior in the Behaviors panel, simply click the "+" button to display the full list of available behaviors, as shown in Figure 8.21. The Show Events For option allows you to specify a target browser. For example, if you choose IE 6.0 as the target browser, Dreamweaver will only allow event handlers that are fully compatible with the selected tag and the target browser to be used with a particular behavior.

FIGURE 8.21

Choosing a Behavior

Once you select a tag, click the "+" button in the Behaviors panel to view all the behaviors that are fully compatible with that tag and the target browser. For example, if you want to create a pop-up window, simply choose the Open Browser Window behavior. This behavior uses the `window.open()` method to create a pop-up window.

FIGURE 8.22

Once you select a behavior, you see a menu of available options for the particular behavior. To open the Against The Clock home page in a pop-up window with a navigation toolbar and location toolbar, you would activate the following options in the Open Browser Window dialog.

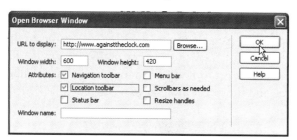

FIGURE 8.23

Specifying the Event Handler

Behaviors are attached to tags through JavaScript event handlers appearing inline as HTML attributes. Once a behavior is attached to a tag, you can view the behavior by choosing the tag and opening the Behaviors panel. The Behaviors panel shows the behaviors in two columns: the left column shows the event handler attached to the tag, and the right column shows the name of the behavior.

FIGURE 8.24

Dreamweaver provides a list of event handlers that are compatible with the selected tag for the target browser. In general, newer browsers offer many more options for event handlers than older browsers. To modify the parameters of a behavior, simply double-click the behavior name in the right column of the Behaviors panel.

Add an Image Swap Behavior in Dreamweaver

1 In Dreamweaver, open imageswap.html from the WIP_08 folder.

2 Single-click the small red lipstick image located in the upper-left corner of the page.

Single-clicking selects the **\<img>** tag and its content.

3 In the Behaviors panel, click the "+" button.

FIGURE 8.25

All the behaviors associated with the **\<img>** tag display.

4 Choose the Swap Image behavior.

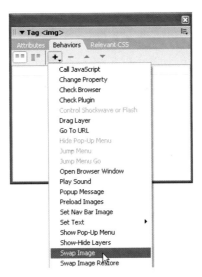

FIGURE 8.26

The Swap Image dialog box appears. From here, you can customize the behavior.

5   Choose the "image detail in layer lgImage" option.

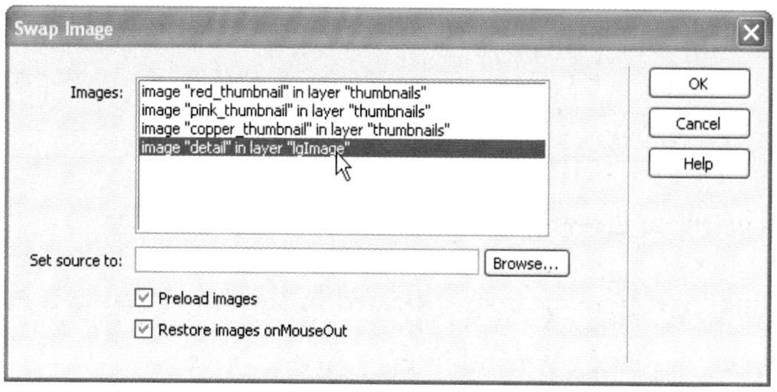

FIGURE 8.27

This option sets the image to swap when the event occurs.

6   **Click Browse to set the source of the image.**

The operating system generates an Open File browser window.

7   **Choose red_lipstick.jpg from the WIP_08>images folder and click OK.**

Assuming you leave the Preload images and Restore images onMouseOut boxes checked, Dreamweaver will add the necessary script to preload images with the page and restore the original image when the user rolls off the thumbnail image.

8   **Click OK.**

The behavior is added to the **<img>** tag.

9   **Look at the Behaviors panel.**

You see two items: Swap Image and Swap Image Restore. You successfully added a swap image behavior.

10   **Save the page. Press the "F12" key to preview the page in your Web browser.**

11   **Roll your mouse over the first thumbnail.**

The large image should change.

12   **Close the file in your browser and close Dreamweaver.**

To Extend Your Knowledge...

DREAMWEAVER BEHAVIORS

To download additional behaviors, simply click the Get More Behaviors option in the Behaviors panel. This option takes you to the Macromedia Exchange Web site. The site allows developers to submit behaviors that other users can download or purchase.

LESSON 6   Writing XHTML-Compliant Scripts

Plans are underway to replace HTML with **_XHTML_**, the eXtensible HyperText Markup Language. XHTML is the natural evolution of HTML. XHTML is designed to align HTML more closely with **_XML_**, the eXtensible Markup Language. XML is similar to HTML, but includes one major difference: XML allows you to define your own tags. For example, a company may define a stock quote as the company symbol (**AAPL**) followed by the current stock price, as shown in the following statement:

```
<stockquote>AAPL, $61.00</stockquote>
```

XML offers several advantages over HTML, including the ability to easily share data between different computer systems or devices. Data sent through XML tends to have small file sizes, and it can be formatted in the same way that CSS can be used to format HTML. The theory behind XML is that it allows devices to download a list of definitions for the tags that are used in a particular document.

XHTML is simply a set of definitions using the XML specification. The browser already contains the XHTML tag definitions, but those definitions could also be downloaded by compatible devices. XHTML is designed to serve as a bridge solution on a migration path to full XML.

XHTML is designed to provide Internet content to equipment that has limited processing resources, including PDA devices and wireless phones. Currently, browsers consist primarily of code that prevents the display of errors generated by poorly written code. Newer devices will consist of simpler browser-type applications because these devices will have limited processing power. This, in turn, will force developers to write cleaner code that will not generate errors.

The W3C needed to define a "stricter" programming language with some added features — a language that would provide an easy migration path from HTML to XML. The resolution to the W3C's problem is XHTML 1.0. Newer browsers support the XHTML 1.0 specification, which is backward compatible with HTML 4.0 and can be viewed in older browsers. Since XHTML is a reformulation of HTML 4.0, it is a straightforward task to turn existing HTML into XHTML-compliant code.

XHTML compliance requires a number of simple steps to upgrade pages and ensure the pages continue to work as the industry moves toward XML adoption. This lesson focuses on XHTML rules that affect the use of JavaScript in various ways.

The Type Attribute and <script> Tags

The **type** attribute should be used in **<script>** tags. The **type** attribute allows the browser to know what type of information is being downloaded in the script. This information is particularly useful when specifying an external JavaScript file to be downloaded by the browser. The **type** attribute is written as **type="text/JavaScript"** when creating JavaScript code. Consider the following example of a **<script>** tag that incorporates an external function using XHTML-compliant code:

```
<script language="JavaScript" type="text/JavaScript"
src="myCodes.js">
```

Strictly speaking, the **type** attribute is not necessary in pages that do not contain external scripts because any embedded scripts will download as part of the text of the page. The XHTML specification, however, requires that all **<script>** tags use the **type** attribute.

Lowercase Tag Names and Attributes

Unlike HTML, XHTML is case sensitive. All tag names and attributes must be written in lowercase characters. When writing XHTML, the following statement would be considered incorrect:

```
<BODY BGColor="#fffff0" TEXT="#000000" onLoad="myFunction()">
```

Instead, you would write the following statement to ensure XHTML compliance:

```
<body bgcolor="#fffff0" text="#000000" onload="myFunction()">
```

JavaScript event handlers used in inline code must be written in all lowercase characters because they, too, are HTML attributes. This requirement is different than JavaScript's standard use of camelback notation. This change occasionally creates compatibility issues in older browsers (even though HTML attributes are supposed to be case insensitive).

Attribute Values and Quotes

You must place attribute values within quotes. The quotes can be single or double, as long as you use matching pairs. For example, the following statement would not be accepted by XHTML, but would work under the older HTML standards:

```
<body bgcolor=#fffff0>
```

You can easily change the code to ensure XHTML compliance:

```
<body bgcolor="#fffff0">
```

Code triggered by inline event handlers must also be placed within quotes.

Embedded Style Sheets/Scripts within the CDATA Section

Scripts that are embedded into Web pages must contain a **CDATA** section. A **CDATA** section starts with **<![CDATA[** and ends with **]]>**. For example:

```
<script language="JavaScript" type="text/javascript">
//<![CDATA[
alert("Hi");
//]]>
</script>
```

Scripts must be included within the **CDATA** section to ensure that the XML parser will not try to interpret the script code. This allows the interpreter to work more efficiently with fewer errors, since scripting languages often include characters that also have meaning in XML or XHTML. For example, consider the less-than comparison operator (**<**) in JavaScript, which signals the beginning of a markup tag in XHTML.

Replace Tag Names with Tag IDs

The purpose of the **name** attribute in a markup tag was to provide a unique identifier for an object. In XHTML 1.0, the **id** attribute serves this purpose, as the **name** attribute is currently being phased out (deprecated). The **name** attribute may be removed completely in the next version of XHTML. In cases such as the **<form>** tag, which requires the **name** attribute to properly pass data to a Web server, the XHTML 1.0 specification recommends that you use both the **name** attribute and the **id** attribute to prevent problems in certain browsers.

Convert a Script to XHTML-Compliant Code

1   **In your text editor, open xhtml.html from your WIP_08 folder.**

2   **Add the `type` attribute to the `<script>` tag and the CDATA tag.**

```
<html xmlns="http://www.w3.org/1999/xhtml">

<head>

<title> Make page XHTML Compliant </title>

<script language="JavaScript" type="text/JavaScript">

//<![CDATA[

function MM_reloadPage(init) {  //reloads the window if Nav4 resized

    if (init==true) with (navigator) {if ((appName=="Netscape")&&
(parseInt(appVersion)==4)) {

...
```

3   **Add the ending portion of the CDATA tag at the end of the script.**

```
...

    if (obj.style) { obj=obj.style;
v=(v=='show')?'visible':(v=='hide')?'hidden':v; }

    obj.visibility=v; }

}

//]]>

</script>

<link href="continents.css" rel="stylesheet" type="text/css" />

...
```

4   **Find the following line of code.**

```
<div ID=northAmerica>
```

This line of code uses the **ID** attribute in uppercase letters. This is a violation of XHTML rules for HTML attributes.

5   **Change the `<div>` tag you found in the previous step to use lowercase letters for the `id` attribute.**

```
<div id=northAmerica>
```

6   **Modify the same `<div>` tag to enclose the attribute value within double quotes.**

```
<div id="northAmerica">
```

Attributes must be written in lowercase letters and the assigned values must be placed within double quotes.

7   **Save the file in your text editor and open the file in your browser.**

Your file is now XHTML compliant. This file creates a DHTML rollover effect with content that changes as you move your mouse over each menu item.

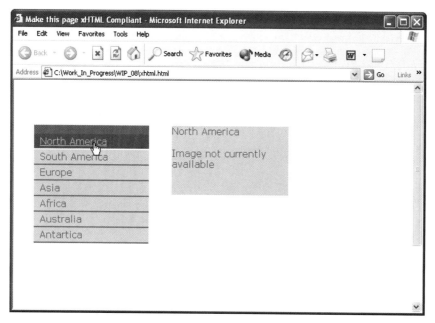

FIGURE 8.28

8   **Close the file in your text editor and browser.**

To Extend Your Knowledge...

XHTML COMPLIANCE

Many developers ignore the **CDATA** tag requirement when creating scripts. Strictly speaking, this requirement is primarily aimed at devices that may not support scripting languages (such as JavaScript) or may support specialty scripting languages in the future (such as a language developed specifically for Internet-enabled digital phones). For best results, include the **CDATA** tag to ensure full XHTML compliance.

S U M M A R Y

In this project, you discovered how to use advanced JavaScript methods to determine a user's computer platform, browser type, and version. You also briefly considered how a Web page can dynamically compensate for different platforms and browsers. This process becomes increasingly complex because of differences in the ways that various browsers report version information.

You found that JavaScript works well as a client-side scripting language, but it shows limitations in the areas of server-side scripting and complex animation. When you use JavaScript with other technologies (such as CGI scripts, Java, and Flash), you can take advantage of the strengths of each technology. This technique allows you to generate far more compelling results than when you use only one of the technologies in isolation. Similarly, you can also use JavaScript to compensate for the limitations of other technologies, including Flash's inability to control various aspects of a browser window.

C A R E E R S   I N   D E S I G N

USE CSS TO ENHANCE YOUR PORTFOLIO

Cascading Style Sheets (CSS) offer a simple and consistent way to build a professional portfolio Web site. When building your first page, create an external file that includes all the styles you need throughout the site. As you create each page, include code that links each page to the external style sheet. This method has several advantages, the most important of which is consistency. Using CSS, you can apply fonts, colors, and styles consistently across all pages in the site. When potential employers see that you apply styles consistently, they will know that you are a careful, detail-oriented designer — an essential quality for landing a job in a design-oriented field.

Other benefits of CSS include allowing you to write source code in an organized fashion, finishing the job in less time, and updating an entire site by making changes to one simple text file — which is an enormous time-saving feature.

KEY TERMS

Applet

Behavior

CGI (Common Gateway
Interface)

Public methods

Public properties

Search/query string

XHTML

XML

CHECKING CONCEPTS AND TERMS

MULTIPLE CHOICE

Circle the letter that matches the correct answer for each of the following questions.

1. What information is returned from the **appName** property of the **navigator** object?

   a. The language of the user's computer

   b. The version of the browser software

   c. The operating system of the user's computer

   d. The company that made the browser

   e. None of the above

2. What information is returned from the **platform** property of the **navigator** object?

   a. The language of the user's computer

   b. The version of the browser software

   c. The operating system of the user's computer

   d. The company that made the browser

   e. None of the above

3. You use the _____ tag to insert a Java applet or a Flash movie into a Web page.

   a. `<element>`

   b. `<plugin>`

   c. `<object>`

   d. `<movie>`

4. Why is it useful to include the **id** attribute when embedding a Flash file or Java applet into a Web page?

   a. It ensures user privacy.

   b. It allows a security certificate to identify the object.

   c. It allows the object to be referenced in JavaScript.

   d. It allows Dreamweaver to apply a behavior to the object.

5. Why is it difficult to write code to determine the exact browser type and browser version being used by a Web surfer?

   a. Many browsers do not support any properties with browser or browser version information.

   b. Security concerns prevent information from being shared by most browsers.

   c. Web browsers report **navigator** properties in different formats.

   d. None of the above.

6. Which of the following browser/s supports the **navigator** object?

   a. Microsoft Internet Explorer

   b. Netscape Navigator and Netscape Communicator

   c. Mozilla Firefox

   d. All of the above

   e. None of the above

7. How can the **getURL()** method in Flash ActionScript be used with JavaScript?

   a. To link an external JavaScript file to ActionScript

   b. To create inline JavaScript code

   c. To trigger a JavaScript function using the **javascript** keyword

   d. None of the above

8. Information can be passed to a JavaScript function by invoking the function using the **getURL()** method in ActionScript.

   a. True

   b. False

9. Which of the following is required by the rules of XHTML compliance?

   a. The **type** attribute must be used within **<script>** tags.

   b. All tag names and attributes must be written in lowercase characters.

   c. Attribute values must be placed within quotes.

   d. All of the above.

   e. None of the above.

10. How are XML and XHTML related?

   a. Both are designed to minimize the need for error-tolerating code in browsers.

   b. XHMTL is meant to transition browsers to the full use of XML.

   c. XHTML is a set of tag definitions using the XML standard.

   d. All of the above.

   e. None of the above.

DISCUSSION QUESTIONS

1. What steps do you follow to insert a Dreamweaver behavior into a Web page?

2. Why is it advantageous to combine JavaScript with other technologies?

3. How do XHTML rules affect JavaScript code?

4. Why is it difficult to extract the exact version number and type of browser from a user's computer?

SKILL DRILL

Skill Drill exercises reinforce project skills. Each skill reinforced is the same, or nearly the same, as a skill presented in the project. Detailed instructions are provided in a step-by-step format. You should work through these exercises in the order provided.

1. Check for a Netscape Browser

In this exercise, you use the **language** property to determine whether a site visitor is using a Netscape-based browser. If this property exists (has a value assigned to it), the visitor must be using this type of browser because the property does not exist in non-Netscape browsers.

1. In your text editor, open skilldetermine.html.

   A script was started for you in the head of the document.

2. Create an **if** statement that determines whether the **language** property of the **navigator** object is equal to **en-US**. If the condition evaluates to **true**, you should output the message, "You are using a Netscape-based browser." If the condition evaluates to **false**, create an **else** statement that says, "You are not using a Netscape-based browser."

3. Save and test your file. If you are using Internet Explorer, you should see the "You are not using a Netscape-based browser" message.

4. If you have a Netscape- or Mozilla-based browser installed on your system, attempt to view the file in that browser. The message you receive should say, "You are using a Netscape-based browser."

5. Save your changes and keep the file open for the next Skill Drill.

2. Check for an Internet Explorer Browser

In this exercise, you use the **userLanguage** property to determine whether a site visitor is using an Internet Explorer-based browser. The **userLanguage** property does not exist in Netscape-based browsers, making this an easy way to determine the type of browser being used.

1. In the open skilldetermine.html, create another **if** statement. This statement should check to see whether the **userLanguage** property of the **navigator** object contains a value of **en-us**.

   Note: the value must be in all lowercase letters to work correctly. You should notice that IE uses a different property and reports the value slightly differently than Netscape browsers by reporting the value in all lowercase letters.

2. If the **if** statement you created in Step 1 evaluates to **true**, output the message, "You must be using Internet Explorer."

3. Create an **else** statement that outputs the message, "You must not be using an Internet Explorer-based browser."

4. Save and test your file.

5. Close the file in your browser and text editor.

3. Make a Script XHTML Compliant

You were asked to update an older Web page, ensuring that it adheres to newer standards. One of your team members started the job. Your job is to finish the necessary steps to modify the existing scripts, ensuring XHTML compliance.

1. In your browser and text editor, open skillxhtml.html from your WIP_08 folder.

2. Test the file by moving your mouse over the image.

    An alert box appears.

3. Find the **<script>** tag in the head of the document. Add the **type** attribute as required by XHTML-compliance rules.

4. Add code to create a **CDATA** section as required by XHTML compliance rules.

5. The image uses the **onMouseOver** event handler, placed inline in the **<img>** tag. Modify this event handler so it uses all lowercase letters to ensure XHTML compliance.

6. Save and close the file in your browser and text editor.

4. Use Dreamweaver to Determine Available Event Handlers

It is often difficult to remember which event handlers can be used with specific HTML tags. For example, older browsers do not allow **onclick** events to be used with **<img>** tags. In this exercise, you use Dreamweaver to determine which events are available for a specific tag in a specific browser. The Dreamweaver application is required for this exercise.

1. In Dreamweaver, open WIP_08>skillsetevents.html.

2. Make sure you are in Design view. Single-click the image shown on the page to select the associated **<img>** tag.

3. Open the Behaviors panel.

    The image already has a behavior that generates a rollover image.

FIGURE 8.29

4.   Click the "+" button and choose Show Events For>IE 3.0.

FIGURE 8.30

5.   Choose another event for the swap image behavior.

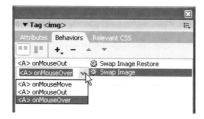

FIGURE 8.31

Since you are using IE 3.0 standards, only three event handlers are available for this tag.

6.   Change the Behaviors panel to show events for IE 6.0.

7.   Change the event handler for the image swap behavior to onClick.

8.   Close setevents.html and close Dreamweaver.

CHALLENGE

Challenge exercises expand on, or are somewhat related to, skills presented in the lessons. Each exercise provides a brief introduction, followed by instructions presented in a numbered-step format that are not as detailed as those in the Skill Drill exercises. You should work through these exercises in order.

1. Determine Specific Browser Version

Properties of the **navigator** object contain clues to the browser type, browser version, and operating system on the user's computer. **Navigator** properties are typically returned as a string. Since different browsers report information in different ways, it is often difficult to extract version information. In this Challenge, you use code to extract the browser name and version information from the string returned from the browser.

1. In your text editor, open browsercheck.js from the WIP_08>browsercheck folder and examine the code. (This file contains a set of functions designed to determine platform, browser type, and version.)

2. In your text editor and browser, open browsercheck.html from the WIP_08>browsercheck folder and examine the code.

    A link to a file named browsercheck.js was already created and functions were invoked from the file to determine the user's operating system.

3. Return to your text editor and find the following comment.

    ```
    // detect browser type and version
    ```

4. Insert the following code below the comment to determine the browser type and version.

    ```
    ...
    // detect browser type and version
    if (detectNetscape()) {
            document.write("Netscape browser detected"+"<br>");
            document.write("version: "+findNetscapeVersion()+"<br>");
            if(findNetscapeVersion()>=5) {
                    document.write("You have a compatible browser.");
            } // end if
      } // end if
    if (detectIE()) {
            document.write("Internet Explorer browser detected"+"<br>");
            document.write("version: "+findIEversion()+"<br>");
            if(findIEversion()>=5) {
                    document.write("You have a compatible browser.");
            } // end if
      } // end if
    // -->
    </script>
    ...
    ```

The code also checks to see if the user has a version 5.0 or higher browser.

5. Save the file in your text editor and refresh your browser.

Your results may differ slightly from the screen shot shown below, depending on which platform, browser, and version you are using.

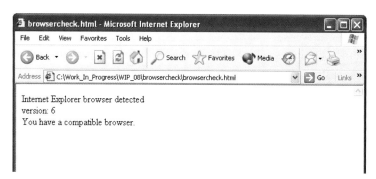

FIGURE 8.32

6. Modify the code to determine whether the user has version 7 or greater of Internet Explorer.

7. Save and test your file.

Your browser should fail the test, assuming you are using version 6 or earlier of Internet Explorer.

8. Close the file in your browser and text editor.

2. Use Dreamweaver to Improve Usability

In this Challenge, you enhance a search form to improve usability. This exercise requires that you use the Dreamweaver application.

1. In Dreamweaver, open challengesearch.html from your WIP_08 folder.

2. Preview the Web page by choosing File>Preview in Browser and choosing your default browser.

3. In the browser, click in the text field.

To enter a search term, you must select and delete the sentence, "What can we help you find?" because this is the default value assigned to this field.

4. In the Dreamweaver window, single-click in the text field to select the **<input>** tag.

5. Select the Set Text of Text Field behavior, which appears under Set Text in the Behaviors panel.

6. Click OK to dismiss the dialog box.

7. Change the event handler associated with this behavior to **onFocus**.

8. Save your changes and preview the page in your browser.

9. Click the text field in the page.

The default text is removed and the field is ready for entry.

10. Close the page in your browser and close Dreamweaver.

3. Work with Dreamweaver Behaviors

In this Challenge, you use Dreamweaver to create a disjointed effect. To accomplish the task, you use the Swap Image behavior. This behavior uses DHTML to turn the visibility of layers on and off in the browser.

1.   In Dreamweaver, open challengeswap.html from your WIP_08 folder.

     This is essentially the same file you used in a previous exercise.

2.   Select the first thumbnail image and examine the attached behaviors.

     The Swap Image behavior was added to this image to create a rollover effect. The rollover effect changes the main image.

3.   Select the second thumbnail, which is the sm_pink_lipstick.jpg image.

4.   Apply the Swap Image behavior to this image. Choose the image named "detail" in the lgImage layer. Set the source to the pink_lipstick.jpg image, located in the WIP_08>images folder.

5.   Select the third thumbnail, which is the sm_copper_lipstick.jpg image.

6.   Repeat Step 4, but use the copper_lipstick.jpg image as the image source.

7.   Save and test your file.

     As you roll over each of the three thumbnails, the main image should change.

8.   Close the file in your browser and close Dreamweaver.

4. Communicate from JavaScript to Flash

Using the **id** attribute, you can access Flash movies through the DOM. In this Challenge, you use the **SetVariable()** method in JavaScript to change the value of a variable that exists within a Flash movie.

1.   In your text editor, open javascript_to_flash.html from your WIP_08>JStoFlash folder.

2.   Insert an **id** attribute into the **<object>** tag and set the **id** equal to "myFlash".

3.   Find the following code.

     The **form** element has been scripted to trigger a JavaScript function.

```
<input type="text" name="sendText" maxlength="45"
onChange="doPassVar(this);">
```

4.   Insert the following function into the script in the head of the document.

```
function doPassVar(args){
     var sendText=args.value;
     window.document.myFlash.SetVariable("myVar", sendText);
}
```

5. Save the file in your text editor and open it in your browser.

6. Enter some text into the HTML form field at the top of the page, and then click your mouse anywhere else on the page to blur this form element.

   The value you enter should appear in the Flash movie.

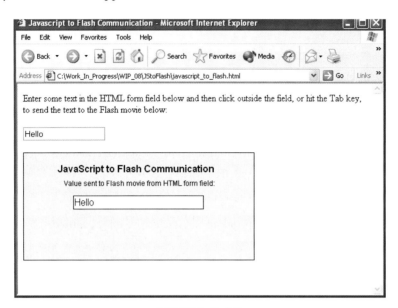

FIGURE 8.33

7. Close the file in your browser and text editor.

   If you want to examine the Flash source file, you can find it in your Resource Folder.

PORTFOLIO BUILDER

Create a Learning Experience

Combining JavaScript with other technologies offers exciting new possibilities for interactivity. Consider a situation where you are teaching children a simple skill, such as counting from 1 to 10. You could use HTML to create a simple, easy-to-understand interface, and then you could use Flash to create a rich media experience. The final step would be to use JavaScript to bridge the gap between those two technologies.

In your browser, open rabbits.html from the WIP_08>Portfolio_Builder_08 folder. This page contains a form field and a cartoon animation of a rabbit jumping across the screen. Your job is to pass a number entered into the form field to the Flash movie. For example, if the user enters the number "4," four rabbits will hop across the screen. The intent of this page is to teach children the numbers 1 through 10.

The Flash file already contains the necessary ActionScript to complete much of the work. A variable named **numRabbits** was created to contain the number of rabbits that move across the screen. A **for** loop was designed to add or remove rabbits when the number of rabbits changes. Flash developers should feel free to examine the source code of the Flash movie, which is included in the WIP_08>Portfolio_Builder_08 folder.

PORTFOLIO BUILDER

Create a Learning Experience (continued)

Your goal is to finish the JavaScript code that will enable communication between the HTML page and the Flash movie. To reach your goal, complete the following tasks:

1. Create an **id** attribute for the Flash movie so it can be addressed from JavaScript as an object.

2. Create the **doPassVar** function that, when invoked, will change the **numRabbits** variable in the Flash movie to the value of the form field. Hint: you can use the code from the Challenge exercise entitled "Communicate from JavaScript to Flash" as a guide.

3. Test the page to make sure the variable value passes to the Flash movie. As soon as you change the value in the form field and click somewhere else, the number of rabbits should change.

4. Modify the JavaScript code so the number entered must be between 1 and 10 before the number is sent to ActionScript. Otherwise, an alert box should be generated and the value in the form field should return to blank, without submitting the number to the Flash movie.

5. Test your script to make sure it performs as expected.

INTEGRATING PROJECT

This Integrating Project is designed to reflect a real-world JavaScript programming job. It draws on the skills that you learned throughout this book, as well as the skills you learned in *Essentials for Design: JavaScript Level 1*. The files you need to complete this project are located in the RF_JavaScript_L2>IP folder.

Southeastern Mortgage Solutions

As a junior Web developer for a small marketing firm, you were asked to use JavaScript commands to enhance and finish a Web site that was only partially completed. The site you will create is a simplified version of Southeastern Mortgage Solutions' actual site, which is located at www.SEMortgageSolutions.com. This site is designed for potential clients who are considering buying a house or refinancing an existing mortgage. The goal of the site is to offer honest and impartial information on the mortgage process. Site visitors can submit preliminary mortgage applications via online forms.

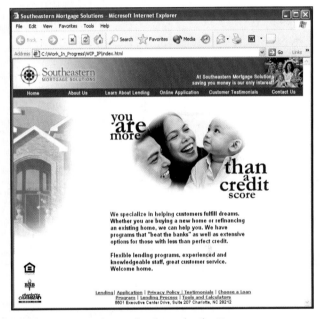

The site is designed for any browser resolution; it uses tables that expand or contract to accommodate resolution changes. The site's structure and design have already been approved by the client. Content has been gathered, and many of the components of the site have been built. Some JavaScript has been incorporated into the site to create rollovers in the top navigation structure. Content pages have also been built. Every page was developed from a standard template to ensure consistency and professionalism.

In addition to creating the content pages, members of the project team also developed a simple Flash animation for the home page that promotes the company's branding strategies, and they added an interactive Flash animation that represents the seven steps of the loan process.

A Tools and Calculators subsection allows mortgage clients to receive preliminary estimates on mortgage loan costs. Plans call for several pages of calculation tools, but the initial site will contain only one page that calculates the monthly mortgage payment. When the user accesses this page and fills out the form, a report will be generated, showing the monthly payment calculated from the supplied information.

Your job is to write the JavaScript code that will create the first mortgage calculator. You will ensure that the form elements are set up correctly, as well as generate JavaScript code that performs specific actions when the user submits the form. As part of this process, you will create functions that validate the data entered into the calculator and complete the necessary calculations. Lastly, you will write JavaScript code to dynamically create a report that displays the results of the calculations.

Set Up and Explore the Site

1 Copy the contents of the RF_JavaScript_L2>IP folder to your Work_In_Progress>WIP_IP folder.

From this point on, when asked to open a file, assume the file is located within the WIP_IP folder.

2 Look at the files to see how the site is organized.

The images folder contains all the images used in the site, and the Flash folder contains all of the Flash files. Pages with address information begin with "add_" as the first part of the file name. Subpages of the library section have "lib_" as the first part of the file name. Notice how the subpages in each section have a standard naming scheme that starts with the same letters. This naming convention groups similar files within the directory structure, allowing for easier site management.

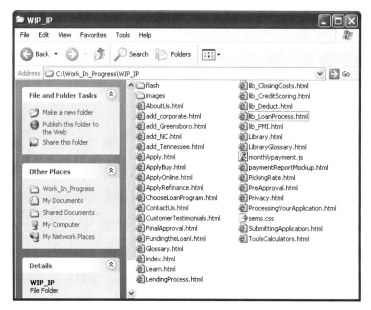

FIGURE IP.1

3 Open WIP_IP>index.html in your browser and explore the completed components of the site.

This is the first page of the Web site. The Flash plug-in (version 4 or higher) is required to see the animation on the opening page. If it is not already loaded on your system, you can download the plug-in from www.macromedia.com.

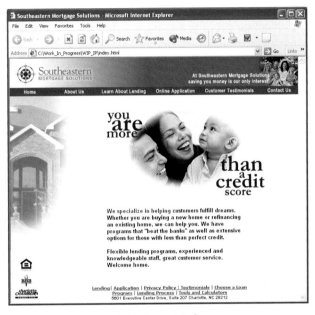

FIGURE IP.2

4 Click various links to access the other pages of the site. The forms do not perform any actions when submitted.

5 Scroll to the bottom of the page and click the Tools and Calculators link. This link takes you to a page that calculates the monthly mortgage payment. The page doesn't work. One of your tasks is to complete the scripting for the mortgage calculator shown on this page.

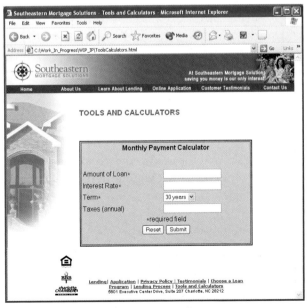

FIGURE IP.3

6 Close the file in your Web browser.

7 In your text editor, open monthlypayment.js from the WIP_IP folder.

You will use these JavaScript functions to finish the mortgage calculator. To minimize the amount of typing necessary to complete the job, the functions were partially written for you. Your task is to complete the process so that the form and external functions work together. You must also complete the external functions.

8 Read the description of each function (shown in the comments at the top of the file), and then scroll through the file and examine the code.

When the form is submitted, your script will extract information from the form, validate the form, complete the mortgage calculations, and write a report of the results.

9 Open paymentReportMockup.html in your Web browser.

Another designer already completed a mock-up of the report that will be generated from your script. Numbers were placed in the mock-up to demonstrate a sample calculation. You are looking at the mock-up in a standard browser window, but the script will create the page in a pop-up window. The report consists of a single table, centered on the page. To create the report, JavaScript will use variables from the calculations and write the HTML dynamically.

FIGURE IP.4

10 Close the file in your text editor.

You are now familiar with the site and the tasks you need to complete. In the next section, you set up the form to interact with the script. Later on, you finish the functions that extract and validate form data and generate a report.

Configure the Form to Work with JavaScript

1   Open the file named ToolsCalculators.html in your text editor.

This page contains the mortgage calculator form.

2   Find the following comment in the head section of the HTML document.

```
<!-- insert code to figure monthly payment -->
```

FIGURE IP.5

3   Insert the following code to create the link to the functions in the external file.

```
...
<meta http-equiv="Content-Type" content="text/html; charset=iso-
8859-1">

<link rel="stylesheet" href="sems" type="text/css">

<!-- insert code to figure monthly payment -->

<script language="JavaScript" type="text/JavaScript" src="monthly-
payment.js">

</script>

<script language="JavaScript" type="text/JavaScript" >

<!--

function MM_swapImgRestore() { //v3.0

...
```

4   Find the following code.

```
<!--********** form starts here************ -->
<form method="post" action="javascript:void(0)">
```

This code starts the form. Notice that a bookmarklet keeps the browser from reloading the page or taking any other action when the form is submitted.

5   Change the code to read as follows.

```
<!--********** form starts here************ -->
<formmethod="post" name="paymentCalc" id="paymentCalc"
action="javascript:void(0)" onsubmit="return validateInfo()">
```

The **onsubmit** handler detects when the form is submitted and stops the submission if the data is entered incorrectly. You assigned a form **name** and **id**, which you can use in JavaScript.

6   Scroll through the code that makes up the form and look for **<input>** tags.

Every **<input>** tag has a **name** and **id** attribute assigned, as shown in the following statement. These attributes allow you to access the form element by name in JavaScript instead of using an array reference such as **elements[1]**.

```
<input name="loanAmount" type="text" id="loanAmount">
```

7   Save the changes to your file and close it in the text editor.

Now that you have set up the event handler for the form and set up the name of each element, you can finish writing the code to extract the data from the form. Once you access the data entered into the form, you can check to see if the information was entered correctly. The event handler controls whether the form is actually submitted. For instance, if the validation code shows the data was entered incorrectly, you can cancel the form submission and return to the form with the values intact. In the next exercise, you write the code to extract data from the form.

Extract Data from the Form

1   Open monthlypayment.js in your text editor and find the following code.

```
//makes sure data is entered correctly
function validateInfo() {
        // extract information from form
```

This function is called when the form is submitted. The function validates the information entered into the form. Start by extracting the information from the form.

2 Enter the following line of code to call on the function that extracts the data.

```
...
//makes sure data is entered correctly
function validateInfo() {
        // extract information from form
        extractFormInfo();
// validate information from form
...
```

The **validateInfo()** function calls on a function that appears before it in the code. The code interpreter scans for functions before interpreting any code, so the position of functions in the code is unimportant.

3 Scroll to the top of the page and find the following code.

```
// extracts data from the paymentCalc form
function extractFormInfo() {
```

This code is the beginning of the function that extracts the form data.

4 Enter the following code to extract the form data and place the information into variables.

```
...
// extracts data from the paymentCalc form
function extractFormInfo() {
        interestRate=document.paymentCalc.interestRate.value;
        loanAmount=document.paymentCalc.loanAmount.value;
        term=document.paymentCalc.term.value;
        annualTaxes=document.paymentCalc.annualTaxes.value;
} // end function
...
```

The **extractFormInfo()** function isn't really necessary, since you can always access the element data by writing statements such as **document.paymentCalc.interestRate.value**. However, it is much simpler to type (and use) the short variable names you created. It is also good practice to divide each step into a simple function.

5 Save your changes and keep the file open in your text editor.

Use a Tracing Alert to Debug

1 In the open monthlypayment.js, enter the following statement directly below the code you entered in the previous exercise.

```
...

        loanAmount=document.paymentCalc.loanAmount.value;

        term=document.paymentCalc.term.value;

        annualTaxes=document.paymentCalc.annualTaxes.value;

        alert("interestRate is : "+interestRate);

} // end function


//makes sure data is entered correctly

...
```

This code allows you to trace the variable value and perform a quick test to see if your code was entered correctly.

2 Save your changes.

3 Open ToolsCalculators.html in your Web browser.

4 Enter a number in the Interest Rate field and click Submit.

An alert box appears, showing the value you entered. You now know that the external functions are being triggered by the form submission. You also know that the extract code is written correctly. If you receive an error message, retrace your steps and look for typing errors or omissions.

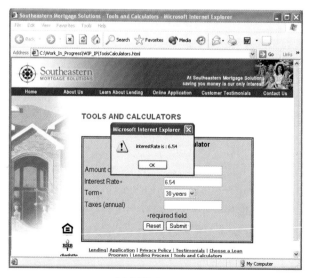

FIGURE IP.6

5   Click OK to acknowledge the alert box.

6   Remove the **alert()** statement you added in Step 1.

7   Save your changes and keep the file open in your text editor.

Use a Function to Validate Form Data

1   In your text editor, find the following code.

```
//makes sure data is entered correctly
function validateInfo() {
        // extract information from form
        extractFormInfo();
        // validate information from form


        // do calculations


} //end function
```

2   Insert the following code.

```
...
// validate information from form
        if (interestRate.indexOf("%")!=-1) {
                alert("Please enter Interest without a % character and
                resubmit.");
                return false;
        } // end if
        // do calculations


} //end function
...
```

This code ensures that users do not enter a percent (%) sign when they enter the interest rate in the form. If a user enters a percent sign, the form-submission process stops, and the user is asked to correct the mistake. As a developer, you could have chosen other means to deal with this potential problem, such as removing the percent sign (if it exists) and converting the value from a string to a number without requiring the user to re-enter the information.

3 Save your changes.

4 Refresh the open ToolsCalculators.html page in your browser.

5 Enter "6.75%" for the interest rate.

6 Click the Submit button.

You receive an alert message that tells you to enter the interest rate without the percent sign and resubmit the form.

FIGURE IP.7

7 Remove the percent sign from the interest rate and resubmit the form.

You should not receive an alert message.

8 Find the following comment in the **validateInfo()** function.

```
// do calculations
```

9 Enter the following statement, which invokes the function to complete the calculations.

```
...
alert("Please enter Interest without a % character and resubmit.");
            return false;
        } // end if
// do calculations
monthlyPayment();
} //end function


// determines monthly payment
function monthlyPayment() {
    ...
```

10 Scroll through the **monthlyPayment()** function.

The formula to generate this payment is extremely complex. To simplify the code and make it easier to find coding mistakes, we divided the code into steps. A loan officer provided the formula to generate the monthly payment, as well as a worksheet that shows each step of the calculation for a set value (such as $50,000 for 30 years at 5%); the code was broken down into the same steps. If necessary, you can insert **alert()** statements to trace the calculations at each step, and you can check your calculations against the sample worksheet to ensure that you designed the code correctly.

At the end of the **monthlyPayment()** function, the function to build the report is invoked with the following code:

```
// call function to generate report
        buildReport();
        return true;
```

So far, you have connected the form and the external script, completed the function that extracts data from the form, and completed the function that validates the form information. The **monthlyPayment()** function will complete the calculations, and the **buildReport()** function will create the report. In the next exercise, you insert the variables into the dynamic code.

Write HTML Code Dynamically from JavaScript

1 Find the following code, which is included at the bottom of the monthlyPayment.js file.

```
// buildReport creates a popup window and writes code dynamically
function buildReport () {
report=window.open("","report","width=455, height=260,
menubar=yes","");
```

This code starts a function that creates a pop-up window, and then it builds the report in the pop-up window. Notice that the **window.open()** statement leaves the browser's menu bar turned on. This allows users to print the report results.

2 Examine the following lines of code (they are directly after the code that you reviewed in Step 1).

```
report.document.write("<html><head>");
report.document.write("<title>Southeastern Mortgage Solutions -
Payment Report</title>");
```

Another developer cut and pasted the mock-up code into a JavaScript function and enclosed each line of code within a **document.write()** statement. Additionally, a Find and Replace command was used in the text editor to replace double quotes in the HTML code with single quotes. This change keeps the JavaScript strings from terminating prematurely.

3 Find the following code.

```
// insert interest rate
report.document.write("5.75%</td></tr>");
```

At this point, the window doesn't show the results of your calculations, but it does show the numbers inserted into the original mock-up. In other words, no matter what numbers you enter, the report will only display the numbers from the mock-up.

4 Change the code you found in Step 3 to the following.

```
// insert interest rate
report.document.write(interestRate+"%</td></tr>");
```

This change allows the code to dynamically write the variable values.

5 Find the following code.

```
// insert term
report.document.write("30 years</td></tr>");
```

6 Change the code you found in Step 5 to the following.

```
// insert term
report.document.write(term+" years</td></tr>");
```

7 Find the following code.

```
// insert monthly tax
report.document.write("100</td></tr>");
```

Don't confuse this code with the code for the **monthlyPayment** variable.

8 Change the code you found in Step 7 to the following.

```
// insert monthly tax
report.document.write(monthlyTax+"</td></tr>");
```

9 Find the following code.

```
// insert monthly payment
report.document.write("391.79</font></td></tr>");
```

10 Change the code you found in Step 9 to the following.

```
// insert monthly payment
report.document.write(monthlyPayment+"</font></td></tr>");
```

11 Find the following code near the bottom of the page.

```
// close window when link is clicked
report.document.write("<a href='#'>close window</a></div>");
```

12 Change the code you found in Step 11 to the following.

```
// close window when link is clicked
report.document.write("<a href='#' onclick='window.close()'>close
window</a></div>");
```

This code inserts an event handler to close the pop-up window when the user clicks the Close Window link.

13 Save the changes to the file.

In the final step, you test the script using a known value. When you already know what the result should be, finding mistakes in your calculations and/or code writing becomes much easier.

Test Using a Known Value

1 Refresh the open ToolsCalculators.html page in your Web browser.

2 Enter "100000" as the Amount of Loan.

3   Enter "30 years" as the Term, enter "5.75" for the Interest Rate, and enter "1200" for the Taxes (annual).

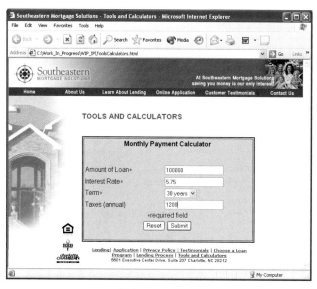

FIGURE IP.8

4   Submit the form.

You should receive $683.57 as the amount of the monthly payment.

FIGURE IP.9

5   Close all open files in your browser and text editor.

Create CSS Rollover Effects for Hyperlinks

1 In your text editor, open sems.css.

FIGURE IP.10

This CSS file creates some of the formatting for the Web site.

2 At the bottom of this document, add the following code.

```
...
h3 {   font-family: Arial, Helvetica, sans-serif;
       font-weight: bold;
       color: #666666;

}
a:hover {

       text-decoration: underline;

       background-color: #FF9900;

}
...
```

3 Save the file in your text editor.

4 Open index.html in your Web browser.

5   Move your mouse over the links at the bottom of the page.

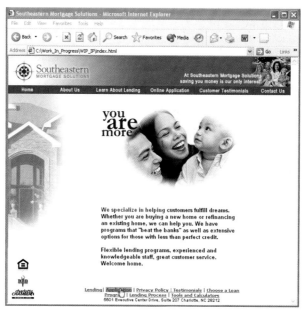

As you move the mouse across each link, an orange highlight appears.

6   Click the links at the bottom of the page to visit the other pages in the site. Move your mouse over the hyperlinks on the other pages.

The style applies to all links on the Web site.

7   Close the file in your browser and text editor.

In this project, you gained a basic understanding of the details involved in constructing a complex script. The actual script used for the Tools and Calculators section of the Southeastern Mortgage Solutions site is larger than what we presented here; it contains additional form validation and formatting code. The SEMortgageSolutions.com site also contains some additional content pages that we did not include in this project.

ECMAScript REFERENCE

Operations

Operator	Description
ARITHMETIC	
+	Adds two numbers.
++	Increments a number.
-	As a unary operator, negates the value of its argument. As a binary operator, subtracts two numbers.
--	Decrements a number.
*	Multiplies two numbers.
/	Divides two numbers.
%	Computes the integer remainder of dividing two numbers.
STRING	
+	Concatenates two strings.
+=	Concatenates two strings and assigns the result to the first operand.
LOGICAL OPERATORS	
&&	(Logical AND) Returns true if both logical operands are true. Otherwise, returns false.
||	(Logical OR) Returns true if either logical expression is true. If both are false, returns false.
!	(Logical negation) If its single operand is true, returns false; otherwise, returns true.
BITWISE OPERATORS	
&	(Bitwise AND) Returns "1" in each bit position if bits of both operands are "1"s.
^	(Bitwise XOR) Returns "1" in a bit position if bits of one but not both operands are "1".
|	(Bitwise OR) Returns "1" in a bit if bits of either operand is "1".
~	(Bitwise NOT) Flips the bits of its operand.
<<	(Left shift) Shifts its first operand in binary representation of the number of bits to the left specified in the second operand, shifting in "0"s from the right.
>>	(Sign-propagating right shift) Shifts the first operand in binary representation of the number of bits to the right specified in the second operand, discarding bits shifted off.
>>>	(Zero-fill right shift) Shifts the first operand in binary representation of the number of bits to the right specified in the second operand, discarding bits shifted off, and shifting in "0"s from the left.

Operations (continued)

Operator	Description
ASSIGNMENT	
=	Assigns the value of the second operand to the first operand.
+=	Adds two numbers and assigns the result to the first.
-=	Subtracts two numbers and assigns the result to the first.
*=	Multiplies two numbers and assigns the result to the first.
/=	Divides two numbers and assigns the result to the first.
%=	Computes the modulus of two numbers and assigns the result to the first.
&=	Performs a bitwise AND and assigns the result to the first operand.
^=	Performs a bitwise XOR and assigns the result to the first operand.
|=	Performs a bitwise OR and assigns the result to the first operand.
<<=	Performs a left shift and assigns the result to the first operand.
>>=	Performs a sign-propagating right shift and assigns the result to the first operand.
>>>=	Performs a zero-fill right shift and assigns the result to the first operand.
COMPARISON	
==	Returns true if the operands are equal.
!=	Returns true if the operands are not equal.
>	Returns true if left operand is greater than right operand.
>=	Returns true if left operand is greater than or equal to right operand.
<	Returns true if left operand is less than right operand.
<=	Returns true if left operand is less than or equal to right operand.
SPECIAL	
?:	Performs simple "if ? then : else".
,	Evaluates two expressions and returns the result of the second expression.
delete	Deletes an object property or an element at a specified index in an array.
new	Creates an instance of an object.
this	Refers to the current object.
typeof	Returns a string indicating the type of the unevaluated operand.
void	Specifies an expression to be evaluated without returning a value.

Statements

Statement	Description
break	Terminates the current while or for loop and transfers program control to the statement following the terminated loop.
continue	Terminates execution of the block of statements in a while or for loop and continues execution of the loop with the next iteration.
delete	Deletes an object's property or an element of an array.
do ... while (*condition*)	Executes its statements until the test condition evaluates to false. Statement is executed at least once.
for (*init; condition; increment*)	A loop that consists of three optional expressions, enclosed in parentheses and separated by semicolons, followed by a block of statements executed in the loop.
for (*var* in *object*)	Iterates a specified variable over all the properties of an object. For each distinct property, JavaScript executes the specified statements.
function	Declares a JavaScript function name with the specified parameters. Acceptable parameters include strings, numbers, and objects.
if (*condition*) ... else	Executes a set of statements if a specified condition is true. If the condition is false, another set of statements can be executed.
labeled	Provides an identifier that can be used with break or continue to indicate where the program should continue execution.
return	Statement that specifies the value to be returned by a function.
switch (*expression*) case label:	Evaluates an expression and attempts to match the expression's value to a case label.
var	Declares a variable, optionally initializing it to a value.
while (*condition*) ...	Creates a loop that evaluates an expression, and if it is true, executes a block of statements.
with (*object*) ...	Establishes the default object for a set of statements.
//	Defines comment until end of the line.
/* ... */	Defines comment within the operators.

Core Objects

Property/Method	Description
ARRAY OBJECT	
length	Size of the array.
index	Position of matched substring (from RegExp object).
input	Original string for matching (from RegExp object).
concat(array1)	Joins two arrays into one array.
join(separator)	Joins array element into a string, separated by separator (Defaults to ",").
pop	Removes last element from an array and returns that element.
push(e1, e2 ...)	Adds one or more elements to the end of the array and returns the last element.
reverse	Reverses the elements in the array.
shift	Removes the first element from an array and returns that element.
slice(begin, end)	Extracts elements from index (begin to end) and returns a new array.
sort	Sorts the elements of an array.
splice	Change content of array by adding and removing elements.
toString	Returns string representation of array.
unshift(e1, e2 ...)	Adds one or more elements to the beginning of the array and returns new array length.
BOOLEAN OBJECT	
toString	Returns string representation of Boolean.

Core Objects (continued)

Property/Method	Description
DATE OBJECT	
getDate	Returns the day of the month.
getDay	Returns the day of the week.
getHours	Returns the hour.
getMinutes	Returns the minutes.
getMonth	Returns the month.
getSeconds	Returns the seconds.
getTime	Returns the numeric value corresponding to the time.
getTimezoneOffset	Returns the time-zone offset in minutes for the current locale.
getYear	Returns the year.
parse	Returns the number of milliseconds in a date string since January 1, 1970, 00:00:00, local time.
setDate	Sets the day of the month.
setHours	Sets the hours.
setMinutes	Sets the minutes.
setMonth	Sets the month.
setSeconds	Sets the seconds.
setTime	Sets the value of a Date object.
setYear	Sets the year.
toGMTString	Converts a date to a string, using the Internet GMT conventions.
toLocaleString	Converts a date to a string, using the current locale's conventions.
UTC	Returns the number of milliseconds in a Date object since January 1, 1970, 00:00:00, Universal Coordinated Time (GMT).

Core Objects (continued)

Property/Method	Description
MATH OBJECT	
E	Euler's constant, approximately 2.718.
LN10	Natural logarithm of 10, approximately 2.302.
LN2	Natural logarithm of 2, approximately 0.693.
LOG10E	Base 10 logarithm of E, approximately 0.434.
PI	Pi, approximately 3.14159.
SQRT1_2	Square root of 1/2, approximately 0.707.
SQRT2	Square root of 2, approximately 1.414.
abs	Returns the absolute value of a number.
acos	Returns the arccosine (in radians) of a number.
asin	Returns the arcsine (in radians) of a number.
atan	Returns the arctangent (in radians) of a number.
atan2	Returns the arctangent of the quotient of its arguments.
ceil	Returns the smallest integer greater than or equal to a number.
cos	Returns the cosine of a number.
exp	Returns E^{number}, where number is the argument, and E is Euler's constant, the base of the natural logarithms.
floor	Returns the largest integer less than or equal to a number.
log	Returns the natural logarithm (base E) of a number.
max	Returns the greater of two numbers.
min	Returns the lesser of two numbers.
pow	Returns base to the exponent power, that is, baseexponent.
random	Returns a pseudo-random number between 0 and 1.
round	Returns the value of a number rounded to the nearest integer.
sin	Returns the sine of a number.
sqrt	Returns the square root of a number.
tan	Returns the tangent of a number.

Core Objects (continued)

Property/Method	Description

NUMBER OBJECT

MAX_VALUE	The largest representable number.
MIN_VALUE	The smallest representable number.
NaN	Not a number value.
NEGATIVE_INFINITY	Negative infinite value for overflow.
POSITIVE_INFINITY	Infinite value for overflow.
toString	Returns string representation of a number.

OBJECT OBJECT

eval	Evaluates a string of ECMAScript in the context of this object.
toString	Returns the string representation of this object.
valueOf	Returns the primitive value of the specified object.

STRING OBJECT

length	Returns length of the string.
charAt	Returns the character at the specified index.
charCodeAt	Returns a number indicating the ISO-Latin-1 codeset value of the character at the given index.
concat	Combines the text of two strings and returns a new string.
fromCharCode	Returns a string from the specified sequence of numbers that are ISO-Latin-1 codeset values.
indexOf	Returns the index within the calling String object of the first occurrence of the specified value.
lastIndexOf	Returns the index within the calling String object of the last occurrence of the specified value.
match	Matches a regular expression against a string.
replace	Finds a match between a regular expression and a string, and replaces the matched substring with a new substring.
search	Executes the search for a match between a regular expression and a specified string.
slice	Extracts a section of a string and returns a new string.
split	Splits a string into an array of strings by separating the string into substrings.
substr	Returns the characters in a string beginning at the specified location through the specified number of characters.
substring	Returns the characters in a string between two indexes into the string.
toLowerCase	Returns the calling string value converted to lowercase.
toUpperCase	Returns the calling string value converted to uppercase.

Core Objects (continued)

Property/Method	Description
REGEXP OBJECT	
$1...$9	Parenthesized substring matches, if any.
global	Whether or not to test the regular expression against all possible matches in a string or only against the first.
ignoreCase	Whether or not to ignore case while attempting a match in a string.
input or $_	The string against which a regular expression is matched.
lastIndex	The index at which to start the next match.
lastMatch or $&	The last matched characters.
lastParen	The last parenthesized substring match, if any.
leftContext or $`	The substring preceding the most recent match.
multiline or $*	Whether or not to search in strings across multiple lines.
right Context or $'	The substring following the most recent match.
source	The text of the pattern.
compile	Compiles a regular expression object.
exec	Executes a search for a match in its string parameter.
test	Tests for a match in its string parameter.

GLOSSARY

absolute path The location of a file or Web page beginning with the root. Includes all necessary information to find the file or page. In the case of a Web page, called "absolute URL." See *relative path*.

absolute positioning Specifying precise coordinates to position any element in an exact position on the screen.

absolute reference The complete path of the file you want to open.

Acrobat A program developed by Adobe Systems, Inc. that allows the conversion of any document from any Macintosh or Windows application to PDF format. It is widely used for distributing documents online.

Acrobat Reader A stand-alone program or Web browser plug-in from Adobe that allows you to view a PDF file. Acrobat Reader is free and can be downloaded from the Adobe Web site.

action The location that receives data from a form.

actions In Macromedia Flash, commands associated with frames, objects, or movie clips that provide control over the behavior of those objects. Written in ActionScript, actions are the building blocks of interactive Flash movies.

ActionScript The scripting language used in Macromedia Flash.

algorithm A specific sequence of mathematical steps to process data. A portion of a computer program that calculates a specific result.

alias Canonical domain names.

anchor A location within an HTML document that can be reached with a hyperlink.

anchor object Represents a text anchor created in the HTML code. Anchor objects can be referenced by the anchors array.

anchors array Represents every text anchor created in the HTML code. For example, anchors[0] represents the first text anchor in the document.

animated GIF A type of sequential file format where multiple bitmap images display one after another.

animation The technique of simulating movement by creating slight changes to an object or objects over time.

anonymous function A function that does not have a name; it is assigned directly to an event handler.

applet Self-contained computer programs, created in the Java programming language, often used on Web sites.

applets array In JavaScript, represents each Java applet or HTML <applet> tag added to an HTML document.

array Variable that holds multiple items of data in numbered or named slots.

ASCII American Standard Code for Information Interchange. Worldwide, standard ASCII text does not include formatting, and therefore can be exchanged and read by most computer systems.

ASP Active Server Pages. A specification for a dynamically created Web page that contain either Visual Basic or JavaScript code. When a browser requests an ASP page, the Web server generates a page with HTML code. Also known as "ASP.net."

aspect ratio The width-to-height proportions of an image.

assignment operator A character or characters that assign a value to a variable.

bandwidth The transmission capacity of a network connection, usually measured in bits per second. See *BPS*.

behavior In Dreamweaver, prewritten JavaScript scripts.

bit (binary digit) A computer's smallest unit of information. Bits can have only two values: 0 or 1.

bit depth A measure of how many colors can be contained in an image. 8-bit color is 256 colors (2 × 2 × 2 × 2 × 2 × 2 × 2 × 2), 16-bit color is 32,768 colors (2 × 2 × 2 × 2 × 2 × 2 × 2 × 2 × 2 × 2 × 2 × 2 × 2 × 2 × 2), and so on.

bitmap image An image constructed of individual dots or pixels set to a grid-like mosaic. The file must contain information about the color and position of each pixel, which requires significant amounts of disk space.

bitwise operators Operators that affect the status of a single bit of computer memory.

blur When keystrokes redirect to another object.

bookmark HTML feature that allows you to save a link to a Web page.

bookmarklet Small chunks of JavaScript code that you can use in place of URLs.

boolean values A data type set to either true or false.

bots Automated programs that explore Web pages, record any hyperlinks used, and index the content of the pages. Short for robots, another term used to describe these programs. See *spider*.

bound When an event handler is attached to an object.

BPS Bits per second. A measurement of how fast data moves from one place to another, usually in thousands of bits per second (Kbps) or million of bits per second (Mbps). A 28.8 modem can transport 28,800 bits per second.

browser　Software program that allows you to surf the Web. The most popular browsers are Netscape Navigator and Microsoft Internet Explorer. The very first browsers, such as Lynx, only allowed users to see text. Also called "Web browser."

browser compatibility　A term that compares the way a Web page functions on different browsers. Incompatibilities often exist due to the way a browser interprets HTML. The differences may be slight or significant.

browser objects　JavaScript objects that control specific aspects of the Web browser.

built-in objects　Objects included in the JavaScript language.

caching　Placing information in the browser's memory.

camelback notation　The process of starting the second word of an event handler or variable name with a capital letter.

canonical domain name　Domain names that can be accessed through the main domain name.

Cascading Style Sheets (CSS)　Part of a Web page that lists properties that affect the appearance of content, the content to which those properties apply, and their values.

case sensitive　Languages that distinguish between uppercase and lowercase letters.

cell padding　The margin around the inside of a cell.

cell spacing　The margin between cells.

CGI　Common Gateway Interface. Protocol that allows scripts to run on a Web server. CGI scripts put the content of a form into an email message, perform a database query, and generate HTML pages on the fly.

CGI script　A CGI program used to process a form or provide other dynamic content.

CGI-bin　The most common name of a directory on a Web server in which CGI scripts are stored.

class　1. In a scripting language (such as JavaScript), represents the definition of an object. 2. In CSS, a style definition that can be added to multiple elements.

client　A computer system or application that requests a service of another computer system on the network.

client-side　Scripting or other actions that take place within the browser, as opposed to the server.

CNAME record　Canonical domain names.

comp　Comprehensive artwork used to present the general color and layout of a page to a client or team.

comparison operators　In computer languages, specific characters or phrases that make comparisons among/between values.

concatenating　Combining two text strings.

constant property　In JavaScript, a property that cannot be changed.

constructor method　A method used to generate a new object.

content-encoding　The type of files being compressed and sent to the browser.

cookie　Information a Web server writes to your computer hard disk via your browser; contains data such as login information and user preferences. This data can be retrieved so Web pages can be customized before they are sent to the visiting browser.

custom class　A rule (or rules) that tell the browser how to display any item to which the selector is applied.

data type　Determines the kind of information the variable can hold.

data type errors　Errors involving data types.

debugging　The process of finding and correcting errors in code.

decision statements　Questions the interpreter must answer based on the relationship of the variables.

declaration　Chunks of CSS that consist of selectors and rules.

decrement　To decrease the value of a variable by 1.

delimiter　A character or sequence of characters marking the beginning or end of a unit of data.

deprecated　The status of a tag or attribute that can still be used, but will eventually be removed. Whenever possible, avoid using deprecated tags.

DHTML　Dynamic HTML. JavaScript programs that dynamically change cascading style sheet properties, allowing parts of a Web page to be hidden, shown, or animated.

DHTML (Dynamic HTML)　A mixture of CSS, HTML, and JavaScript.

directories option　Allows developers to specify whether directory buttons appear in Web browsers.

disjointed rollover　Changing the event handler associated with a change to an image object; allows a developer to automatically change one image when the user rolls over a different image.

div　A block of content that can be positioned on the page. See *absolute positioning* and *relative positioning*.

DNS　Domain name server or domain name system. Maps IP numbers to a more easily remembered name. When you type http://www.somedomain.com into a browser, the DNS searches for a matching IP address (228.28.202.95).

do while statement　Allows looping of certain code segments until a value changes.

DOCTYPE　Specification of the DTD that applies to a page.

document The general term for a computer file containing text and/or graphics.

document object Represents the HTML document loaded into the browser window. Allow the developer to control aspects of HTML and cascading style sheet (CSS) code.

document root The main directory for a Web site.

DOM Document Object Model. The most useful part of the complete object model; provides direct control over HTML and CSS coding.

domain name A unique name used to identify a Web site, FTP site, and/or email server. A domain name always points to one specific server, even though the server may host many domain names.

dot syntax Periods used within the JavaScript code to note how items relate to one another.

down state An image that displays when you click the button.

download Transfering data from a server to your computer's hard disk.

dpi Dots per inch. The measurement of resolution for page printers, phototype-setting machines, and graphics screens. Currently graphics screens use resolutions of 72 to 96 dpi; standard desktop laser printers work at 600 dpi.

drag To position the pointer on an object, press and hold down the mouse button, move the mouse, and then release the button.

DSL Digital subscriber line. A means for gaining high-speed access to the Internet using phone wiring and a specialized phone connection.

DSN Data source name. Used to access a database.

dynamic Content that changes according to client- or server-side scripting.

dynamic document When changes occur in a document, according to user choices or changing conditions.

ECMA The European Computer Manufacturers Association.

ECMAScript An official standardized version of JavaScript maintained by the ECMA.

e-commerce Electronic commerce. Conducting business online, including product display, online ordering, and inventory management. The software, which works in conjunction with online payment systems to process payments, resides on a commerce server.

element Each slot or piece of information.

element object Individual fields in a form.

email address An electronic mail address, in the form user@domain.com.

embedded style sheet CSS rules are defined in the HTML document using the <style> tag.

embedding Including a complete copy of a text file or image within a document, with or without a link.

empty string A unit of zero characters.

end-of-loop test A condition that is evaluated to determine when the loop stops executing.

equality operator The "==" operator, which means "are the values equal?"

escape character Marks the beginning of an escape sequence.

escape sequence Codes within JavaScript that represent characters that would normally create syntax errors.

event handler A keyword that allows the computer to detect an event.

exclusive OR operator (^) Returns a value of true if, and only if, one of the values is true.

external CSS file CSS styling information included in a separate (external) file that controls the appearance of a Web page.

external style sheet Style information included in a separate file referenced by a Web page. Allows a Web designer to control the formatting of an entire Web site from one external file.

external URL A page outside the local Web site.

features Attributes of the browser window.

features parameter Allows developers to turn on menu bars, toolbars, and scroll bars, as well as control the width and height aspects of the pop-up window within the open() method.

FIFO First In-First Out; queue where the most recently stored item is the first item retrieved.

file A specific collection of information stored on the computer disk, separate from all other information. Can be randomly accessed by the computer.

file extension The suffix used to identify file types under the Macintosh and Windows operating systems, separated from the rest of the file name by a period.

file:/// A protocol used by browsers to access information available on the local computer.

fires When an event occurs, programmers say that it "fires."

fixed positioning Images remain unaffected when the page on which they reside scrolls up or down.

flag A Boolean variable that determines whether an event has occurred.

flowchart A diagram that shows how a script progresses during execution.

flow-of-control statement When the computer stops the execution of a command long enough to evaluate a condition, and then follows specific commands based on the result.

focus The state of being active. Usually the last object clicked has focus.

folder The digital equivalent of a paper file folder. Double-clicking a folder icon opens the folder to reveal the files stored inside.

font The complete collection of all the characters (numbers, uppercase and lowercase letters, and in some cases, small caps and symbols) of a given typeface in a specific style; for example, Helvetica Bold.

font class In Web design, the type of font (serif, sans serif, monospace, cursive, or fantasy) that will be used if the user's computer does not have any of the font-family members. See *Cascading Style Sheets*.

font family In Web design, a grouping of (supposedly) similar fonts, used to display text in the Web page.

form A page that enables a user to type information and send it to a site via form elements such as text boxes and pull-down menus.

form element Objects that represent one portion of a form — such as a radio button or text area.

form method See *get* and *post*.

form object Represents a form in the HTML document.

form validation The process of making certain a Web form contains all required data and no invalid data.

forms array Collection of objects that represent every <form> tag encountered in an HTML document.

frame An HTML page, displayed with other HTML pages in a single browser window.

frame action An action attached to an individual frame in the Timeline.

frame rate The number of successive images that are displayed in one second, designated fps (frames per second).

frameset HTML file that divides the browser window into sections and displays various HTML files in the sections, which are known as frames.

FTP File Transfer Protocol. Method of transferring files through the Internet from one computer to another. FTP allows you to download files from another computer, as well as upload files from your computer to a remote computer.

functions Named, reusable sections of code that can exist in the head or body section of an HTML document or in an external file.

get A method for sending form data by appending it to the URL of the action. See *post*.

GIF Graphics Interchange Format. A popular graphics format for online clip art and drawn graphics. Graphics in this format are acceptable at low resolution. See *JPEG*.

global scope Variables that can be used anywhere.

global variables Variables declared outside functions.

header Small amount of text containing specific instructions for the Web browser.

height option Used to specify a value for the height of a browser window.

hex values Numbers specified in the hexadecimal system, commonly used for specifying colors on Web pages.

hexadecimal number Method of writing numbers where each digit represents a number between 1 and 16. Also known as "base-16."

history object JavaScript object that represents the browser's history list. Used to return to pages previously visited by the browser.

home page Main page of a Web site. A Web site containing only one page is also called a home page.

HTTPS Secure HyperText Transport Protocol; ensures that all information transmitted between Web browsers and Web servers is encrypted.

hyperlink An HTML tag that directs the computer to a different anchor or URL. A hyperlink can be a word, phrase, sentence, graphic, or icon. A hyperlink can also cause an action, such as opening or downloading a file.

hypertext Organization of content that enables the user to select related content.

hypertext reference Synonymous with URL (Uniform Resource Locator), which represents the location of a document.

ID selector Used to create a single element that can be referenced in JavaScript or other scripting languages.

if-then statement A programming construction that executes one section of code if a particular expression is true, and a second section if it is false.

IIS Internet Information Server. Microsoft's Web server that runs on Windows NT platforms. IIS comes bundled with Windows NT 4.0. IIS is tightly integrated with the operating system, so it is relatively easy to administer.

image map A graphic containing "hot spots," or areas of an image defined as links. When a viewer clicks a hot spot, he is actually clicking a link.

increment To increase the value of a variable by 1.

index Each entry in an array.

index date 12 a.m., January 1, 1970, Greenwich Mean Time (GMT). Often used in time calculations.

inequality operator The "!=" operator, which means "the values are not equal."

initialize To assign a beginning value to a variable.

inline code A single JavaScript command or multiple commands that appear inside an HTML tag.

inline style sheet   Works as an attribute within an HTML tag.

input   An element, such as a text box, that receives information from the user.

internal style sheet   Style information included within a Web page.

Internet   A global system of interconnected computers.

interpreter   The program that executes instructions in a computer language.

Java   A platform-independent programming language invented by Sun Microsystems that Web developers use to create applets. Java-enabled Web pages include animations, calculators, scrolling text, sound effects, games, and more.

JavaScript   A scripting language, originally designed by Netscape, that you can embed into HTML documents.

JavaScript Object Model   A map of how objects are categorized in JavaScript.

JPEG   A compression algorithm that reduces the file size of bitmapped images, named for the Joint Photographic Experts Group that created the standard. JPEG is "lossy" compression; image quality is reduced in direct proportion to the amount of compression.

Jscript   Microsoft's version of JavaScript.

keyboard event   Refers to a group of events related to keys pressed on the keyboard.

keyframe animation   A series of still images played in rapid succession.

keywords   A word or words that identifies the content of a Web page and can be used by search engines as part of their process of determining the results of searches.

language   The common set of words, including definitions and pronunciations, and the methods of combining those words shared for the purpose of communication among a group of people.

language attribute   Specifies the scripting language that appears within an HTML <script> tag.

layer   Use of CSS elements with absolute positioning and z-index values.

LIFO   Last In-First Out; stacking method where the most recently stored item is the first item retrieved.

link object   Object that represents a hyperlink.

linked style sheet   See *external style sheet*.

links array   The array that stores information about hyperlinks in an HTML document.

listener   Another term for event handler.

LiveScript   The original name for JavaScript.

local scope   A variable that only exists within a function.

local variable   A variable created within a function, only available within the function.

location   The address of a particular Web page or file.

location object   Allows you to change the browser's URL or reload the current document.

location option   Includes the URL location box.

location property   Holds the address of the current HTML document. Changing the location property forces the Web browser to load the page stored in the new address.

logic error   The code does one thing, but it was intended to do something else.

logical AND operator   Evaluates whether both variables are set to true.

logical NOT operator   Negates a Boolean value.

logical operators   Special operators designed to compare two true or false values.

logical OR operator   Returns a value of true if any of the variables compared is equal to true.

loosely typed language   Since JavaScript does not require you to declare the data type when you create the variable, the JavaScript language is described as a loosely typed language.

mailto: A protocol used to tell the browser to create a new email message.

math object   Used to complete various calculations.

MB   Megabyte. A unit of measure of stored data equaling 1,024 kilobytes, or 1,048,576 bytes. Also Abbreviated as M.

Mbps   Megabits per second. Measure of data throughput in millions of bits per second.

menubar option   Turns on the browser's menu bar.

meta tag   An optional HTML tag that specifies information about a Web document. Some search engines index Web pages by reading the information contained within meta tags.

methods   Commands that perform actions.

millisecond   1/1000th of a second.

MIME   Multipurpose Internet Mail Extensions. Standard for attaching non-text files (formatted word-processing files, spreadsheets, pictures, executable files) to email messages.

MIME type   An indication of the kind of data being sent to the browser. Used by the browser so it knows what to do with the data.

modify condition statement   Changes the variable each time a loop executes.

modulus operator   Used find the remainder left over after division.

mouseover The event triggered at the moment the user rolls the mouse (cursor) over an area or item on a Web page. Typically used to tell the browser to do something, such as execute a rollover script.

multidimensional array An array stored within an array.

multimedia The combination of text, sound, and video images to create an interactive document, program, or presentation.

named target A frame that has a designated name, allowing links to specify that content should be displayed within that frame.

naming convention A standard way to create variable names.

negated Opposite.

nested frameset A frameset contained within another frameset.

nested tag A tag contained within another tag.

normal state The image that displays when the user is not interacting with the button.

null Means the property or value exists, but has no assigned value.

object A reference to a collection of properties and methods.

object method A function executed by an object.

object model A map of the organizational structure of an OOP environment.

object property A unit of information about an object.

objects As a simple analogy, think of objects as nouns that you can use in a scripting language.

ODBC connectivity A standard database access method developed by Microsoft. The goal of ODBC is to make it possible to access any data from any application, regardless of which database management system (DBMS) handles the data.

OOP Object-oriented programming. A style of programming that relies on reusing objects in multiple computer programs.

OS Operating system. The software that allows your computer to function. Examples of operating systems include Mac OS X and Microsoft Windows XP.

over state The image that displays when the user moves the mouse pointer over an image.

page properties In Web design, the characteristics of a layout page, including default background and text colors, page width, and background image.

page title Text that appears in the title bar of the user's browser when he views a page.

parsing When you view a Web page in a browser, an interpreter decides how to display the HTML or JavaScript code, then returns information to the screen.

pathname The location of the file relative to the domain name.

Perl Practical Extraction and Report Language. A powerful computer language, especially used for writing CGI scripts that handle input/output actions on Web pages.

persistent state The browser can record and retrieve information, even when the user leaves a page and then returns to that page.

PHP A server-side HTML-embedded scripting language used to create dynamic Web pages. The strength of PHP lies in its compatibility with many types of databases. PHP can talk across networks using IMAP, SNMP, NNTP, POP3, and HTTP.

PNG Portable Network Graphics. PNG is a graphics format similar to GIF. Not widely supported by older browsers.

pop Removing the last element in an array.

populating The process of inserting data into an array.

pop-under windows Using various JavaScript techniques, designers often create pop-up windows that display behind the main browser window.

pop-up blockers Software packages designed to stop scripts from generating pop-up windows without the user's permission.

pop-up menu A Web-page form element, with which users can choose one item from a specific set of options.

pop-up windows Used for a variety of purposes in Web development, the most common being online advertisements.

post A method for sending form data using headers. See *get*.

precedence The order in which operations are completed.

precedence error When steps in a solution execute in the wrong order.

preload Loading the file before the user sees the image.

program A sequence of instructions, encoded in a specific computer language, for performing predetermined tasks.

programmer's comments Messages that programmers insert directly into their source code to explain how the code was written.

property An aspect or quality of an object.

protocol A set of rules and conventions that describe the behavior computers must follow in order to understand each other.

pseudo-class Situations that do not exist in HTML.

public methods In the Java programming language, methods that can be accessed from anywhere, including JavaScript.

public properties In the Java programming language, properties that can be accessed from anywhere, including JavaScript.

push   A method that adds an element to the end of an array.

queue   An array where the first item to be retrieved is the item stored earliest.

radio button   A Web-page form field; users can choose one of several defined options.

redefining HTML tags   When HTML tag names are used as selectors, the rule applied overwrites the default display styles of the tag.

redirect   To cause the browser to load a different page without intervention from the user. A particular HTML code in the heading of a Web page seamlessly redirects the visitor to another Web page.

refresh   To reload.

relative path   The location of a file or Web page that uses the location of the current file or page as a reference. In the case of a Web page, called "relative URL." See *absolute path*.

relative positioning   Allows you to offset an element relative to where it would normally appear in the document.

relative reference   When a path to a file is written relative to the current document.

reserved words   Names of commands used in the programming language.

resizable option   Determines whether the user is allowed to resize the window once it is opened.

reverse   Reverses the order of the elements in an array object.

RGB   1. The colors of projected light from a computer monitor (Red, Green, and Blue) that, when combined, simulate a subset of the visual spectrum. 2. The color mode of most digital artwork.

robots   See *bots, spider*.

rollover   A Web-page element that changes appearance based on the position of the user's mouse cursor.

root   1. Top-level directory from which all other directories branch out. 2. On a UNIX system, the system administrator's account (also called the "superuser account"). For security reasons, only the system administrator is allowed to log in as root.

rule   Consists of an attribute and a value.

rules of precedence   Determine how complex forumlas are computed.

screen object   Represents the user's computer screen; allows developers to determine the current size of the user's screen.

script   Written document that tells the computer or browser what to do.

script tag   Allows JavaScript to be inserted into an HTML document.

scripting   The process of adding programming capabilities to a program (AppleScript), file (ActionScript), or Web page (JavaScript).

scripting language   Similar to a traditional programming language, but is usually less powerful and often designed for a specific function.

scrollbars option   Determines whether the scroll bars appear.

search engine   A Web site that allows users to search for keywords on Web pages. Every search engine has its own strategy for collecting data.

search engine optimization   When creating a Web site, adding descriptive keywords and alt text to maximize the likelihood that search engines will find the site.

security certificate   A license to use digital encryption.

select list   A list of potential choices that displays as a menu or as a box with its own scroll bar.

select option   A potential choice listed in a select list.

selection   The currently active objects in a window. Often made by clicking with the mouse or dragging a marquee around the desired object/s.

selector   Can be an HTML tag that you are redefining; it can also be a special situation (a pseudo-class), which is a name you assign to a rule that you can apply to specific HTML elements.

self   When using frames, a value for the target attribute. This causes the browser to place the linked content into the frame containing the current document when the user follows the associated link.

server-side scripting   When the Web server (not the user's computer) processes the JavaScript.

setup condition   A variable that initializes to create the beginning state of the loop.

shift   Removes an item from the beginning of the array instead of from the end.

shopping cart   A piece of software that acts as the interface between a company's Web site and its deeper infrastructure, allowing consumers to select merchandise, review what they selected, make necessary modifications or additions, and purchase the merchandise.

spider   Also known as a robot or bot, a program used by search engines to index Web sites. Spiders search the Web to find URLs that match the given query string.

stack   Refers to a section of memory where the most recently stored item is the first to be retrieved.

state   An image that displays when a particular event occurs; the current condition or situation.

stateless   HTML does not collect (or remember) the actions you perform while browsing the Web.

static document   Pages do not change with user choices or changing conditions.

static positioning   When the browser positions elements on a Web page in the order they appear in the source code.

status option Turns on the browser's status bar, which appears at the bottom of the window in most browsers.

strictly typed languages Require you to specify the data type used with a specific variable when you create the variable.

string method Provide a number of useful functions, such as convertng text to all uppercase or all lowercase letters, searching through text for a particular sequence of characters, or splitting a text string into multiple pieces of information.

string object Any object that holds text.

string variables Variables that possess string values.

style sheet A defined set of formatting instructions for font and paragraph attributes, tabs, and other properties of text.

sub-object Part of another object.

swapping depths The process of changing the stacking order of objects.

syntax The set of rules that dictates how the language is written.

syntax error Errors in the grammatical rules of JavaScript.

target The page or part of a page to which a link points.

TCP/IP Transmission Control Protocol/Internet Protocol. A suite of communications protocols that defines the way information transmits over the Internet.

text The characters and words that form the main body of a publication.

text box A box into which users can type.

text editor An application used to create or make changes to text files.

text field A Web page form element in which users can enter information, such as name, address, or other data.

timer Used to set a waiting period before an action executes or to repeat an action at specific intervals.

tokens Keywords or other items that have significance to the interpreter.

toolbar option Used to specify whether the window displays toolbars.

top When using frames, a value for the target attribute. This value causes the browser to place the linked content into the current browser window, rather than an individual frame, when the user follows the associated link.

tracing The process of examining the status of variables as the program executes.

unshift Adds a new element to the start of the array and moves other elements up by one position.

uppercase The capital letters of a typeface as opposed to the lowercase (small) letters. When type was hand-composited, the capital letters resided in the upper part of the type case.

URL Uniform resource locator. Address of any resource on the Web.

URL parameter Passes information from one page to another by including a question mark and additional information at the end of a URL in a hyperlink.

usability The ease with which a user can access, navigate, and achieve goals on a Web site.

user-defined objects Created by programmers to bring consistent structure to specific programming tasks.

validate To ensure that the user entered information completely and correctly and that the information is in the proper format.

validation Making certain that input fields, particular types of information, and/or information are in the correct format for that form to be successfully submitted.

value In a rule, the value assigned to the property.

variable A unit of information that can be referred to by name.

VBScript A Microsoft scripting language used for client-side scripting.

vector graphics Graphics defined by coordinate points and mathematically drawn lines and curves, which may be freely scaled and rotated without image degradation in the final output.

W3C World Wide Web Consortium. The group responsible for defining HTML standards (http://www.w3c.org).

Web designer The aesthetic and navigational architect of a Web site who determines how the site looks, the site design, and what components the site contains.

Web developer A person who builds the technical architecture of Web sites, providing the programming required for a particular Web product to work.

Web directory A site that contains categorized listings of Web sites.

Web host A company that provides access to a server on which you can place Web site content. This server is connected to the Internet, allowing the general public to access the Web site.

Web page A single file or Web address containing HTML or XHTML information. Web pages typically include text and images, but may include links to other pages and other media.

Web site A collection of HTML files and other content that visitors can access by means of a URL and view with a Web browser.

Webmaster The person responsible for the Web server (usually the sysadmin).

Web-safe color The Web-safe color palette is a specific set of colors that accurately displays on most computer operating systems and monitors.

while statement Performs an action repeatedly until the condition becomes false.

white space Includes tabs and spaces; often used to make code easier to read. Areas on a Web page that contain no images or type. Proper use of white space is critical to a well-balanced design.

width option Specifies a value for the width of a browser window.

window object Represents the browser window.

World Wide Web Client-server hypertext system for retrieving information across the Internet.

WYSIWYG Web page editor A Web page editor that allows an author to directly manipulate items on a page, so that "what you see is what you get."

x coordinate In JavaScript, represents the number of pixels from the left corner of the screen.

XHTML An acronym for eXtensible HyperText Markup Language. The reformulization of HTML 4.01 in XML.

XHTML elements An emerging specification for defining the handling of events on a Web page.

XHTML frameset A version of XHTML that includes all tags that are part of HTML 4.01, including those involving frames.

XHTML strict A version of XHTML that does not include any presentational tags or attributes.

XHTML transitional The most common version of XHTML. Includes all tags and attributes that are part of HTML 4.01 except those involving frames.

XML eXtensible Markup Language.

XOR The exclusive OR operator appears in virtually every programming language, but may look slightly different from one language to the next. Programmers typically refer to this operator as XOR, which is pronounced "ex or."

XSL eXtensible Stylesheet Language.

y coordinate In JavaScript, represents the number of pixels from the top of the screen.

z-index Value used for determining which of a set of overlapping layers will be displayed.

INDEX